THE AMERICAN NEGRO

HIS HISTORY AND LITERATURE

A NEW NEGRO

FOR

A NEW CENTURY

Booker T. Washington, N. B. Wood,
and Fannie Barrier Williams

ARNO PRESS and THE NEW YORK TIMES
NEW YORK 1969

General Editor
WILLIAM LOREN KATZ

In 1900, when "A New Negro for a New Century" was published, the United States was rapidly changing from a provincial to a mature country, an industrial colossus. To the average black man, the forces arrayed against his advancement were so formidable as to almost exclude hope. With Reconstruction a shattered dream, with black men caught in the grip of an ever-increasing and solidifying Jim Crow, it seemed to many that solace might be found in Booker T. Washington's offer to southern whites of the fidelity and love of his people for a promise of a fair economic relationship. "In all things that are purely social we can be as separate as the fingers," he said in 1895, "Yet," he went on hopefully, "one as the hand in all things essential to mutual progress."

It is not surprising that Booker T. Washington, in the context of that repressed era, would make such a speech. Only a few voices were critical of it in 1895; even W. E. B. DuBois asked that Washington's offer be given a fair chance. But by 1900, when it was clear that Washington's accommodationism had failed to produce the desired results, when it was evident that the tide had turned the other way, many black leaders found it deplorable that he not only continued in this direction but used his considerable power to silence his black critics. He chose to ignore the facts: in 1896, *Plessy* v. *Ferguson* in effect legalized and nationalized separate-but-equal customs; between 1890 and 1900 the number of southern Negro illiterates only dropped from 2,883,216 to 2,717,606; the death rate showed no appreciable decline (it was still double that of the whites); crime convictions in the South for blacks were 29 per 1,000 as against 6 per 1,000 whites, and even worse in the North; in 1890, 90 Afro-Americans were lynched, in 1900, 107; in 1890, the American Federation of Labor was still courted by black labor, but by the end of World War I it was hostile.

In other words, John Hope's lonely words in 1896, that it was "cowardly and dishonest for any of our colored men to tell white people and colored people that we are not struggling for equality," were prophetically true. As C. Vann Woodward has demonstrated, between 1895 and 1903, not only was the black man disfranchised but he was relegated to the position of a member of a subordinate caste.

It is within this framework that we must weigh the essays in *A New Negro for a New Century*. True enough, as Washington pointed out with regard to the Spanish-American War, most wars between nations had had a basis in self-interest or in sentiment. He understood that the Spanish-American War, in which black soldiers so bravely fought, was precipitated by a feeling of revenge and retaliation, more than as a matter of justice for the struggling Cubans. But, somehow, in transferring the lessons he observed in that war to the American scene, he could not free himself from a black "Social Darwinist" posture. In spite of the increased hardening of segregation, and such events as the bloody riot in 1898 in Wilmington, North Carolina, and the brutal attacks on blacks in New York City in 1900, he persisted in maintaining that he was right and the critics not only wrong but dangerous. Though it should have been apparent that the black community needed leaders and teachers, he applauded General Armstrong's narrowly conceived emphasis on vocational direction. This had been laid down at Hampton Institute in 1867. In Washington's words:

> There has been a marked tendency of late years to make the education conform more to the industrial lines laid by General Armstrong. This is a healthy sign, as the more practical education is the better, especially as the tendency of modern industrialism is more and more towards specialization in all departments of learning and activity of whatever sort; and this

iv

is said without intending in the least to depreciate or underrate what is regarded as the higher education.

He concluded, meaningfully, "All education is good, but assuredly that is the best which enables a man to fit in most readily with the conditions of life in which he finds himself."

In the same vein, Fannie Barrier Williams, a well-known black clubwoman, not only described the characteristics of Afro-American womanhood but asserted that the mission of the first National Convention of Colored Women in 1895 was to state that the race "must begin to help itself to live better, strive for a higher standard of social purity, to exercise a more helpful sympathy with the many of the race who are without guides and enlightenment in the ways of social righteousness." The black woman, she claimed, was "the real new woman in American life." This woman, in her words, had "succeeded in lifting herself as completely from the stain and meanness of slavery as if a century had elapsed since the day of emancipation."

A New Negro for a New Century was one of the earliest attempts to picture the New Negro. For Washington, the bravery of the Afro-American soldier and his ability to fit into the industrial system, via vocational educational, were worthy of applause. For Reverend Wood, a description of the conditions

under which the black man suffered and the heroes
who had developed led to his concept of the New
Negro. For Mrs. Williams saw a message of courage
and inspiration transmitted by Afro-American
womanhood. But, above all, there was an emphasis
on the economic accomplishments of the Negro, on
the efforts for self-help and self-betterment, and the
clear assumption that these were the signs of the
New Negro. While these signs were indeed present,
it is possible that the Washington-Williams inter-
pretation did not tell the whole story. The transition
from plantation to ghetto, from dependence to independence, from slavery to freedom, was only then
beginning. They ignored Frederick Douglass' ad-
monition more than a half century earlier that only
in struggle is there progress. One must recall W. E.
B. DuBois' words of 1903 describing Washington's
"mistakes and shortcomings,"

> So far as [Washington] apologizes for injustice
> . . . does not rightly value the privilege and
> duty of voting, belittles the emasculating effects
> of caste distinctions, and opposes the higher
> training and ambition of our brighter minds
> . . . we must unceasingly and firmly oppose
> them.

And one must remember that, more than a century after the Emancipation and almost seven dec-
ades after the optimistic message of *A New Negro*

for a New Century, the black American is still asking "Freedom? When?" and still looking forward to that day when, with Martin Luther King, Jr., we will all say "God almighty, Freedom, at last."

Daniel Walden
PROFESSOR OF AMERICAN STUDIES
PENNSYLVANIA STATE UNIVERSITY

A NEW NEGRO FOR A
NEW CENTURY

BOOKER T. WASHINGTON.

A NEW NEGRO FOR A NEW CENTURY

AN ACCURATE AND UP-TO-DATE RECORD OF THE UPWARD STRUGGLES OF THE NEGRO RACE

The Spanish-American War, Causes of It; Vivid Descriptions of Fierce Battles; Superb Heroism and Daring Deeds of the Negro Soldier

"COLORED OFFICERS OR NO COLORED SOLDIERS"
THE CLOSING OF THE WAR AND THE PEACE TREATY

EDUCATION
INDUSTRIAL SCHOOLS, COLLEGES, UNIVERSITIES AND THEIR RELATIONSHIP TO THE RACE PROBLEM

BY

PROF. BOOKER T. WASHINGTON

RECONSTRUCTION AND INDUSTRIAL ADVANCEMENT
BY
N. B. WOOD, THE HISTORIAN

THE COLORED WOMAN AND HER PART IN RACE REGENERATION
The Names and Location of the Clubs in the National Association of Colored Women of the United States and their Benefits to Our Sisters in Black

BY THE FAMOUS CLUB WOMAN, WRITER AND AUTHOR

FANNIE BARRIER WILLIAMS

MAGNIFICENTLY ILLUSTRATED

MANUFACTURED BY
AMERICAN PUBLISHING HOUSE
352, 354, 356 DEARBORN STREET
CHICAGO, ILL.

INTRODUCTION.

This book has been rightly named "A NEW NEGRO FOR A NEW CENTURY." The Negro of to-day is in every phase of life far advanced over the Negro of 30 years ago. In the following pages the progressive life of the Afro-American people has been written in the light of achievements that will be surprising to people who are ignorant of the enlarging life of these remarkable people.

In the succeeding pages, both History and Reminiscence of the Afro-American have been collected in attractive form. The stories given have been gathered from the lips of the heroes themselves. Stories, which once woven into the text-books of the Nation, will obtain for the brave contemporaries of our own times places in history along with those of our heroic forefathers. To these reminiscences gathered fresh from the field, the colored pupil and historian of this new Century must turn for their narrative.

Sectionalism, which threatened the disruption of the Union in 1861, has been banished forever. The cries of an enthralled and afflicted people have been answered and humanity has been redeemed.

The numberless histories of the Spanish-American War that have been published and which all have given national praise to the white soldiers, the patriotism, the valor and bravery of the colored soldiers has scarcely, if ever, been mentioned. I hope that these chapters will be accepted as an authentic statement of the thrilling experiences and daring acts of the brave black men, both regulars and volunteers, who faced the perilous exploits of war with indomitable courage and have made what ought to be an imperishable impress upon the whole country, teaching a lesson in patriotism, which speaks volumes for the stability of our struggling race.

The stand that our colored soldiers took throughout the war is discussed pro and con in the following pages.   All the colored regiments and officers that were sent to Cuba, as well as the regiments and officers which were afterwards sent to the Philippine Islands, are carefully and correctly listed herein.

The section on Education is especially apt at a time when the American people have begun to speculate as to the value of the last 30 years of education among the colored people.   As on all questions relative to the race problem, Prof. Booker T. Washington is especially original and helpful in giving the right point of view in estimating the value of the education already given to the Negro and the kind of education most needed.   The race is fortunate in having so masterful a man to present these subjects with a thoroughness and authority of an Historian.

Mr. Wood's chapters reciting the achievements of the Negro from the days of reconstruction are full of interest and happy surprises.

The club movement among the colored women of the country, written by Mrs. Fannie Barrier Williams, the well-known club woman and newspaper correspondent, will be found to be one of the most interesting parts of the book.   Nothing in the whole book represents so distinctively the new life of this progressive race as the ambitions, the social energy, and achievements of colored women in the organized efforts for social betterment.

This is the first attempt to publish in permanent form a history of the progressive life of the colored women of America, with the names and locations of all the clubs belonging to the National Association. These clubs are composed of some of the best women in the country and their location will prove of inestimable value to women traveling unprotected or as strangers in any part of the country. We have been frequently requested to furnish just such a helpful directory of women's clubs.

The photographs contained in this book make a most pleasing gallery of intelligent and progressive men, and strong, intellectual and charming women.

J. E. MacB.

CONTENTS.

ILLUSTRATIONS.

A NEW NEGRO FOR A NEW CENTURY.

CHAPTER I.

CAUSE OF THE SPANISH-AMERICAN WAR.

At bottom it will be found that most wars between nations have had a basis in self-interest or in sentiment. Territorial encroachment in one phase and another has been the provocation of most wars in Europe and Asia and Africa since the breaking up of the Roman Empire, which itself had been built up and consolidated by the systematic conquest of weaker tribes and nations. The wars of the Crusaders, the War of the Reformation, and the French Revolution in its initial stages, were exceptions to the rule. They were primarily wars based on sentiment—religious sentiment, humane sentiment, "the rights of man," as some of the demagogues—of whom the American, Thomas Paine, was one of the most forceful, conspicuous and industrious—of the French Revolution were wont to characterize it.

Our own War of the Rebellion, one of the greatest wars of modern times, when the numbers engaged in it and the extent of territory affected are considered, was primarily a war based on sentiment. The long but peaceful contest of the Abolitionists against the Slave Power had aroused the whole country, so that everywhere, in every State in the Union, there was a sharp division of opinion among the people, often extending to the home circle; but it is highly probable that the question would still have remained unsettled, and that we should now be agitating it, if the Slave Power had been content to allow slave territory to remain restricted to the Southern States. When it reached out to invade free soil through the Fugitive Slave Law and to force Kansas into the Union as a slave State, for the purpose of keeping even the balance of political power between the free and slave States, then the question passed beyond the stage of sentiment, in which the slave was little thought of or considered, and became one of selfish interest on the part both of the North and the South. The free labor of the Northern States, and all the States not in the slave group are so considered here, would not tolerate the competition of slave labor, and upon this issue the contending sections came to open conflict.

It is true always, however, that "God makes the wrath of man to serve him," and out of the War of the Rebellion the slave fought his way to freedom. What a glorious record the Afro-American made in that war! It is one of the brightest pages in all history. In the early stages of the war he was not even allowed to drive the teams or to throw up breastworks for the Union army; before the close of the war he was a regularly enlisted soldier to the number of 200,000, who had fought with such valor, such heroism, from Battery Wagner to Fort Fisher, from Newmarket Heights to Petersburg, that when the victorious Union army at last

CHAS. E. YOUNG,
First Lieutenant of Regular Army, Graduate of West Point
Academy, and Major of Volunteers in Cuba.
13

marched into Richmond, the fallen and deserted capitol of the Lost Cause, he was accorded the place of honor at the head of the column!   In the sententious language of General Benjamin F. Butler—who first declared the straggling refugees to be "contraband of war" and put them to work— "the colored troops fought nobly."   So they did; so nobly that never more in the lifetime of our grand Republic will a patriotic white soldier refuse to allow a black soldier to drink out of his canteen, as Colonel Theodore Roosevelt of the Rough Riders expressed it, after fateful San Juan Hill, thirty-six years after Colonel Robert Gould Shaw was "buried with his 'niggers' " in the silver sands of Morris Island.

The Spanish-American war was precipitated by a sentiment of revenge and retaliation, more than as a matter of justice to the struggling Cubans. It would be too much to say that the United States would not have been forced ultimately to put a period to Spanish rule on the American continent, as the nature of that rule was not only barbarous and inhuman to the last degree, "the open sore of the century," but it was a heavy expense to this country in the necessity it entailed of preserving the neutrality laws—policing the coast to prevent blockade running with munitions of war and the like—and in the interruption to commerce which the periodical uprising of the Cubans against Spanish rule it made necessary.   How expensive to this country this constant interruption of trade relations was for more than half a century, it is not easy to estimate, but it is one of the impelling considerations in the declaration of war which cannot be overlooked. Of course, at bottom, the savage methods of warfare adopted by the Spaniards against the Cubans not only shocked the people of the United States, but of the world, and did more to create sympathy for the struggling Cubans than anything else. Weylerism became the synonym of barbarous warfare all over the globe, and will perhaps secure a permanent place in the copious lierature of brutality.

Then the heroic struggles of the Cubans for independence in the Ten Years' War, beginning in 1868, and the last war begun in 1895, appealed to all that is chivalric and noble in the American character. Maximo Gomez, the grand old commander-in-chief of the Cuban forces, and Antonio Maceo, the Phil Sheridan of the Cubans, the invincible mulatto leader, who gave his life for Cuba as his eight brothers have done before him, and Quintin Bandera, "the black thunderbolt," and Jose Marti and a hundred others, by their brilliancy and tenacity and humanity, invited the sympathy of Christian mankind everywhere. What a magnificent galaxy of military heroes the Cubans have furnished to the history of Liberty! It is unmatched in the annals of any land, except our own. It will forever remain the chief pride and glory of the people of Cuba, whatever fate the future may have in store for them, and they deserve the best.

But the American people were reluctant to take any part in the internal affairs of a friendly power, such as Spain was. They could not do so, in the absence of justifiable provocation, without exciting the suspicion and perhaps the open antagonism of European powers in sympathy with the Spanish crown and jealous of the growing power of the United States. Great pressure was brought to bear on President Grant in the Ten Years' War to interpose the power of the United States between the belligerents, but he steered clear of entangling alliances, contenting himself with cleaving close to the advice given by George Washington when he retired to Mount Vernon, and insisting upon a strict observance of the Monroe Doctrine, both of which, as a result of the Spanish-American War, have got "lost in the shuffle," so to speak, whether for national weal or woe remains to be seen. When the war of 1895 broke out it was not expected that it would last long, and the people of the United States were disposed to allow Spain a reasonable time to suppress it. President Cleveland was decidedly opposed to interference on the part of the United States between Spain and the insurgents. Nevertheless, in February, 1896, Congress passed the following joint resolutions:

"Be it resolved by the Senate and the House of Representatives of the United States of America, that in the opinion of Congress a condition of public war exists between the Government of Spain and the Government for some time maintained by force of arms by the people of Cuba; and that the United States should maintain a strict neutrality between the contending powers, according to each all the rights of belligerents in the ports and territory of the United States.

"Resolved, further, that the friendly offices of the United States should be offered by the President to the Spanish Government for the recognition of the independence of Cuba."

GEN. MAXIMO GOMEZ,
Commander-in-Chief of the Cuban Army in the **Struggle**
for Freedom.

The two years intervening between 1896, when the joint resolution was adopted, and 1898, were years of momentous events in Cuba and of diplomatic friction between the United States and Spain, of which the recall of the Spanish minister, De Lome, in February, for writing a disparaging letter about President McKinley, was an incident. Indeed the tension between the two countries grew more and more strained as the conflict in Cuba proceeded. A large section of the American people and press insisted upon American intervention, which clamor was persistently resented by the haughty Spanish Government. But President McKinley, like President Cleveland, was determined to avert war if possible. He used the great powers of his high office in the cause of peace. But there is "a Divinity that shapes our ends, rough hew them as we may."

On the 25th of January, 1898, the battleship Maine glided into the harbor of Havana. She went there on an errand of peace as the representative of a friendly power. She was located in the harbor by representatives of the Spanish Government, who knew where the torpedo mines were located. On the 15th of February the battleship Maine was blown to atoms by a floating mine, together with 266 American sailors, of whom more than thirty were Afro-Americans. A chronicler of the incident says: "A wave of horror and indignation swept over the country. The belief was instinctive that the act was the product of treachery. The fury of the people was restrained only by the urgent request of the Captain of the Maine in a dispatch to the Navy Department, that "judgment be suspended until an official investigation could be had."

The board of inquiry appointed by the President reported that "the loss of the Maine was not in any respect due to fault or negligence on the part of any of the officers or members of her crew; that the ship was destroyed by an explosion of a submarine mine, which caused the partial explosion of two or more of her forward magazines; and that no evidence has been obtained fixing the responsibility for the destruction of the Maine upon any person or persons." By the time this report was submitted the war fever was intense. Congress had appropriated $50,000,000 for the national defense, and the President fought for delay in order that the country might be prepared when the issue should be joined. March 28 the President submitted to Congress the findings of the board of inquiry in the destruction of the Maine. Consul-General Lee left Havana April 10, thus severing diplomatic relations with the Spanish authority in the island. April 18, 1898, Congress adopted the following declaration of war, which was signed by the President April 20:

"Whereas, The abhorrent conditions which have existed for more than three years in the Island of Cuba, so near our own borders, have shocked the moral sense of the people of the United States, have been a disgrace to Christian civilization, culminating as they have in the destruction of a United States battleship with 266 of its officers and crew, while on a friendly visit in the harbor of Havana, and cannot longer be endured, as has been set forth by the President of the United States in his mes-

sage to Congress of April 11, 1898, upon which the
action of Congress was invited; therefore,

"Resolved, By the Senate and House of Representatives of the United States of America, in Congress assembled—

"First—That the people of the Island of Cuba
are, and of right ought to be, free and independent.

"Second—That it is the duty of the United
States to demand, and the Government of the
United States does hereby demand, that the Government of Spain at once relinquish its authority
and government in the Island of Cuba, and withdraw its land and naval forces from Cuba and
Cuban waters.

"Third—That the President of the United States
be, and he hereby is, directed and empowered to
use the entire land and naval forces of the United
States, and to call into the actual service of the
United States the militia of the several States, to
such extent as may be necessary to carry these resolutions into effect.

"Fourth—That the United States hereby dis-
claims any disposition or intention to exercise
sovereignty, jurisdiction or control over said island,
except for the pacification thereof, and asserts its
determination when that is completed to leave the
government and control of the island to its people."

Minister Stewart L. Woodford was not allowed
by the Spanish Government to present the ultima-
tum of the United States, his passports having been
handed to him at 7 o'clock in the morning of April
21, and he left Madrid, from which severance of
diplomatic relations dates the actual beginning of

LIEUTENANT JOHN H. ALEXANDER,
Graduate of West Point.

the war. April 24 the Queen Regent formally communicated to the Spanish Cortes the existence of war. April 25 the American Congress passed the following bill without a division:

"Be it enacted by the Senate and House of Representatives of the United States of America in Congress assembled—

"First—That war be, and the same is hereby declared to exist, and that war has existed since the 21st day of April, A. D. 1898, including said day, between the United States of America and the Kingdom of Spain.

"Second—That the President of the United States be, and he hereby is, directed and empowered to use the entire land and naval forces of the United States, and to call into the actual service of the United States the militia of the several States, to such extent as may be necessary to carry this act into effect."

April 21 the blockade of the ports of Cuba was proclaimed and Admiral Sampson's squadron was ordered to enforce it, and on April 23 a call for 125,000 volunteers was issued. June 9 the House passed a war revenue act and the Senate concurred in it June 10. The first decisive battle of the war was fought in Manila Bay, Philippine Islands, May 1, 1898, when Admiral George Dewey's fleet destroyed the Spanish fleet.

CHAPTER II.

AFRO-AMERICAN VOLUNTEERS.

Never before since the war of 1812 had the Republic had an opportunity to test the temper of the people as to their loyalty in facing a foreign enemy. The Civil War had estranged the sections almost as much as the agitation of the slave question had; for it left a bitterness in its results—such as the manumission and enfranchisement of the late slaves and the reconstruction policy, forced upon the country by that uncompromising radical, Representative Thaddeus Stevens, of Pennsylvania —which seemed to be intensified rather than tempered by time. The white people of the Southern States resented the entire policy forced upon them as the result of the war, and combined against the Northern States in politics, State and National, for the purpose of bringing to naught, as far as such combination could effect it the policy so forced upon them. The bitterness rankled in their souls all the more as the war had destroyed well nigh all their wealth, along with it their slave property, which had become co-equal in citizenship; a transformation in itself of the most radical and provoking character, from the standpoint of those who, for two centuries and more, had been taught to and did regard the African as less than human, as simply property.

But the declaration of war with Spain was responded to with a fervor and enthusiasm in every

State of the Union, among all the race elements of
the population, that put at rest forever any linger-
ing suspicion that the Republic would be divided in
sentiment in the face of a foreign foe.   Nowhere
in the country was more enthusiasm displayed than
in the Southern States.   The old flag, the stars
and stripes, for the first time since 1860 was displayed everywhere in the Southern States.   This
was, too all the more surprising, when it is remembered that of the total Cuban population of 1,631,-
687, 528,998 are classed as negroes and mulattoes,
and that these latter, in all the revolutions in Cuba,
have been, for the most part, the inspiration in
council and backbone in the field, for no one will
dispute the power and influence in civil life of such
men as the brilliant journalist and agitator, Juan
Guelberto Gomez, who lived in exile as much as in
Cuba, and in military life of such men as General
Antonio Maceo and his eight brothers, General
Flores Crombet, a veteran of the Ten Years' War,
who was killed early in the war of 1895, General
Quintin Bandera and a host of others, less re-
nowned but equally devoted to the cause of Cuba
and its independence of Spanish tyranny.   When
these facts are properly weighed against the pronounced prejudice of the Southern whites against
people of the African race, the enthusiasm with
which the whites of the Southern States espoused
the cause of the Cubans and responded to the
President's call for State troops and volunteers
would seem to be inexplicable, and is upon the
surface.

It may be that the course pursued in the first
instance by President McKinley in retaining Gen-

GENERAL ANTONIO MACEO.
This late General was second in command of the Cuban
Army.

eral Fitz'iugh Lee, of Virginia, who was appointed
by President Cleveland, as Consul-General at
Havana, when Republicans all over the country
were clamoring for his removal, had much to do
with arousing the enthusiasm of the white people
of the Southern States in the Cuban "war for independence and humanity."   Very true it is that the
President's course in retaining General Lee at
Havana, and in other acts of liberalism shown by
him towards the white people of the Southern
States, did much to enlist the active sympathy and
support of the Southern Senators and Representatives in Congress in the war policy, most of them
voting the $50,000,000 war credit and supporting
other ne essary measures for the successful prosecution of the war.

Then in the distribution of military honors the
President was extremely generous to the whites
of the South, who were given three of the Major-
Generals of Volunteers, viz.:   General Fitzhugh
Lee, General Joseph Wheeler, General M. C. Butler.   They also fared equally well in the distribution of all the other military appointments.   Because of all these reasons, creditable alike to the
President and the white men of the South, the bitterness engendered by the Civil War, which had
so long estranged the sections, was greatly soft-
ened, and made the Spanish-American War one of
the most popular in the history of the country.
The white South saw that it was treated as fairly
as the white North, and when men have that conviction they are always liable to display a magna-
nimity and enthusiasm in a given cause which are
the best portents of its probable success.   At any

rate, it proved to be so in the Spanish-American War, as in all our wars of the past, and will do so in all our wars of the future. A people numerically as strong and sustained by such inexhaustible and diversified material resources as those of the United States, when moved by a common purpose and acting together, must prove, all things being equal, invincible in a conflict with any existing single foreign power. It has always been so in the past— in the two wars with Great Britain, in the Mexican War and in the Spanish-American War.

The white people of the Southern States, although uniformly opposed in politics to the administration of President McKinley, have no room whatever for complaint in the matter of their treatment in the Spanish War. They were given their full share of the military and naval honors, of high and low degree, and the quotas of their States were accepted upon an equal footing with those of the other States of the Union. Nor was this confidence misplaced. As Consul-General at Havana, General Lee sustained the honor and dignity of the Republic with marked courage and ability; Major-General Joseph Wheeler came out of the conflict as one of the heroes of the war, as did also Lieutenant Henry Pearson Hobson, whose sinking of the Merrimac at the mouth of Santiago harbor was one of the most daring and heroic exploits in naval warfare. It is interesting to note here that in the Santiago campaign Major-General Wheeler had in his command one squadron of four troops each of the fighting black Ninth and Tenth Cavalry, United States Regulars. Thirty-six years before the little General was leading Confederate soldiers in the effort to perpetuate the slavery of black men and giving scant quarter to black soldiers in the uniform of the United States who came his way. There was no more significant feature in the Spanish-American War than General Wheeler leading black regulars against the Spaniards to free black Cubans.

The Afro-American citizens of the United States were as enthusiastic as others to enlist and fight. Everywhere, in the North and the South, they showed willingness and eagerness to enlist. There were no cowards among them, as there had been none in the Civil War, and as there will be none in any other crisis the Republic may be called upon to face. But they were to be subjected to very great and mortifying disappointment. Under the conditions of the first call for volunteers only the organized militia of the States was acceptable. This rule barred the Afro-American out entirely. And the President had not designated any Afro-Americans to be general staff or line officers. In the Northern and Western States the Afro-Americans are so relatively few in number that comparatively few of them are connected with the State militia, those in so great a State as New York, for instance, being without any representation whatever. A few were represented in other Northern States, to whom appropriate reference will be made at the proper time.

The Afro-Americans of the Northern and Western States who thus found themselves excluded from participation in the war, because they were not represented, except in isolated instances, in the State militia, more generally styled the National Guard, made frantic and heroic efforts to break through the stone wall and get into the war anyhow. Volunteer regiments were raised in many instances, and first offered to the State authorities, which, under the law governing the National Guard, they could not accept. Tender was then made to the President direct, who referred all such applications to the War Department, and they were not heard of any more. The War Department was not in a position to accept volunteers who were not designated by the States. Congress undertook to remedy the defect by authorizing the formation of ten immune regiments, but this came to naught, because the War Department insisted upon giving the staff and line officers (above the grade of second lieutenants) to white men. The Afro-Americans would not tolerate this; consequently only four Afro-American regiments were recruited under this act—the Seventh, Eighth, Ninth and Tenth—and they were officered by white men under protest and threats of rebellion on the part of the men. None of these regiments saw active service, although some of them did a little garrison duty in Cuba.

This question of officering Afro-American troops became a burning one during the existence of the war, and it is one now. It is doubtful if a regiment so officered could be recruited in any State by State or Federal authority.

The writer of this history is under obligation to Congressman George H. White, of North Carolina, for securing a complete list of the Afro-American volunteers mustered into the service from the Ad-

jutant-General of the United States Army, which
is as follows:

Third Alabama Volunteer Infantry, First Brigade, second division, Fourth Army Corps.

Eighth Illinois Volunteer Infantry, not brigaded.

Companies A and B, Indiana Volunteer Infantry, not brigaded.

Thirty-third Kansas Volunteer Infantry, not
brigaded.

Ninth Ohio Battalion, Volunteer Infantry, Second Brigade, first division, Second Army Corps.

Sixth Virginia Volunteer Infantry, Third Brigade, second division, First Army Corps (transferred
later to the Third Brigade, first division, First
Army Corps.)

Seventh United States Volunteer Infantry, Third
Brigade, first division, First Army Corps.

Eighth United States Volunteer Infantry, not
brigaded.

Ninth United States Volunteer Infantry, not
brigaded.

Tenth United States Volunteer Infantry, First
Brigade, third division, First Army Corps.

The Third North Carolina Volunteer Infantry
was called out by Governor Russell and went into
camp at Camp Russell, but it was not mustered into
the United States service. It was officered
throughout by Afro-Americans, James H. Young
being the colonel commanding. The only other
regiment so officered was the Eighth Illinois, Colonel J. R. Marshall commanding. This regiment
did garrison duty in the Province of Santiago for
some time after the war, and Colonel Marshall
acted for a time as governor of San Luis. The

JAMES H. YOUNG,
Colonel Third North Carolina Volunteer Infantry, Raleigh,
N. C.

Ninth Ohio Battalion was commanded by Brevet Major Charles Young, a lieutenant in the regular army, and the only Afro-American holding such a position in the regular army. He is a graduate of the West Point Military Academy. His command was stationed first at Camp Alger, Va., and then transferred to Camp Meade, Pa., and from there to Summerville, S. C., where it was finally mustered out. The Twenty-third Kansas was officered by Afro-Americans, with the exception of colonel and lieutenant colonel. The best-known captain of the regiment, which did garrison duty in Cuba for a short while, was John L. Waller, ex-United States Consul to Madagascar, who got into trouble with the French authorities after he was superseded in the consulship by a Mr. Witte, of Georgia, presumably because of a valuable concession of rubber land which he had secured from the Queen of Madagascar before the French assumed the protectorate of the island. The Third Alabama and Sixth Virginia battalions were mustered into the service with Afro-American officers, but for some unexplained reason these were changed for white officers, and the action came near causing a riot in both regiments. The four immune regiments were officered by white men, with the exception of the second lieutenants.

Company L, Sixth Massachusetts Volunteer Infantry, has the distinction of being the only Afro-American company mustered into the service as a part of a white regiment. It was commanded by Captain Williams, and went to Porto Rico with the expedition commanded by Major-General Nelson A. Miles.

The President commissioned about one hundred Afro-American second lieutenants in the volunteer service. Two paymasters were appointed, with the rank of major—John R. Lynch, of Mississippi, an ex-Congressman and ex-Fourth Auditor of the Treasury, and Richard R. Wright of Georgia, President of the State Agricultural and Mechanical College. Mr. Wright resigned after the war, but Major Lynch has been continued in the service. Rev. C. T. Walker, of Georgia, and Rev. Richard Carroll, of South Carolina, were commissioned as chaplains in the volunteer service.

The absence of Afro-American troops from the quotas of the Southern States will be noted. The explanation is that it is not the policy of those States to comprehend such troops in their militia. Virginia, South Carolina, North Carolina, Georgia and Alabama were exceptions.

The governors of Virginia, North Carolina and Alabama offered these troops, with their Afro-American officers, when it was necessary to fill out the quotas of their States called for by the President. Those of Virginia and Alabama were mustered into the United States service, but the officers were finally changed to white men. The North Carolina regiment was not mustered into the service of the United States. The governors of South Carolina and Georgia refused to offer any such troops, with the proviso that they would do so when there were no longer any white troops to offer.

We hope the colored troops in the Philippines, which are the Twenty-fourth and Twenty-fifth Infantry, portions of the Ninth and Tenth Cavalry, and the Forty-eighth and Forty-ninth Volunteer Regiments, officered by colored men, will give a good account of themselves.

There is no room for doubt that if the war had been prolonged and Afro-American volunteers could have faced the enemy, they would have given a good account of themselves, as did the volunteers in the Civil War and the four regiments of regulars in the Santiago campaign under Major-General William R. Shafter.

COL. JOHN R. MARSHALL,
Colonel of the Eighth Illinois Infantry in the Spanish-
American War.

CHAPTER III.

There are four regiments of Afro-American soldiers in the regular army of the United States. They are the Twenty-fourth and Twenty-fifth Infantry and the Ninth and Tenth Cavalry. These four regiments or parts of them were fortunate enough to go to Cuba and to participate in all the hard fighting there from the beginning to the end of the brief campaign. They did not go to Cuba to win glory or to demonstrate the courage and capacity of their race in the tent and the field. They went to Cuba already covered with glory, earned in a hundred battles in the Civil War and in all the Indian wars in the far West, from 1866, when the regiments were first mustered in the service at New Orleans, to the battle of San Juan Hill, thirty-two years later, in 1898.

It seems incredible, in view of the record these regiments have made in the regular army, and the record the Afro-American regiments made in the Civil War, a record any race may well be proud of, that there should have been any one in the Republic who doubted the capacity and courage of Afro-American soldiers; and yet there were plenty of people who did so, and who were greatly surprised and taken back when these veterans in Cuba, these "smoked Yankees," as the affrighted Spaniards called them—

"Storm'd at with shot and shell,
While horse and hero fell,
They who had fought so well,
Came through the jaws of Death,
Back from the mouth of Hell,
All that was left of them—"

emerging on the top of El Caney and San Juan
Hill, in a mad charge, singing as they mowed down
the enemy: "There'll Be a Hot Time in the Old
Town To-night." The incredulity can only be ac-
counted for upon the theory that in the main one
generation is ignorant of what another did, despite
the activity of the daily and periodical press and of
the making of books without number. Then, too,
there is a deep-seated disposition among the white
Americans to discredit the Afro-Americans, however worthily they acquit themselves, in war or
peace. This disposition was shown in a very
marked and provoking degree in the news dis-
patches from Cuba during the days of active hostilities, when the part taken by Afro-American soldiers was minimized or slurred over, except in rare
instances. It was not until after the war was over,
and those who took part in it returned to the
United States and gave their side of the story that
the truth and the whole truth came out.

On the morning of the 24th of June, 1898, the
convoy of the Fifth Army Corps arrived off Guan-
tanamo Bay, and on June 22 the disembarkation
was begun at Baiquiri. By the evening of the
24th the troops were all ashore. The Fifth Army
Corps was divided into the following brigades:

THE SANTIAGO CAMPAIGN.

Fifth Army Corps, Major-General William R. Shafter commanding. First Division, Major-General J. F. Kent commanding.

First Brigade—Sixth and Sixteenth United States Infantry and Seventy-first New York Volunteer Infantry.

Second Brigade—Second, Tenth and Twenty-first United States Infantry.

Third Brigade—Ninth, Thirteenth and Twenty-fourth United States Infantry.

Second Division, Major-General H. W. Lawton commanding.

First Brigade—Eighth and Twenty-second United States Infantry and Second Massachusetts Volunteer Infantry.

Second Brigade—First, Fourth and Twenty-fifth United States Infantry.

Third Brigade—Seventh, Twelfth and Seventeenth United States Infantry.

Division of dismounted cavalry, Major-General Joseph Wheeler commanding.

One squadron of four troops drawn from the Second, Third, Fifth, Sixth, Ninth and Tenth United States Cavalry.

One squadron of four troops drawn from the First United States Volunteer Cavalry (Rough Riders).

The artillery consisted of Light Batteries E and K, First United States Artillery, and Batteries A and F, Second United States Artillery, commanded by Major J. W. Dillenback.

Reinforcements composed of General Duffield's

DR. J. WEBB CURTIS,
Physician and Assistant Surgeon of the Eighth Illinois in
Cuba and the Forty-eighth United States Volun-
teers in the Philippines.

brigade joined General Shafter later, and consisted of the Thirty-third and Thirty-fourth Michigan Volunteer Infantry, and parts of two dismounted squadrons of cavalry. Lomia's battery of heavy artillery from the Fifth Regiment, United States Artillery, also arrived with six siege mortars, but they were not disembarked.

The number of officers in the expedition was 815, and 16,072 men.

The Spanish troops offered but slight resistance, and General Lawton's division reached Siboney June 23; they pushed forward, and the following day the place was occupied by General Kent's division. The orders were that Lawton's division should, on June 24, take up a defensive position between Siboney and Santiago; Kent's division was to be held near Santiago; General Bates was to support General Lawton; General Wheeler's cavalry division was to occupy the rear on the road to Baiquiri. General Young's brigade of Wheeler's division, consisting of part of the Tenth United States Cavalry and two battalions of the First Volunteer Cavalry (known as the Rough Riders), passed Lawton on the night of the 23-24, and was in consequence in advance on the morning of the 24th. On the Santiago road, some three miles from Siboney, there is a strong natural position called Las Guasimas. The Spaniards were posted here in considerable strength, and Young's brigade was taken by surprise. After a short but fierce engagement the enemy was driven from its position.

It was in this engagement that, it is said, the Tenth Cavalry saved the Rough Riders from annihilation, but Colonel Theodore Roosevelt in his story of his regiment denies this, and also that there was any surprise. A great many members of the Tenth make the claim and many privates among the Rough Riders allowed it. In his story of the engagement Colonel Roosevelt says: "Our men behaved very well indeed—white regulars, colored regulars and Rough Riders alike. The newspaper press failed to do full justice to the white regulars, in my opinion, from the simple reason that everybody knew they would fight, whereas there had been a good deal of question as to how the Rough Riders, who were volunteer troops, and the Tenth Cavalry, who were colored, would behave; so there was a tendency to exalt our deeds at the expense of those of the First Regiment, whose courage and good conduct were taken for granted."

Captain Charles G. Ayers made the following report to General Young, June 27, 1898 (annual report of the Major-General commanding the army, 1898, p. 355):

"Sir: I have the honor to report that on the 24th instant two commissioned officers and fifty-three enlisted men of Troop E, Tenth Cavalry, went into action, with other troops of the brigade, against the regular Spanish infantry, and were placed by General Young in person in support of Captain J. W. Watson's (Tenth Cavalry) two Hotchkiss guns, and also to support the troops in our front should they need it. The position was in plain view of the Spaniards, who occupied a high ridge and had the exact range; but pursuant to their instructions they held their position one hour and a quarter without firing a shot, for fear of firing upon their own men. Their coolness and fine discipline were superb.

"In connection herewith, it gives me great pleasure to call attention to the great gallantry of Second Lieutenant George Vidmer, Tenth Cavalry, and Privates Burr Neal, W. R. Nelson, Augustus Walby and A. C. White, who, under a heavy fire, came to my assistance in carrying Major Bell, First Cavalry, to a place of safety, he being shot through the leg below the knee and his leg broken."

The Rough Riders occupied the left column, while the regulars, including one squadron of the Tenth and one of the First Cavalry, occupied the right column; of the latter Brigadier-General B. M. Young says (annual report of the Major-General commanding, p. 333): "The fine discipline of these particular troops was almost perfect. The ammunition expended by the two squadrons engaged in an incessant advance for one hour and fifteen minutes averaged less than ten rounds per man. The fine quality of these troops is also shown by the fact that there was not a single straggler, and in not one instance was an attempt made by any soldier to fall out in the advance to assist the wounded or carry back the dead."

General Joseph Wheeler says (Ibid. 163): "I was immediately with the troops of the First and Tenth Regular Cavalry, dismounted and personally noticed their brave and good conduct, which will be specially mentioned by General Young."

This Las Guasimas engagement cleared the way to Santiago, 964 American troops having dislodged

COL. W. A. PLEDGER,
Orator and Editor, Atlanta, Ga.

4,000 Spaniards, with the loss of 16 killed and 52 wounded.

From June 24 to June 30 the time was spent in concentrating the American troops in preparing for the advance towards Santiago, the objective point. El Caney is a small village to the northeast of Santiago, and three miles away, on the same side, were the San Juan Hills and blockhouses. The approach to the town was by that route. Lawton's, Kent's divisions and Grimes' battery were ordered to move on the hills. The dispositions were made June 30, and on the morning of July 1, at 6 o'clock, the conflict opened, with Lawton in position, Chaffee's brigade on the right, Ludlow's on the left, and Miles' in the center. The conflict soon became general. The naturally strong position of the enemy was made more so by the stone blockhouses and forts. After two hours' fighting Bates' brigade was ordered from the rear to Lawton's support. The Spaniards fought with great courage and pertinacity, but were slowly driven from their entrenchments and forced to retire. From the heights Grimes' battery played upon the San Juan blockhouses with great effect. The Spaniards used smokeless powder, and it was difficult to locate them. Wheeler's and Kent's divisions were now ordered to deploy, Wheeler to the right and Kent to the left. General Shafter tells the story of the remainder of the fighting as follows:

In the meantime Kent's division, with the exception of two regiments of Hawkins' brigade, being thus uncovered, moved rapidly to the front from the forks previously mentioned in the road, utilizing both trails, but more especially the one to the left, and, crossing the creek, formed for attack in front of San Juan Hill. During this formation the Second Brigade suffered severely. While personally superintending this movement its gallant commander, Colonel Wykoff, was killed. The command of the brigade then devolved upon Lieutenant-Colonel Worth, Thirteenth Infantry, who was soon severely wounded, and next upon Lieutenant-Colonel Liscomb, Twenty-fourth Infantry, who, five minutes later, also fell under the terrible fire of the enemy, and the command of the brigade then devolved upon Lieutenant-Colonel Ewers, Ninth Infantry.

"While the formation just described was taking place, General Kent took measures to hurry forward his rear brigade. The Tenth and Second Infantry were ordered to follow Wykoff's brigade, while the Twenty-first was sent on the right-hand road to support the First Brigade, under General Hawkins, who had crossed the stream and formed on the right of the division. The Second and Tenth Infantry, Colonel E. P. Pearson, commanding, moved forward in good order on the left of the division, passed over a green knoll, and drove the enemy back toward his trenches.

After completing their formation under a destructive fire, and advancing a short distance, both divisions found in their front a wide bottom, in which had been placed a barbed-wire entanglement, and beyond which there was a high hill, along the crest of which the enemy was strongly posted. Nothing daunted, these gallant men pushed on to drive the enemy from his chosen position, both divisions losing heavily. In this assault Colonel Hamilton, Lieutenants Smith and Shipp were killed, and Colonel Carroll, Lieutenants Thayer and Myer, all in the cavalry, were wounded."

The day closed with the Americans holding all they had gained. The fight was renewed on the morning of the 2d and the day closed with the American positions well advanced. July 3, in the morning, the fight was opened anew, but the enemy soon gave way and the firing was discontinued. At 8:30 o'clock General Shafter demanded the surrender of the Spanish army, and on July 17 this was done, there having been no fighting in the interval, pending the negotiations for the surrender. The Spanish troops surrendered numbered 22,000.

The American losses in the three days' fighting —July 1, 2 and 3—were as follows: Twenty-two officers and 208 men killed; 81 officers and 1,203 men wounded; 79 missing.

Some of the exploits of the Afro-American troopers will be told in the following chapter.

CHAPTER IV.

THE AFRO-AMERICAN REGULARS IN CUBA.

In all the fierce fighting of July 1, 2 and 3, in assaulting and carrying by storm the heights of El Caney and the blockhouses on the top of the San Juan hills the members of the four Afro-American regiments displayed a courage and heroism equal to that of their white comrades in arms. The writer has searched in vain through the reports of staff and line officers, published in the annual report of the Major-General commanding, for an instance of cowardice or infraction of discipline. They all uniformly report that men and officers alike shared the hazards and the glory of the conflict with the courage, intrepidity and cheerfulness which have always marked the regular soldiers of the army of the United States. In all the voluminous reports there is but one discordant note, and that was the failure of the Seventy-first New York Volunteers to move into action as ordered, owing to the conduct of their officers, all of whom have since been removed from their commands. But not a murmur against the conduct of the black regulars is to be found in the reports; on the contrary, there are words upon words of praise from their gallant commanders, all of them whites, and graduates of the West Point Military Academy, who displayed a pardonable and praiseworthy pride in the conduct of the brave men in their commands. This high and unimpeachable testimony is a priceless legacy not only to the Afro-American people, who have so many prejudices to fight down, but to the white American people, whose honor and glory and safety and pride are wrapped up in the brave sons who wear the uniform of the Republic, on land and sea, who go forth to fight the enemy.

Colonel Leonard Wood, commanding Second Brigade, Cavalry Division, says (Major-General's Report, p. 343): "In regard to the conduct of the brigade as a whole, I can only say that it was superb. That dismounted cavalry should have been able to charge regular infantry in strong position, supported by artillery and the general lay of the land, seems almost incredible, yet this is exactly what the Cavalry Division of the Fifth Army Corps did in this fight, passing over a long zone of fire and charging steep hills, topped with works and blockhouses."

Lieutenant-Colonel A. S. Daggett, Twenty-fifth Infantry, commanding, says (Ibid, p. 386): "All officers and men behaved gallantly." (Ibid, 388): "The Twenty-fifth Infantry caused the surrender of the stone fort." General Chaffee disputes this (Ibid, p. 388), and awards the credit to the Twelfth Infantry. He says: "The troops arriving at the stone fort (El Caney) were there in the following order: Twelfth Infantry, which took the place; the command of General Bates, some minutes later; the Twenty-fifth Infantry. A captain of the Twenty-fifth Infantry claimed the capture of the place from me at the time and on the ground, and I told him then that his proposition was absurd, and stated to him the order in which the troops arrived." At any rate, the three commanders must have reached the fort pretty close together.

PAUL LAURENCE DUNBAR,
The Poet-Laureate of the Negro Race.

Captain A. C. Markley, Twenty-fourth Infantry, commanding regiment, says (Ibid, 434): "On the march to the front this regiment was the rear one of the three in its brigade. After coming under fire, it was ordered to take a position on the left, and marched about a mile by the flank, under fire, to its place; advanced over the flat the same as the other regiments assisting in the capture of Fort San Juan, getting on the top of the hill among the first, with a creditable number of men of its small companies, and in time to get men killed and to silence one gun by volley fire." Captain Henry Wygant, Twenty-fourth Infantry, commanding Second Battalion, says (Ibid., 435): The gallantry and bearing shown by the officers and soldiers of the regiment under this trying ordeal was such that it has every reason to be proud of its record."

At the Lenox Lyceum, in New York, October 14, 1898, Colonel Theodore Roosevelt (First United States Volunteer Cavalry, the "Rough Riders"), speaking to a mass meeting favorable to his candidacy for governor of New York, said: "Now a word as to the colored man in military life. I'm glad to see here one or two men in uniform. (Cheers.) In fact, I rather think that however any other colored man may vote, you won't get a trooper of the Ninth or Tenth Cavalry to vote against a Rough Rider. (Great cheering.) And the feeling is reciprocated. As I heard one of the Rough Riders say after the charge at San Juan: 'Well, the Ninth and Tenth men are all right. They can drink out of our canteens.'

"That night my men had lain in reserve for an

uncomfortable hour, got the order to go forward, and we struck the Ninth Cavalry and in the first charge, on what we called Kettle Hill, they and we went up absolutely intermingled, so that no one could tell whether it was the Rough Riders or the men of the Ninth who came forward with the greater courage to offer their lives in the service of their country. One or two other cavalry regiments joined us on the hill and we turned our attention to the San Juan blockhouse and began volley firing until we took that. Eventually I found myself on the hill nearest the city, the highest officer there, and in command of sections of a number of cavalry regiments, including portions of the Ninth and Tenth. That night we took spades and worked at the trenches shoulder to shoulder, white and colored men together. So I had opportunities of seeing the colored troops under all circumstances—charging, lying under fire, digging in the trenches, advancing with us."

"Never did anything but advance did you?" shouted a man in the rear, and the query was greeted with applause and laughter, which increased when Colonel Roosevelt replied with a whimsical expression of face:

"Well, now that you remind me of it, I don't think we did go in the opposite direction very much. When you've been under fire with a man," he continued, "and fought side by side with him, and eaten with him when you had anything to eat, and hungered with him when you hadn't, you feel a sort of comradeship that you don't feel for any man that you have been associated with in other ways, and I don't think that any Rough Rider will ever forget the tie that binds us to the Ninth and Tenth Cavalry. (Cheers.) As I say, that gives you a sense of comradeship that nothing else can give. Of course, we feel that for all who fought with us there, regular or volunteer, and the reason why we feel that enthusiasm toward our fellow-soldiers is one which should have equal weight in civil life. It wasn't because the colored troopers were colored that we admired them any more than it was because the white cavalrymen of the First, Third and Sixth were white that we admired them. In each case it was because they were brave men, worthy of respect.

"And now, in civil life, it should be the same. I don't want to see any of our citizens claiming or receiving favors because he is of a certain race, color or creed, but I want to see every American citizen treated on his merits as a man. As the men of the Ninth and Tenth Cavalry reflected honor not only on the entire American people, but especially on those of their own race, so I hope and believe that you will honor yourselves and all your fellow-Americans by fearless and honorable discharge of the obligations of citizenship in these times of peace and if you so do your duty it is your right that you should receive the same treatment in every respect as other citizens without respect to race or creed."

In view of this pronouncement there was a very great deal of surprise when, in his story of the Rough Riders (Scribner's Magazine, April, 1899, pp. 435-436), Colonel Roosevelt published the following:

"On the hill-slope immediately around me I had

a mixed force composed of members of most of the cavalry regiments, and a few infantrymen. There was about fifty of my Rough Riders, with Lieutenants Goodrich and Carr. Among the rest were perhaps a score of colored infantrymen, but, as it happened, at this particular point, without any of their officers. No troops could have behaved better than the colored soldiers had behaved so far; but they are, of course, peculiarly dependent upon their white officers. Occasionally they produce non-commissioned officers who can take the initiative and accept responsibility precisely like the best class of whites; but this cannot be expected normally, nor is it fair to expect it. With the colored troops there should always be some of their own officers; whereas, with the white regulars, as with my own Rough Riders, experience showed that the non-commissioned officers could usually carry on the fight by themselves if they were once started, no matter whether their officers were killed or not.

*   *   *   *

"None of the white regulars or Rough Riders showed the slightest sign of weakening; but under the strain the colored infantrymen (who had none of their officers) began to get a little uneasy and to drift to the rear, either helping wounded men, or saying that they wished to find their own regiments. This I could not allow, as it was depleting my line, so I jumped up, and, walking a few yards to the rear, drew my revolver, halted the retreating soldiers, and called out to them that I appreciated the gallantry with which they had fought and would be sorry to hurt them, but that I should shoot the first man who, on any pretense whatever, went to the rear. My own men had all sat up and were watching my movements with the utmost interest; so was Captain Howze. I ended my statement to the colored soldiers by saying: 'Now, I shall be very sorry to hurt you, and you don't know whether or not I will keep my word, but my men can tell you that I always do;' whereupon my cow-punchers, hunters, and miners solemnly nodded their heads and commented in chorus, exactly as if in a comic opera, 'He always does; he always does.' This ended the trouble."

This makes very nice reading, but it is not history, in which it is always hazardous to sacrifice truth "to make a period round." It is therefore fortunate that one of the Afro-Americans who was with Colonel Roosevelt at the time and knows all about the scandalous incident he relates should write a correction of the Rough Rider's statements. Sergeant Presley Holliday, Troop B, Tenth Cavalry, says (New York Age, May 11, 1899):

"In the beginning I wish to say that from what I saw of Colonel Roosevelt in Cuba and the impression his frank countenance made on me, I cannot believe that he made the statement maliciously. I believe the Colonel thought he spoke the exact truth. But did he know that of the four officers connected with two certain troops of the Tenth Cavalry one was killed and three were so seriously wounded as to cause them to be carried from the field and the command of these two troops fell to their first sergeants, who led them triumphantly to the front? Does he know that both at La Guasimas and at San Juan Hill, the greater part of

ALEXANDER MILES,
One of the Founders of the City of Duluth, Minnesota; Successful Business Man; Head of The United Brotherhood, the First Fraternal Insurance Company to Be Organized Among Colored People.

Troop B of the Tenth Cavalry was separated from its commanding officer by the accidents of battle and was led to the front by its first sergeant?

"When we reached the enemy's works on San Juan Hill our organizations were very badly mixed, few company commanders having their whole companies or none of somebody else's company. As it was, Captain Watson, my troop commander, reached the crest of the hill with about eight or ten men of his troop, all the rest having been accidentally separated from him by the thick underbrush during the advance, and being at that time, as was subsequently shown, on the firing line under some one else, pushing to the front. We kept up the forward movement and finally halted on the heights overlooking Santiago, where Colonel Roosevelt, with a very thin line, had preceded us, and was holding the hill. Here Captain Watson told us to remain while he went to another part of the line to look for the rest of his troop. He did not come to that part of the field again.

"The Colonel made a slight error when he said his mixed command contained some colored infantry. All the colored troops in that command were cavalrymen. His command consisted mostly of Rough Riders, with an aggregate of about one troop of the Tenth Cavalry, a few of the Ninth and a few of the First Regular Cavalry, with a half-dozen officers. Every few minutes brought men from the rear, everybody seeming to be anxious to get to the firing line. For a while we kept up a desultory fire, but as we could not locate the enemy (which all the time kept up a hot fire on our position), we became disgusted and lay down and kept silent. Private Marshall was here seriously wounded while standing in plain view of the enemy trying to point them out to his comrades.

"There were frequent calls for men to carry the wounded to the rear, to go for ammunition, and as night came on, to go for rations and entrenching tools. A few colored soldiers volunteered, as did some from the Rough Riders. It then happened that two men of the Tenth were ordered to the rear by Lieutenant Fleming, Tenth Cavalry, who was then present with part of his troop, for the purpose of bringing either rations or entrenching tools, and Colonel Roosevelt, seeing so many men going to the rear, shouted to them to come back, jumped up and drew his revolver, and told the men of the Tenth that he would shoot the first man who attempted to shirk duty by going to the rear, that he had orders to hold that line and he would do so if he had to shoot every man there to do it. His own men immediately informed him that 'you won't have to shoot those men, Colonel. We know those boys.' He was also assured by Lieutenant Flemming of the Tenth that he would have no trouble keeping them there, and some of our men shouted, in which I joined, that 'we will stay with you, Colonel.' Everyone who saw the incident knew the Colonel was mistaken about our men trying to shirk duty, but well knew that he could not admit of any heavy detail from his command, so no one thought ill of the matter. Inasmuch as the Colonel came to the line of the Tenth the next day and told the men of his threat to shoot some of their members and, as he expressed it, he had seen his mistake and found them to be far different men from what he supposed, I thought he was sufficiently conscious of his error not to make so ungrateful a statement about us at a time when the nation is about to recognize our past service.

"Had the Colonel desired to note the fact he would have seen that when orders came the next day to relieve the detachment of the Tenth from that part of the field, he commanded just as many colored men at that time as he commanded at any other time during the twenty-four hours we were under his command, although colored as well as white soldiers were going and coming all day, and they knew perfectly well where the Tenth Cavalry was posted, and that it was on a line about four hundred yards further from the enemy than Colonel Roosevelt's line. Still when they obtained permission to go to the rear they almost invariably came back to the same position. Two men of my troop were wounded while at the rear for water and taken to the hospital and, of course, could not come back.

"Our men always made it a rule to join the nearest command when separated from our own, and those who had been so unfortunate as to lose their way altogether were, both colored and white, straggling up from the time the line was established until far into the night, showing their determination to reach the front.

"In explaining the desire of our men to go back to look for their comrades it should be stated that from the contour of the ground the Rough Riders were so much in advance of the Tenth Cavalry that to reach the latter regiment from the former one had really to go straight to the rear and then turn sharply to the right; and further, it is a well-known fact in this country most persons of color feel out of place when they are by force compelled to mingle with white persons, especially strangers, and although we knew we were doing our duty and would be treated well as long as we stood to the front and fought, unfortunately some of our men (and these were all recruits with less than six months' service) felt so much out of place that when the firing lulled often showed their desire to be with their commands. None of our older men did this. We knew perfectly well that we could give as much assistance there as anywhere else and that it was our duty to remain until relieved. And we did. White soldiers do not, as a rule, share this feeling with colored soldiers. The fact that a white man knows how well he can make a place for himself among colored people need not be discussed here.

"I remember an incident of a recruit of my troop with less than two months' service who had come up to our position during the evening of the 1st, having been separated from the troop during the attack on San Juan Hill. The next morning before the firing began, having seen an officer of the Tenth who had been sent to Colonel Roosevelt with a message, returning to the regiment, he signified his intention of going back with him, saying he could thus find the regiment. I remonstrated with him without avail and was only able to keep him from going by informing him of the Colonel's threat of the day before. There was no desire on the part of this soldier to shirk duty. He simply didn't know that he should not leave any part of the firing line without orders. Later, while lying in reserve behind the firing line, I had to use as much persuasion to keep him from firing over the heads of his enemies as I had to keep him with us. He remained with us until he was shot in the shoulder and had to be sent to the rear.

"I could give many other incidents of our men's devotion to duty, of their determination to stay until the death, but what's the use? Colonel Roosevelt has said they shirked, and the reading public will take the Colonel at his word and go on thinking they shirked. His statement was uncalled for and uncharitable, and considering the moral and physical effect the advance of the Tenth Cavalry had in weakening the forces opposed to the Colonel's regiment both at Las Guasimas and San Juan Hill, altogether ungrateful, and has done us an immeasurable lot of harm.

"And, further, as to our lack of qualifications for command, I will say that when our soldiers who can and will write history sever their connections with the regular army and thus release themselves from their voluntary status of military lockjaw and tell what they saw, those who now preach that the negro is not fit to exercise command over troops and will go no further than he is led by white officers, will see in print held up for public gaze, much to their chargin, tales of those Cuban battles that have never been told outside the tent and the barrack room, tales that it will not be agreeable for some of them to hear. The public will then learn that not every troop or company of colored soldiers who took part in the assaults on San Juan

HON. J. FRANK WHEATON,
Lawyer and First Colored Man to Be Honored by Election
to the State Legislature of Minnesota.

Hill or El Caney was led or urged forward by its white officer.

"It is unfortunate that we had no colored officers in that campaign, and this thing of white officers for colored troops is exasperating, and I join with The Age in saying our motto for the future must be: 'Colored officers or no colored soldiers.'"

So much for Colonel Roosevelt's statements.

First Sergeant M. W. Sadler, Company D, Twenty-fifth Infantry, furnished the following graphic account to the New York Age of the part his regiment had in the capture of El Caney:

"Santiago de Cuba, July 30.—I wish to call attention to the heroic part the Twenty-fifth United State Infantry played in compelling the surrender of Santiago. We have no reporter in our division and it appears that we are coming up unrepresented.

"On the morning of July 1 our regiment, after having slept a part of the night with stones for pillows and heads resting on hands, arose at the dawn of day, without a morsel to eat, formed line, and after a half-day of hard marching succeeded in reaching the bloody battleground of El Caney. We were in the last brigade of our division. As we were marching up we met regiments of our comrades in white retreating from the Spanish stronghold. As we pressed forward all the reply that came from the retiring soldiers was: 'There is no use to advance further! The Spaniards are intrenched and in blockhouses. You are running to sudden death.' But without a falter did our brave men continue to press to the front.

"In a few moments the desired position was

reached. The first battalion of the Twenty-fifth Infantry, composed of Companies C, D, G and H, were ordered to form the firing line, in preference to other regiments, though their commanders were senior to ours. But no sooner was the command given than the execution began. A thousand yards distant to the north lay the enemy, 2,000 strong, in intrenchments hewn out of solid stone. On each end of the breastwork were stone blockhouses. Our regiment numbered 507 men all told. We advanced about 200 yards, under cover of jungles and ravines. Then came the trying moments. The clear battlefield was reached. The enemy began showering down on us volleys from their strong fortifications and numberless sharpshooters hid away in palm trees and other places of conceal-ment. Our men began to fall, many of them never to rise again, but so steady was the advance and so effective was our fire that the Spaniards became unnerved and began over-shooting us. When they saw we were 'colored soldiers' they knew their doom was sealed. They were afraid to put their heads above the brink of the intrenchments, for every time a head was raised there was one Span-iard less.

"The advance was continued until we were with-in about 150 yards of the intrenchments; then came the solemn command, 'Charge.' Every man was up and rushing forward at headlong speed over the barbed wire and into the intrenchments, and the Twenty-fifth carried the much-coveted position.

"Our losses were as follows: Company A— Wounded, Sergeant Stephen H. Brown, Private William Clark. Company B—Killed, Private

French Payne; wounded, Private Thomas Brown. Company C—Wounded, Privates Joseph L. Johnson, Samuel W. Holley, John H. Boyd. Company D—Killed, Privates Tom Howe, John B. Phelps, John W. Steele; wounded, Sergeant Hayden Richards, Privates Robert Goodwin, Andrew Smith. Company E—Wounded, Privates Hugh Swann, David Gilligin, John Sadler and James Howard. Company F—Wounded, First Sergeant Frank Coleman, Private William Lafayette. Company G —Killed, Private Aaron Leftwich; wounded, Privates Alvin Daniels, Benjamin Douglass, George P. Cooper and John Thomas. Company H—Killed, Corporal Benjamin Cousins, Private Albert Strothers; wounded, Henry Gilbert, William Bevels and Edward Foreman. Officers—Killed, Second Lieutenant H. L. McCorkle; wounded, Captain Eaton A. Edwards, Lieutenants Kennison and Murdock.

"So great was the loss of officers that Company C had to be commanded by its first sergeant, S. W. Taliaferro, the gallant aspirant for a commission from the ranks, the facts of which are yet fresh in the minds of reading Afro-Americans. The company's commander was wounded early in the action by the explosion of a bombshell.

"Thus our people can now see that the coolness and bravery that characterized our fathers in the 60's have been handed down to their sons in the 90's. If any one doubts the fitness of a colored soldier for active field service, when the cry of musketry, the booming of cannons and bursting of shells seem to make the earth tremble, ask the regimental commanders of the Twenty-fourth and Twenty-

H. T. KEALING, A. M.,
Educator and Editor of the A. M. E. Review, Philadelphia, Pa.

fifth Infantries, and the Ninth and Tenth Cavalries; ask Generals Kent and Wheeler, of whose divisions these regiments formed a part.

"The Spaniards call us 'Negeretter Soldados,' and say there is no use shooting at us, for steel and powder will not stop us. We only hope that our brethren will come over and help us to show to the world that true patriotism is in the minds of the sons of Ham. All we need is leaders of our own race to make war records, so that their names may go down in history as a reward for the price of our precious blood."

Sergeant-Major Benjamin F. Sayre, Company C, Twenty-fourth Infantry, furnished in a letter to a friend the following pen picture of the part his regiment took in capturing the San Juan Heights:

"Siboney, Cuba, July 19, 1898.—The war is ended, at least in these parts; we possess the ancient and beautiful city of Santiago. Our flag was raised with impressive ceremonies, bands playing and cannons booming on the plaza of the city yesterday. The Spanish soldiery are bivouacked under guard behind the intrenchments, where a few days ago we were crouching, engaged in a stubborn and sanguinary struggle with them. The Cubans are pouring in from their retreats and shelters in the mountains by thousands, whole families whose only subsistence for months has been mangroves, roots, land crabs, etc., emaciated, pale and wan, but with their eyes glowing with a new light of hope, their faces illumined with hope and thanksgiving for the new era of life, freedom and prosperity for their beloved isle.

"The Twenty-fourth Regiment has made a record for itself that will live as long as the world lasts. It was our regiment that took the fortified ridge of San Juan, the last stronghold of the enemy, before Santiago, after the Ninth and Thirteenth had been repulsed and were retreating. Seven of our officers were laid low and thirteen of our non-commissioned officers before we had gone one hundred yards after fording the river; but we went right at them with a yell, every man shooting straight to kill. The steady advance of the black troops under their withering fire nonplussed the enemy; they became panic-stricken and leaping out of their entrenchments fled shamefully. In a few minutes we were on the heights firing down on them as they ran and dodged about among the trees and high grass. The hill-top, blockhouse and trenches were literally filled with their dead and wounded, some of them shot to pieces. Everywhere the name of the Twenty-fourth Regiment is on everyone's lips. Soldiers and Cubans alike vie with each other in doing honor to any Twenty-fourth man whenever they meet one.

"The men were relieved two days ago and marched to the little seaside village of Siboney, where the hospitals are, and here we witnessed all the pathetic aftermath that is the sequel of every battle and the poor unfortunate victims of man's inhumanity to man. The first report was 200 killed on our side and 1,300 wounded and missing. The death-rate has increased by an average of six or eight every day since. Men are dying off like sheep, for the fever has broken out among them, and if they do not get our troops away pretty quick hundreds will die. No one knows who will be next to go.   Every precaution has been taken; every old building has been burned to the ground, our drinking water is boiled, and every article of bedding and wearing apparel thoroughly aired and sunned all day when the skies are not pouring down floods of water.   Notwithstanding, men are falling down as if struck on the head with a sledge hammer, who a few minutes before were apparently in the best of health, and every morning a silent squad of men go out to dig three or four graves. The spread of canvas for our hospitals alone covers the area of a small city, and, besides this place, there is another five miles down the coast and a steamship moored out in the sea, while hundreds of wounded men have been shipped to Atlanta, Ga., and New York City.   War is a terrible expedient, and it is only those who have not experienced it who would urge it on two nations, unless every other possible method of adjustment had been resorted to without avail.

"After all, I am glad I had a hand in it; that charge was magnificent and I would not exchange that thrill of exultation which I felt when I reached the crust of that volcano of rifle pits among the first of my comrades and raised a shout at the fleeing Spaniards for any consideration.   I was detailed to go in search of the colors, which I succeeded in recovering, although, at times, I found myself in unpleasant proximity to the whistling of Mauser bullets.   It was a dangerous tour along the fighting line, for which service I was highly complimented and promoted to the rank of sergeant-major."

After remaining forty days in the trenches and in the field, the Twenty-fourth Infantry was or-

S. LAING WILLIAMS, A. B. AND M. L.,
Is an Alumnus of the University of Michigan and Columbian
Law School, and Member of the Chicago Bar.

dered to Siboney, where the yellow fever had
broken out among the volunteer troops, July 15,
for hospital service. On reaching Siboney, the
following day, the regiment (numbering 15 officers
and 456 men) was requested to furnish 65 men to
do service at the pest camp. Volunteers were called
for. "This was the crucial test," says Major A. C.
Markley, Twenty-fourth Infantry, commanding,
(Major-General's Report, pp. 450, 451, 452, 453)
"of the mettle of the men and an anxious moment,
indeed. In preparation for it an interview had been
had with Captain A. A. Augur, commanding Company H, a man of high and strong character, and
a course of action decided on. Captain Augur then
explained matters to his men and called for volunteers for the pest camp. Fifteen gallant fellows
responded from his company, and this fine example
soon produced more than were needed for all purposes."

Thus, in the field, in the camp, and in the hospital, facing Mauser bullets, or what not, and Yellow Jack, the deadliest of foes, these black troopers,
Americans all and true, without the incentive of
ever being promoted beyond a non-commissioned
officer's rank, acquitted themselves as heroes, as
all men should who are citizens of our grand but not
always just Republic. A few of these brave men
were promoted to be second lieutenants* and as-

---

* Six colored non-commissioned officers who rendered
particularly gallant and meritorious services in the face of
the enemy in the actions around Santiago on the 1st and 2d
inst. were appointed second lieutenants in the two colored
immune regiments organized under special act of Congress.
These men are Sergeants William Washington, Troop F,
and John C. Proctor, Troop I, of the Ninth Cavalry, and

signed to immune regiments, but all of them have
now been mustered out of the service—turned out
on the cold world in their old age and with their
honors full upon them, as not good enough to be
officers in the regular army of the Republic!

All honor to the heroic brave who fought and
still live! And to the heroic dead, "they are resting
well," may they have not died in vain.

Sergeants William McBryar, Company H; Wyatt Hoffman,
Company G; Macon Russell, Company H, and Andrew
J. Smith, Company B, of the Twenty-fifth Infantry, com-
manded by Colonel Daggett. These two regiments were
in the thick of the fiercest fighting at El Caney and San
Juan and won high praise for their courage and efficiency.
The Ninth Cavalry was also with the Rough Riders at Las
Guasimas.

CHAPTER V.

THE PEACE TREATY.

It was a long time before the American people could bring themselves to the point of interfering in the domestic affairs of a friendly power, a step at which all nations, for obvious reasons, hesitate. The long-continued abuse of Spanish rule in Cuba, which had become a scandal to Christendom, however, at last became so intolerable that they could no longer be excused and endured without a stigma attaching to the honor and humanity of the American Republic. When the national conscience had reached this conclusion, in February, 1896, Congress passed a resolution recognizing a condition of war between Spain and Cuba, and the friendly offices of the United States were offered to Spain for the recognition of Cuban independence. But nothing in the interest of peace had been accomplished, the public mind of both nations had been further exasperated, up to February 15, 1898, when the warship Maine, on a friendly visit, was destroyed in the harbor of Havana, whether by accident or connivance of the Spanish authorities has never been determined. In the explosion 266 of the crew of the Maine lost their lives. This catastrophe was so appalling as to make war inevitable. The joint resolution declaring war between the United States and Spain was passed by Congress April 13 and was signed by President Mc-

T. THOMAS FORTUNE,
Editor of the New York Age, and Brilliant Politician,
Author and Speaker.

Kinley April 20, 1898, at 11:24 o'clock A. M., and Spain followed suit April 24. May 1 Admiral Dewey destroyed the Spanish Asiatic fleet in the harbor of Manila. The American army of invasion, 16,000 strong, under Major-General W. R. Shafter, landed at Baiquira June 20-22, and began to move at once on Santiago, where the enemy was intrenched in force. Admiral Cervera's fleet, in attempting to escape from the harbor of Santiago, was destroyed, July 3, by the American fleet. On the same day General Shafter, having fought his way, without one repulse, to the gates of Santiago, demanded the surrender of that stronghold. July 28, General Nelson A. Miles, heading the American army of invasion, landed at Guanica, Porto Rico.

The Spanish Government, through the French Ambassador, M. Cambon, asked for terms of peace, which were submitted by the President, July 30, and were formally accepted by Spain August 9, the peace protocol being signed, armistice proclaimed and the blockade of Cuba raised August 12. August 13 Manila surrendered to the Americans.

September 9 the following Peace Commission on the part of the United States was announced: William R. Day, of Ohio, ex-Secretary of State; Cushman K. Davis, of Minnesota, United States Senator; George Gray, of Delaware, United States Senator; Whitelaw Reid, of New York. On the part of Spain: Eugene Montero Rios, President of the Senate; Beunaventura Abarzuza; M. W. Z. de Villaurrutia; General R. Cerero; M. J. de Garcia. The American commission sailed for France September 17, and the conferences of the Joint Commission began in Paris, October 1. The treaty of peace was signed at Paris, December 10, at 8:45 o'clock P. M.

The following is a synopsis of the Treaty of Paris:

Article 1 provides for the relinquishment of Cuba.

Article 2 provides for the cession of Porto Rico.

Article 3 provides for the cession of the Philippines for $20,000,000 as compensation.

Article 4 embraces the plans for the cession of the Philippines, including the return of Spanish prisoners in the hands of the Tagalos.

Article 5 deals with the cession of barracks, war materials, arms, stores, buildings, and all property appertaining to the Spanish administration in the Philippines.

Article 6 is a renunciation by both nations of their respective claims against each other and the citizens of each other.

Article 7 grants to Spanish trade and shipping in the Philippines the same treatment as American trade and shipping for a period of ten years.

Article 8 provides for the release of all prisoners of war held by Spain and of all prisoners held by her for political offences committed in the colonies acquired by the United States.

Article 9 guarantees the legal rights of Spaniards remaining in Cuba.

Article 10 establishes religious freedom in the Philippines and guarantees to all churches equal rights.

Article 11 provides for the compensation of courts and other tribunals in Porto Rico and Cuba.

Article 12 provides for the administration of justice in Porto Rico and Cuba.

Article 13 provides for the continuance for five years of Spanish copyrights in the ceded territories, giving Spanish books admittance free of duty.

Article 14 provides for the establishment of consulates by Spain in the ceded territories.

Article 15 grants to Spanish commerce in Cuba, Porto Rico and the Philippines the same treatment as to American for ten years, Spanish shipping to be treated as coasting vessels.

Article 16 stipulates that the obligations of the United States to Spanish citizens and property in Cuba shall terminate with the withdrawal of the United States authorities from the island.

Article 17 provides that the treaty must be ratified within six months from the date of signing by the respective Governments in order to be binding.

Under the supervision of the Evacuation Commissioners, the removal of the Spanish troops from Cuba and Porto Rico began immediately after the arrival of the American commissioners in those islands. The complete evacution of Porto Rico was accomplished by October 17, and on October 18 the United States flag was hoisted at San Juan and the United States came into formal possession of the island.

The evacuation of Cuba by the Spaniards was begun in December, 1898.

President McKinley issued a proclamation April 11, 1899, ratifying the work of the commission. And thus ended the rule of Spain in North America, which her sailors had discovered and which

EDWARD WILSON,
Graduate of Williams College, and Successful Member of the
Chicago Bar.

77

her chivalric and adventurous soldiers did so much to conquer. She went into the war with great pride and confidence; she emerged from it with her navy destroyed; her army discredited and her West Indian and Asiatic colonies forever lost to her! "O what a fall was there!"

CHAPTER VI.

AFRO-AMERICAN EDUCATION.

That the age of prophecy, like that of chivalry, has passed away was never more signally shown than in the utter breaking down of all the predictions that followed the Afro-American people out of the house of bondage into the home, the church and the school-house of freedom. It was confidently predicted by his enemies that he was incapable of mastering the common rudiments of education, and the idea that he could master the higher education was laughed out of court. When the war came to a close in 1865 a large portion of the American people regarded the Afro-American people "as less than man, yet more than brute." They had no faith in the possibility of his mental or moral regeneration.

And yet, in those early days when the race was enslaved, there appeared among them men of great piety and learning, who devoted themselves, where they were allowed to do so, to the education of such of their fellows as were classed as "free negroes." Such pioneers in the work of education were Rev. Daniel Alexander Payne of South Carolina, Rev. J. W. Hood of North Carolina, Rev. John Peterson of New York, George B. Vashin of Missouri—men who illustrated in their lives and work those higher virtues of capacity, industry, devotion to race, which were to have such a splendid army of emulators in the after years and under more favoring conditions.

No sufficient tribute has ever been paid to General O. O. Howard, who laid the foundation of the Afro-American educational work while he had charge of the important work of the Freedman's Bureau. It is meet that General Samuel Chapman Armstrong, the founder of the Hampton Normal and Agricultural Institute, should pay him such a tribute. General Armstrong said:

"General Howard and the Freedmen's Bureau did for the ex-slaves, from 1865 to 1870, a marvelous work, for which due credit has not been given; among other things, giving to their education an impulse and a foundation, by granting three and a half millions of dollars for schoolhouses, salaries, etc., promoting the education of about a million colored children. The principal negro educational institutions of to-day, then starting, were liberally aided, at a time of vital need. Hampton received over $50,000 through General Howard for building and improvements."

But it is not alone in the money expended by General Howard as the representative of the Government in the direction indicated by General Armstrong are we indebted to this great soldier and philanthropist; out of his private purse he founded Howard University at the capital of the nation and endowed it with a princely domain, which must to-day be worth $5,000,000 in the open market. It was through no fault of General Howard's that this endowment was scattered to the winds.

General Armstrong was also one of the pioneers in this educational work, having been placed by

DR. DANIEL H. WILLIAMS,
Chicago, Ill., Founder of Provident Hospital and Training
School, Chicago; Appointed by President Cleveland as
Surgeon-in-Chief of the Great Freedman's Hospital, Washington, D. C. By his profession
he has amassed a large fortune; as
Physician and Surgeon he has
few equals of any race
or country.

General Howard, Commissioner of the Freedman's Bureau, in charge of ten counties in Eastern Virginia, with headquarters at Hampton, the great "contraband" camp, "to manage negro affairs and to adjust, if possible, the relations of the races." How the Hampton work, one of the best and strongest, was planted, is best told in the language of General Armstrong himself:

"On relieving my predecessor, Captain C. B. Wilder, of Boston, at the Hampton headquarters, I found an active, excellent educational work going on under the American Missionary Association of New York, which, in 1862, had opened, in the vicinity, the first school for freedmen in the South, in charge of an ex-slave, Mrs. Mary Peake. Over 1,500 children were gathering daily; some in old hospital barracks—for here was Camp Hamilton, the base hospital of the Army of the James, where, during the war, thousands of sick and wounded soldiers had been cared for, and where now over 6,000 lie buried in a beautiful national cemetery. The largest class was in the 'Butler School' building, since replaced by the 'John G. Whittier school-house.'

"Close at hand the pioneer settlers of America and the first slaves landed on this continent; here Powhatan reigned; here the Indian child was baptized; here freedom was first given the slave by General Butler's 'contraband' order; in sight of this shore the battle of the Merrimac and Monitor saved the Union and revolutionized naval warfare; here General Grant based the operations of his final campaign.   *   *   *

"I soon felt the fitness of this historic and

strategic spot for a permanent and great educational work. The suggestion was cordially received by the American Missionary Association, which authorized the purchase, in June, 1867, of 'Little Scotland,' and estate of 125 acres (since increased to 190), on Hampton River, looking out over Hampton Roads. Not expecting to have charge, but only to help, I was surprised one day by a letter from Secretary E. P. Smith of the A. M. A., stating that the man selected for the place had declined, and asking me if I could take it. I replied 'Yes.' Till then my own future had been blind; it had only been clear that there was a work to do for the ex-slaves, and where and how it should be done.

"A day-dream of the Hampton school nearly as it is had come to me during the war a few times; once in camp during the siege of Richmond, and once one beautiful evening on the Gulf of Mexico, while on the wheel-house of the transport steamship Illinois en route for Texas with the Twenty-fifth Army (negro) Corps, for frontier duty on the Rio Grande River, whither it had been ordered, under General Sheridan, to watch and if necessary defeat Maximilian in his attempted conquest of Mexico.

"The thing to be done was clear: To train selected negro youth who should go out at once and teach and lead their people, first by example, by getting land and homes; to give them not a dollar that they could not earn for themselves; to teach respect for labor; to replace stupid drudgery with skilled hands; and, to these ends, to build up an industrial system, for the sake not only of self-support and intelligent labor, but also for the sake of character. And it seemed equally clear that the people of the country would support a wise work for the freedmen. I think so still."

They have done it. From the small seed planted at Hampton, and as an outgrowth of the work of the Freedman's Bureau, schools of elementary and higher education rapidly sprang up in every State. The enthusiasm with which these schools were filled, not only by the young, but by the adults, astonished not only the people of the North, but those of the South. Many who watched the phenomenon, and who had their doubts about the capacity of the Afro-American people to receive mental discipline and to continue in well doing, said that when the novelty should wear off these schoolhouses would be emptied of their eager disciples. But they were not. Each succeeding year has seen the grand army of school children grow larger and larger and more earnest in enthusiasm; and the numerous academies, seminaries, institutes and colleges have been and are overcrowded.

In the early stages of the work there were very few Afro-Americans competent to teach and there were no funds to carry on the work, as the common school system in the Southern States had not been inaugurated; it was to come later, after the work of foundation-laying had been done under the inspiration of the Freedman's Bureau and the organized missionary associations of the North. But where were the teachers to come from? Unfortunately, I think, as events have demonstrated, the whites were indisposed to undertake this necessary work, and were in many instances hostile to

PROF. W. E. B. DUBOIS,
Sociologist and Writer, Atlanta, Ga.

those who did do it. There are few brighter pages in the missionary history of the world than that which records the readiness and willingness with which the white men and women of the Northern States went into the South, into its large cities and its waste places, and labored year in and year out, to lay the foundation of the Afro-American's religious and educational character, and the unparalleled financial support which was given them, and is continued to this day, by the philanthropic people of the North. It is estimated that in the maintenance of the educational work among the Afro-American people of the South the philanthropists of the North, directly and through organized associations like the American Missionary Association and the Peabody Fund, have expended annually an average of one million dollars since 1867, making a grand total of $32,000,000. Fully a hundred colleges, institutes, and the like have been established and maintained, and are to-day doing a marvelous work. A majority of these schools have white management, but all of them are represented in their faculties by their graduates. A great many of them are managed in all their departments by Afro-Americans.

As has been said, these schools of higher learning are maintained, for the most part, by the organized charities and individual philanthropists of the North. There are two funds set apart for this work, besides the Peabody Fund, of which the whites receive a large share—the John F. Slater Fund and the Hand Fund, of a million dollars each, the income of which is applied to helping these Afro-American schools.

PROF. W. H. COUNCILL,
President Agricultural and Mechanical College, Normal, Ala.

Mention should be made here of the fact that Hon. Jonathan C. Gibbs, one of the first Afro-American graduates of Dartmouth College, was one of the State Superintendents of Education of Florida in the Reconstruction era, and died while holding that position. His son, Hon. Thomas V. Gibbs, died in 1898, after having done much as its secretary and treasurer, in connection with President T. DeS. Tucker, to place the State Normal and Agricultural College, at Tallahassee on a prosperous foundation.

With the inauguration of the public school system in the Southern States the voluntary schools were gradually absorbed and their Northern teachers displaced by those they had prepared. The extent and importance of their work may be judged by the fact that when they entered the field in 1866-7 there were comparatively few Afro-American teachers in the South, whereas to-day there are no fewer than 25,000 employed in the public schools. Baltimore, I believe, is the only Southern city in which white teachers are now employed in these schools. Any unbiased person must admit that this is not only a creditable but a remarkable showing, one alike creditable to the race and to those who lavished upon it time and money to effect it.

Most of the Southern States maintain normal and agricultural schools for the education of Afro-American youths. Alabama not only does this, but makes a generous appropriation for the work of the Tuskegee Normal and Industrial Institute. Prof. Richard R. Wright, president of the State Normal College, at College, Ga., is perhaps

PROF. W. S. SCARABOROUGH, A. M., LL. D., PH. D.,
Vice-President Wilberforce University. Has written a Greek
Grammar, and many treatises on Greek. Is also
a member of seven Educational Societies.

the best known of the presidents of these State institutions. The one in North Carolina, presided over by James B. Dudley, at Greensboro, also has a good reputation. In South Carolina, ex-Congressman Thomas E. Miller has charge of the State School at Orangeburgh. A very excellent work is being done by Prof. S. G. Atkins, at the Slater Academy, at Winston, N. C., one of the few schools of its kind in the South supported in large part by the native whites.

The African Methodist Episcopal and the African Methodist Episcopal Zion Churches maintain a large number of schools. The main school of the former is located at Wilberforce, Ohio, with S. T. Mitchell as president. Prof. W. S. Scarborough, who has written a Greek grammar and many treatises on Greek subjects, is connected with the school—Wilberforce University. The main school the latter is located at Salisbury, N. C., W. H. Goler being president. The school was built up in its earlier stages by Rev. Joseph C. Price, who had the reputation in his lifetime of being one of the most eloquent men in the Republic. The Baptist denomination also maintains a large number of schools.

Among the schools of higher learning which have an assured standing may be mentioned Lincoln University, in Chester County, Pa.; Howard University, Washington, D. C.; Shaw University, Raleigh, N. C.; Claflin University, Orangeburgh, S. C.; Atlanta and Clark Universities, Morris Brown College, Gammon Theological Seminary and Spelman Seminary, all of Atlanta; Fisk, Roger Williams and Central Tennessee Colleges at Nash-

PROF. HIRAM E. ARCHER, M. S.,
Director of the Department of Science and Assistant Principal in the Agricultural and Mechanical College, Normal, Alabama.

ville, Tenn.; Knoxville College, Knoxville, Tenn.; Berea College, where both races are educated, at Berea, Ky.

Among the normal and industrial schools Hampton Institute and its offspring, the Tuskegee Institute, at Tuskegee, Ala., head the list; the Calhoun School, at Calhoun, Ala.; the Mt. Meigs School, at Mt. Meigs, Ala.; the Gloucester School, at Gloucester, Va., with the State industrial schools in most of the Southern States.

The educational work in the Southern States is accomplishing wonders in the moral and intellectual uplift of the people, which has already been felt in the life of the South, and must be felt in larger measure in the years to come. There has been a marked tendency of late years to make the education conform more to the industrial lines laid by General Armstrong. This is a healthy sign, as the more practical education is the better, especially as the tendency of modern industrialism is more and more towards specialization in all departments of learning and activity of whatever sort; and this is said without intending in the least to depreciate or underrate what is regarded as the higher education. All education is good, but assuredly that is the best which enables a man to fit in most readily with the conditions of life in which he finds himself.

CHAPTER VII.

SLAVERY IN THE COLONIES.

The first African slaves were brought to the New World in the year 1565, in the English ship "Jesus," commanded by Sir John Hawkins, under the patronage of "Good Queen Bess." Thus we find that exactly three hundred years from the landing of this first cargo of two hundred and fifty chained slaves at St. Domingo, our martyred President went to his God bearing the shackles of four million freedmen.

The demand for these slaves grew out of the fact that Spanish cruelty had exterminated the inoffensive Indians found on the islands, and it was found necessary to have Negro slaves to cultivate the plantations.

The hearty sons of Africa not only survived the oppressive cruelty of their heartless task-masters, but in time they rebelled against them, and under their invincible "Black Prince," Toussaint, killed them in battle or drove them from the island. Thus, as Bancroft well says, "Hayti, the first spot in America that received African Slaves, was the first to set the example of African Liberty."

He also says the sovereigns of England, especially Elizabeth and Anne, "participated in the hazard, the profits and the crimes, and became at once smugglers and slave merchants."

We are horrified at this depravity, and yet history is repeating itself; Christian England and America are to-day, with the approval of their rulers, sending opium to China and rum to Africa.

As we purpose showing how slavery spread to the different colonies, we will take a hasty glance at each of them, in the order of its introduction.

Virginia, 1619:—It seems to be a mooted question among historians, as to whether the Dutch ship landed the first slaves of the thirteen original colonies at Jamestown, Virginia, in 1619 or 1620. We find as much authority for the one year as the other; but upon the whole we are inclined, with Ridpath, Williams and others, to favor 1619 as the correct date.

However, the first slaves that landed in what is now the United States, were brought to Florida at the founding of St. Augustine in 1565, by Pedro Menendez de Aviles, who entered into a compact with his sovereign, Philip II. of Spain, in which he obligated himself to take with him five hundred slaves.

In Virginia the institution of slavery grew very slowly at first, and the Negroes were regarded as chattels; but an act was passed in 1705 declaring them to be real estate.

The slaves had no personal rights, and could not leave the plantation to which they belonged, without a written pass from their master. If one dared to lift a hand against a Christian (?) or white man, he received thirty lashes, and if he resisted punishment, was liable to be killed with impunity,

REV. N. B. WOOD,
Historian and Lecturer.

and his murderer was guiltless in the eyes of the law. Trial by jury was denied him, and more than five meeting together was considered felony, and punishable by death.

We read of slaves given in part payment to clergymen for preaching to whites, but no record of any one preaching to Negroes. A few Negroes were emancipated for meritorious services, but a law passed in 1699 required them to leave the colony within six months of securing their liberty.

New York, 1628:—Slavery was introduced at this time; but the kind-hearted Dutch treated their Negro slaves with much humanity. The institution was mainly patriarchal. Manumission of slaves for meritorious services, or prompted by justice, was quite frequent. Under this mild system the Negroes were correspondingly happy. They married and were given in marriage, they sowed and reaped a good share of the fruits of their labor. While there were no schools for them, there were no laws against their receiving instruction when their work was done.

There is not found in all history a greater contrast than is presented by the treatment accorded these slaves by the humane Dutch, and that of their English conquerors. In 1702 an act was passed making it unlawful to trade with Negro slaves, on pain of fine or imprisonment.

"Not above three slaves were allowed to meet together, on pain of being whipped by a justice of the peace, or sent to jail."

In 1710 the city of New York passed an ordinance forbidding slaves appearing in the streets after dark without a lighted lantern, on penalty of being locked up in the watch-house that night, and sent to prison the next day until the master paid the fine; after which the slave received fifty lashes and was discharged.

A slave market was erected at the foot of Wall Street, where slaves were sold daily to the highest bidder. Negroes had no family relation, but lived together by common consent. Even free Negroes had no property, land, schools or other privileges. Thus their lives were spent in a huge sepulcher and they were buried in a common ditch after death. This horrible state of affairs culminated in the so-called "Negro plot" of 1741. In February of that year the house of Robert Hogg, a merchant of New York City, was robbed of fine linen, medals, silver coin, etc. The case was given to the officers of the law to arrest and punish the guilty parties. They pushed the case with such zeal that aided by a "diseased public conscience, inflamed by religious bigotry, accelerated by hired liars, and consummated in the blind and bloody action of a court and jury who imagined themselves sitting over a powder magazine," they perpetrated in the name of law the darkest and most cruel deed in American history.

From May 11th to August 29th, one hundred and fifty-four Negroes were cast into prison, fourteen of whom were burned at the stake, eighteen hanged, seventy-one transported, and the remainder pardoned. All because a few Negroes stole goods from a prominent merchant, "and the people imagined a vain thing," namely, that a plot was made by the Negroes to murder the whites and burn the city. Some of the poor wretches

resorted to accusing others, hoping so to obtain
pardon thereby, until the jail was filled to over-
flowing.   The slightest accusation of this kind
was welcomed, and distorted into positive proof
of guilt.   Moreover, it must be remembered that
the "Negroes were considered heathen, and therefore not sworn by the court; that they were not
allowed counsel; that the evidence was indirect,
contradictory, and malicious; while the trials were
hasty and unfair."

In time all believers in the "Negro Plot" were
converted to the opinion that the zeal of the
magistrates had not been "according to knowledge," and that there was no competent evidence
to show that there had been an organized plot.
Every fair historian now condemns the heartless
and bloodthirsty magistrates.

Every law passed by the legislature of New
York prior to the Revolution, tended to curtail
the Negroes' rights, until their condition was
little removed from the brute.   Nor did "Our
Brother in Black" fare much better in the other
colonies.

Massachusetts, 1633:—We come now to consider slavery in the "Old Bay State."   It must
have been introduced before 1633, for we read
that during that year some Pequod Indians found
a Negro up in a tree who was lost and trying to
find his way home.   The Indians were frightened,
so ran to the white settlement and reported they
had seen the Devil.

As early as 1637 some of the Pequod Indians,
"who would not endure the yoke or be obedient
servants," were sent to the Bermudas and ex-

changed for Negroes. Sometimes slaves received kind treatment, but as often cruel; depending entirely upon the disposition of the master.

"Negro children were considered an incumbrance in the family, and when weaned, were given away like young puppies," as we learn from the famous Dr. Dunlap.

The great and good missionary to the Indians, John Eliot, "had long lamented with a bleeding and burning passion, that the English used their Negroes but as their horses or their oxen, and that so little care was taken about their immortal souls;" therefore he requested their masters for several miles around to send their slaves to him that he might instruct them "in things of their Everlasting Peace." But he did not live long enough to make much progress in this noble work.

As might have been expected in cultured Massachusetts, there were those wise and humane enough to realize that a Negro with learning, was a more valuable slave for the acquisition.

Richard Dalton, of Boston, a ripe scholar and great linguist, becoming afflicted with weak eyes, determined to teach his Negro boy Cæsar to read Greek So proficient did the boy become, that he could read aloud to his master any Greek author almost as readily as English.

The "Boston Chronicle" of September 21st, 1769, has the following advertisement: "To be sold, a likely little Negro boy, who can speak the French language, and very fit for a valet."

Emboldened by this evidence of capacity for mental culture, and fitness for citizenship, the Negroes demanded the privilege of British subjects.

As there was imminent prospect for war with the mother country, the colonists were conciliatory to them, knowing they would prove a factor for or against them in case of war.

The famous decision of Lord Mansfield about this time, in the Summersett case, tended to inspire a hope in the breast of the slaves of Massachusetts. It may be briefly stated as follows: Charles Stewart, of Boston, was in London with his Negro slave, James Summersett, when the slave was taken sick, and abandoned by his master, who seemingly did not care whether he lived or died. The Negro, recovering, obtained employment. When the master heard of it, he had him arrested and put on board a ship about to sail for Jamaica, where he was to be sold.

Some friends of the Negro made affidavits, and obtained a writ of *habeas corpus*. In the ensuing trial Lord Mansfield gave his decision in the following words: "The state of slavery is of such a nature that it is incapable of being introduced on any reasons, moral or political, but only by positive law, which preserves its force long after the reasons, occasions, and time itself from whence it was created is erased from memory. It is so odious that nothing can be suffered to support it but positive law. Whatever inconveniences, therefore, may follow from the decision, I cannot say this case is allowed or approved by the law of England, and therefore the Black must be discharged."

Of course this decision produced universal joy among the Colonial Negroes, and it caused the question to arise, as to whether the Colonial governments could pass acts legalizing that which was contrary to the law of England.

Maryland, 1634:—This colony was united with Virginia until 1630; consequently slavery was regulated by the laws of the "Old Dominion" up to that time. Thus when the English Catholics under Lord Baltimore settled Maryland in 1634, they found slavery had preceded them.

The slaves here were worked in a great variety of employments, such as cultivating tobacco, chopping, learning the different mechanical trades, handling light crafts along the water courses, fishing and taking oysters. This created a great demand for Negroes, and their number increased very rapidly. The period of one hundred and forty-four years, from the founding of the Colony to the Revolution, is described as "one long starless night of oppression and outrage."

As a sample of the brutality of the laws governing Negroes, an Act was passed in 1723, where the penalty of a Negro or other slave striking a white person was to have his ears "cropt on order of a justice." The Mosaic law taught "an eye for an eye and a tooth for a tooth," but in this code both ears were forfeited for one blow. In 1729 a still more inhuman Act was passed, by which Negroes and other slaves found guilty of certain crimes, should be hanged, and afterwards the bodies quartered and exposed to public view. Cannibals would go only one step further; they would eat them after being quartered.

They capped the climax in 1752 by passing an Act forbidding emancipation by "last will and testament, or giving freedom to Negro slaves in any way." Thus, like the horse or ox, the Negro of Maryland was absolute property for life. He was simply in the eyes of the law an upright, reasoning, talking animal; nothing more nor less.

Delaware, 1636:—Vincint, the historian of this Colony, shows that slavery existed on the Delaware River as early as 1636.

The record shows that Peter Alricks, Calvert, D'Hinoyossa, and two Indian chiefs, met in council in September, 1661, to arrange a treaty. At this time it was agreed to furnish the Dutch every year three thousand hogsheads of tobacco, provided the Dutch would "supply them with Negroes and other commodities." Thus we find an inter-Colonial traffic in slaves established.

We infer that slaves were frequently manumitted in this Colony, from the fact that an Act was passed in 1739 providing that good security should be given in case of manumission, that the county should not be at any charge by reason of sickness or incapacity for self-support on the part of said slave. Upon the whole, the Negro fared better in Delaware than in some of the other colonies. But even here he had no rights of any kind.

Connecticut, 1646:—There is a strong presumptive evidence that slavery existed here from the beginning, certainly since 1646, in spite of a law passed in 1642, which read as follows: "If any man stealeth a man or mankind, he shall be put to death. Exodus XXI. 16."

Of course this law was a dead letter, but the growth of slavery in this colony was very gradual.

It is refreshing to read of an Act passed in 1702

JOHN G. MITCHELL,
The Aggressive Editor of the Richmond Planet.

for the benefit of a certain class of slaves. It seems that certain heartless masters were in the habit of working their slaves until they were decrepit and worn out in their service, and when they were no longer profitable, emancipated them to live on charity or starve. They would then pose as those who had done noble deeds. But the law-makers were not deceived, and passed an Act compelling the owners of such slaves, or their heirs, to provide for them in their old age, even if they had liberated them by turning them out like an old horse to die.

We are glad to note that the law was rigidly enforced. But let no man imagine that a slave life in this Colony was "a flowery bed of ease."

Often was he publicly flogged for the high crime and misdemeanor of being out the night before without a pass from his master. And to make matters worse, if he used any strong epithets, or gave vent to his feelings in defamatory language, while undergoing punishment, he was subject to a double dose of the same medicine, by special Act passed in 1730.

Perhaps, like a man we have heard of, he comforted himself with the thought that he could not do such a law justice, and therefore said nothing. The man referred to was a proverbial record-breaker in profanity. He was drawing a load of apples up a steep hill, when the end board came out and all the apples rolled out of the wagon pell-mell to the bottom of the hill. Thinking he could not do the occasion justice, the man simply folded his arms and said nothing.

When the mutterings of the impending war

were heard in the distance, the colonists were aroused to the inconsistency of fighting for freedom while holding slaves in cruel bondage. Nor were they blind to the fact that their Negroes could be induced by kind treatment to help them against the common enemy. Accordingly the following Act was passed in 1774: "No Indian, Negro or mulatto slave shall at any time hereafter be brought or imported into this state, by sea or land, from any place or places whatsoever, to be disposed of, left or sold, within this state." Thus we find that Connecticut tried to alleviate the condition of her slaves, and legislate against the nefarious traffic.

She should have taken one more step and liberated the slaves she had at this time, but had she done so, doubtless England would have repealed the Act, as she did in the case of Pennsylvania and New Hampshire. We think it might be recorded of Connecticut, "She hath done what she could." Her sable sons showed their appreciation of her kindness by fighting nobly to free their masters in the Revolutionary struggle.

Rhode Island, 1647:—It is supposed slavery was introduced in this year. It remained for this liberty-loving little colony to pass the first positive Act against slavery recorded in modern history. It was passed in 1652 by the General Court, and is worded as follows: "Whereas, there is a common course practiced among Englishmen to buy Ne-gers, to that end they may have them for service or slaves forever; for the preventinge of such practices among us, let it be ordered that no blacke mankind or white being forced by covenant bond, or otherwise, to serve any man or his assignees longer than ten years, or until they come to bee twenty-four years of age, if they bee taken in under fourteen, from the time of their cominge within the liberties of this Collonie. And at the end or terme of ten years to sett them free, as the manner is with the English servants. And that man that will not let them goe free, or shall sell them away elsewhere, to that end that they may bee enslaved to others for a long time, hee or they shall forfeit to the Collonie forty pounds."

We rejoice that this little Colony, founded by Roger Williams, the friend of the oppressed, the defender of civil and religious liberty, should put herself on record in this manner. It is about the kind of law one would expect from "Little Rhodie." But it is deplorable that it was abortive and became a dead letter, since it was not backed up by public sentiment, either in the Colony or the mother country. For it is notoriously true that slavery flourished here even with this law upon the statute books.

No doubt some good came of the law, for as Bancroft well says, "the law was not enforced, but the principle lived among the people." For we read that when Acts were passed imposing fines on "housekeepers" for entertaining slaves after nine o'clock at night, they paid their fines cheerfully and continued to treat the slaves kindly. This shows that the leaven of the anti-slavery law was permeating the Colony.

New Jersey, 1664:—Slavery was introduced here before the formation of a separate colony, and probably near the same time it appeared in New Netherlands.

The record of early history in New Jersey in meager, but enough is known to show the slaves received kinder treatment here than in any of the other colonies. This was the invariable rule where the population was composed largely of Quakers and Dutch. With the exception of an Act protecting slaves from drunkenness, by punishing those who sold or gave them rum, few laws of importance touching slavery were passed for many years.

An Act passed by the Legislature of East Jersey in 1664 provided for the trial of "Negroes and other slaves for felonies punishable with death," to be by a jury of twelve persons before three justices of the peace; for theft, before two justices; the punishment by whipping. To the glory of New Jersey be it said this was the only Colony that gave to the Negro that coveted boon, the right of trial by jury. In most of the other colonies the Negro was convicted even before the mock trial, often without the shadow of justice. But here I doubt not he had both shadow and substance. Verily in this Colony, "the lines had fallen unto him in pleasant places."

The example of the Quakers for teaching the colored people was contagious, for others gave them instruction, and encouraged the preaching of the gospel unto them. It is believed that free Negroes were enlisted in military companies of this Colony. And the law of 1760 implies that slaves for life could be enlisted by obtaining permission from their masters.

South Carolina, 1665:—The entire slave population of South Carolina was regarded as chattel property absolutely. The solemnity of a jury was never allowed them. But in case of "burglary, robbery, burning of houses, killing or stealing of any meat or other cattle, or other petty injuries, as maiming one of another, stealing of fowls, provisions, or such like trespass, or injuries," he was tried for his life before two justices and three freeholders, who often sentenced him to death for the most trivial offence.

The code of laws of South Carolina for the correction of slaves stands without a parallel for cruelty. For striking a white man, he was severely whipped for the first offence, for the second whipped still more severely, had his nose slit, and face burned, and for the third offence a cruel death was his portion. If any Negro, slave or free, tried to persuade some other slave to run off out of the colony, he received on conviction forty lashes and was branded on the forehead with a red-hot iron, that "the mark thereof might remain." Any white man meeting a Negro might demand of him to show his ticket; and on refusal could "beat, maim or assault him." And if such slave could not be taken, to "kill him."

Such codes trained the white people into a brood of tyrants. Even the "poor white trash," who did not own a Negro, would knock them down, and throw them off the sidewalk in wanton cruelty; while the overseer who was most disposed to beat and torture the poor Negro received the highest salary. The young white boys took their cue from their fathers and overseers, and it was a common sight to see them in their sports, whip in hand, threatening or punishing the little Negroes.

In time a reaction took place, for it dawned

upon the planters that a Negro could do more labor with less abuse, especially where it was bestowed by those having no authority. A law existed against teaching a Negro to read or write, but for obvious reasons there was more leniency shown them some years before the Revolution.

North Carolina, 1669:—The code of laws proposed by Dracho for Athens is said to have been written in blood, because of its severity. The constitution and code of laws drafted by John Locke for the government of North Carolina, might be described as written in blood with a goose-quill. Surely a more brutal, unwieldy and asinine code was never proposed for the government of a crude young colony, but little removed from a backwoods settlement, in the world's history. All of the insoluble problems of political economy of the past, much of the visionary speculation of the future, was dumped into a common heap by this absurd instrument. In short, it might be defined as a conglomeration of heterogeneous inconsistencies. The poet assures us that,

"Kings and Lords may flourish or may fade,
A breath can make them as a breath has made,
But the honest yeomanry, the country's pride,
When once destroyed can never be supplied."

The Locke constitution was an insult to humanity and designed to wrest from the yeomanry what few rights were conferred by the Magna Charta.

We read that "no elective franchise could be conferred upon a freeholder of less than fifty acres," while "all executive power was vested in the proprietors themselves, or the nobility."

According to Bancroft: "The instinct of aristocracy dreads the moral power of a proprietary yeomanry; the perpetual degradation of the cultivators of the soil was enacted. The leet-men or tenants, holding ten acres of land at a fixed rent, were not only destitute of political franchise, but were adscripts of the soil; under the jurisdiction of the lord without appeal; and it was added, 'all the children of leet-men shall be leet-men, and so to all generations.'" It seems, then, that tenants were but little more then serfs or slaves; and if they, Anglo Saxons as they were, received such treatment at the hands of these petty lords, so-called, what mercy could the poor Negro expect? "If they have called the master of the house Beelzebub, how much more shall they call them of his household?"

By way of numbering largely and for political purposes, they received the Negro slaves into the established church. But in the constitution we find this language: "Every freeman of Carolina shall have absolute power and authority over his Negro slaves of what opinion or religion soever;" thus his humanity was conceded, and a little regard had for his soul, but his body was the absolute property of a brutal owner who "neither feared God nor regarded man." While Negroes were received into the church, there is no record of any effort made in or out of the church to give them instruction or banish their dark clouds of ignorance, superstition and crime.

While traveling from one plantation to another, a Negro was required to take the most frequented road or path; and if found in any other, except in the company of a white man, he was liable to be seized by the owner of the land through which he was passing, and hit forty lashes. If one Negro enter- tained another from a different plantation, at night, the only time they could visit, he was sub- ject to twenty lashes on his bare back, while the guest received forty in the same manner. Still there was one clause of humanity in this code which is commendable. In case a poor half- starved slave was found guilty of stealing hogs or corn, damages could be recovered against his master in the county or general court. But we turn from this to a brutal act where a slave guilty of giving false testimony, "should have one ear nailed to the pillory, and there stand for the space of one hour, the said ear to be cut off, and there- after the other ear nailed in like manner, and cut off at the expiration of one other hour." The Locke constitution seemed to create an insatiable thirst for blood, so much so, and the murder of slaves became so frequent, that the Legislature was forced to call a halt, by refusing to pay for the slaves killed.

New Hampshire, 1679:—Public sentiment of this Colony was decidedly opposed to Negro slavery, and the Governor used his authority to manumit a slave March 14, 1684. Belknap's History of New Hampshire thus records the fact: "The governor tould Mr. Jeffery's Negro hee might goe from his master, hee would clere him under hande and sele, so the fello no more attends his mas- ter's conscernes." In their criminal code we find this article: "If any man stealeth mankind, he shall be put to death, or otherwise grievously punished." It is safe to infer that this law would not have been a dead letter in this Colony as it was in Massachusetts and Connecticut; but unfortunately England rejected the whole code as "fanatical and absurd." The Governor of this Colony, backed by public sentiment, determined to do all he could to prevent legal recognition of slaves; but in this he was opposed by the authority of the Crown, as the following order of 1761 would indicate: "You are not to give your assent to, or pass any law imposing duties on Negroes imported into New Hampshire."

The severe climate mitigated against their profitable use; so few Negroes found their way into the Colony. While some were treated with great kindness, others through neglect, poorly clad and fed, were often hurried to premature graves. This called for an Act in 1718 for restraining inhuman severities inflicted upon servants and slaves; a portion of which we quote from "Freedom and Bondage," as follows: "If any man smite out the eye or tooth of his man servant or maid servant, or otherwise maim or disfigure them much, unless it be by mere casualty, he shall let him or her go free from his service. If any person or persons whatever in this province shall willfully kill his Indian or Negro servant or servants, he shall be punished with death." Probably this is the only Colony that ever passed a law inflicting the death penalty on a man for murdering a Negro slave.

Pennsylvania, 1681:—It is to the credit of the Quakers that one of their number, Francis Daniel Pastorius, drafted the first protest against slavery issued by any religious body in America. This

JUDSON W. LYONS,
Register of the Treasury, Washington, D. C., who has to
sign Uncle Sam's money to make it good.

113

was written in 1688, and adopted by the German-town Friends, and by them sent to the monthly meeting, and thence to the yearly meeting at Philadelphia. The original of this remarkable document was found by Nathan Kite of Philadelphia in 1844. Referring to the slaves it said: "Have not these Negroes as much right to fight for their freedom as you have to keep them slaves?" It prophesied the time would come,

> "When from the gallery to the farthest seat,
> Slave and slave owner shall no longer meet,
> But all sit equal at the Master's feet."

It also boldly denounced "the buying, selling, and holding men in slavery, as inconsistent with the Christian religion." But when this memorial came for action before the yearly meeting, it was voted "not proper then to give a positive judgment in the case." Still in 1696 the yearly meeting pronounced in unmistakable language against importing more slaves, and adopted measures tending to the moral improvement of those in the Colony. George Keith denounced slavery "as contrary to the religion of Christ, the rights of man, and sound reason and policy."

The pious philanthropist, William Penn, tried in vain to embody his anti-slavery sentiments into the law of the province.

He encouraged his people by example and influence to treat the poor Negro with great kindness and justice, and we see the Society of Friends did more to ameliorate the condition of slaves than any other religious body. On the seventh of June, 1712, a bill was passed emancipating slaves by law, but was repealed by Queen Anne, the notorious slave merchant.

Georgia, 1732:—General John Oglethorpe, the founder and first Governor of Georgia, has received much unmerited praise from the casual reader of history because he opposed the introduction of slavery into that Colony. But his opposition was based on political and prudential motives, rather than philanthropy. Dr. Stevens, the Georgia historian, informs us that even Oglethorpe owned a plantation and Negroes in South Carolina, about forty miles above Savannah.

England was anxious to have a strong settlement of white men on her southern boundary, to protect her from the Spanish Colony on the south, and the Indians on the west; so it was thought the introduction of Negroes would be unfavorable to this scheme, as they were apt to desert to the Spanish. But the reasons assigned by the trustees for prohibiting slavery were: "1. Its expense, both in buying and keeping a Negro slave. 2. It would induce to idleness and render labor degrading. 3. The settlers being freeholders of fifty acres each, requiring only one or two extra hands for their cultivation, the German servants would be more profitable than black."

Moreover, it was claimed that the cultivation of silk and wine requiring skill rather than strength and endurance, whites were better adapted to it than Negroes.

As the colony grew, England became determined to carry out her original policy; but the settlers were equally resolved to have Negroes. The constant toast of the authorities was "the one thing needful," Negroes; they even smuggled them into the Colony. The opposition weakened, and in 1748

Rev. Martin Bolzins wrote to the trustees as follows: "Things being now in such a melancholy state, I must humbly beseech your honors not to regard our, or our friends petition against Negroes." Even the great George Whitefield used his utmost influence in favor of bringing Negroes into the Colony. It seems that he had a visionary scheme to build an orphanage in Georgia for the benefit of Indian children.

Through the bounty of his friends, Whitefield owned two small plantations; one in South Carolina, where slaves were employed, the other in Georgia, where only free help was used. In his letter to the trustees of Georgia, he rejoices in the success of the plantation in South Carolina, enabling him to support a great many orphans, but deplores the fact that the one in Georgia was a failure, and concludes by saying: "This confirms me in the opinion I have entertained for a long time, that Georgia never can or will be a flourishing province without Negroes are allowed." What a contrast is presented by Whitefield's view and that of a nobler and grander contemporary reformer, John Wesley, whose name will be fragrant while time lasts. Said he: "Slavery is, in and of itself, the execrable sum of all villainies."

We wonder if Whitefield ever considered that one reason why his South Carolina plantation was profitable, was because it was run on the economical plan of half starving and overworking the poor slaves, stimulated as they were by the overseer's lash We wonder, too, if he considered that slavery was the prime cause of making an orphanage necessary, since this cruel system produced more orphans among the Indians and Negroes than all other agencies combined. Did he take into account the character of labor then used on Georgia plantations, such as were obtained by emptying the jails and almshouses of England; men who were by nature and practice crminals and vagrants, of whom it might have been said, "they toil not, neither do they spin?" Lastly, we wonder if this great preacher ever noticed closely the language of his Lord, "One is your Master, even Christ; and all ye are brethren." Under the influence of Whitefield and others, slavery was introduced in 1749. Thus the seeds of slavery were sown in this the youngest and fairest of the original thirteen colonies. Some of the terrible harvest was reaped by the swords of Sherman's army in that never to be forgotten march through the state; during which they burned and wasted the country, "sixty miles in latitude, three hundred to the main." Verily, "God is not mocked: for whatsoever a man soweth, that shall he also reap."

CHAPTER VIII.

NEGRO SOLDIERS IN THE REVOLUTION.

It was said that Marshal Ney fought five hundred battles for France, and not one against her, and yet he was shot as a traitor to his country. So in reading the annals of history, we see the Negro fought to gain and perpetuate the liberty of this country, in every prominent war, from the French and Indian to the Rebellion, while he himself was forced to remain in bondage.

We read of no greater inconsistency or more indefensible farce, than to call this the land of freedom, when millions of her people were slaves, including some of the most gallant defenders of this country or their descendants.

When we meet together on "the day we celebrate," our orators are prone to ring the changes on the American eagle, Washington and the brave patriots of '76; but who ever heard a Fourth of July orator refer to La Fayette and the French, or the other brave foreigners, but for whom our cause would probably have failed?

When was a reference in such a speech, made to the part performed by the black men in that glorious struggle for freedom? It would almost seem that a systematic effort was made to consign these swarthy heroes to oblivion, and obliterate their very names from the page of history. But we are glad to know that the effort was a futile one. Still, while our datas are somewhat fragmentary, they are ample for a sketch, and we doubt not, the greater part of the story which perhaps will never be known was fully equal to this sample: —

There is positive proof that at least two Negroes of Virginia, Israel Titus and Samuel Jenkins, fought under Braddock and Washington in the French and Indian war. The first died at Williamstown, Massachusetts, in 1855, about one hundred and ten years of age. A sketch of his life was published in the Springfield *Republican* of about that date. Samuel Jenkins is thought to have been about one hundred and fifteen years old when he died at Lancaster, Ohio, in 1849. The Lancaster Gazette of that period gave a brief sketch of his life, remarkable in many respects.

There were doubtless others in this war who lived and died unknown to fame, their names and records having been lost.

The protomartyr of the Revolutionary war was Crispus Attucks, a Negro, who was the leader in the Boston massacre on that memorable 5th of March, 1770. Attucks led the citizens in the charge, shouting, "The way to get rid of these idlers is to attack the main guard; strike at the root; this is the nest!" These were perhaps his last words, as his men threw a shower of clubs, stones and brickbats at the soldiers, which they returned with a galling fire. Attucks was the first to fall, being conspicuous on account of his height, which was six feet and two inches, and the still more important fact that he was in advance of his men. Two others, Samuel Gray and Jonas Caldwell, were killed, while Samuel Maverick and Patrick Carr, an Irishman, were mortally wounded. Attucks and Caldwell were buried from Faneuil Hall, afterwards called the "Cradle of Liberty," the other two from their homes, but all four in one common grave, with the following epitaph on their monument.

"Long as in freedom's cause the wise contend,
Dear to your country shall your fame extend;
While to the world the lettered stone shall tell,
Where Caldwell, Attucks, Gray and Maverick fell."

Crispus Attucks was a man of some learning, and sometime before his tragic death indited the following letter to the Tory Governor of Massachusetts:

"To Thomas Hutchinson:—You will hear from us with astonishment. You ought to hear from us with horror. You are chargeable before God and man with our blood. The soldiers were but passive instruments, were machines; neither moral nor voluntary agents in our destruction, more than the leaden pellets with which we were wounded. You were a free agent. You acted coolly, deliberately, with all that premeditated malice, not against us in particular, but against the people in general, which, in the sight of the law, is an ingredient in the composition of murder. You will hear further from us hereafter.

"Crispus Attucks"

And he did hear, and the world has heard of this liberty-loving hero and patriot. For by his death and that of his fellow patriots the torch of liberty was kindled in Boston never to be extinguished.

Every schoolboy has read of Major Pitcairn, who commanded the British regulars in the fight at Lexington and Concord, April 19, 1775, shouting to the militia: "Disperse, you rebels; lay down your arms and disperse!" And when they stood their ground, how he ordered his men to fire, which command they obeyed, killing seven of the patriots, the first martyrs of the Revolution. But it is not as well known that one of those who fell that day was a Negro; and that his death and that of his fellow martyrs was avenged by another Negro, the brave Peter Salem, who killed Major Pitcairn while leading his men in the charge at the battle of Bunker Hill.

This Peter Salem was born and lived at Farmington, Massachusetts, and was probably a slave until the beginning of the Revolution. He served faithfully throughout the entire war.

There were quite a number of the sons of Africa fighting side by side with their countrymen of the white race at Bunker Hill, several of whom were conspicuous for their bravery, among them Salem Poor, Titus Coburn, Alexander Ames, Barzilai Lew, and Cato Howe each of whom received a pension. This fact is established by the painting of Colonel Trumbull, who witnessed this battle from Roxbury and reproduced it upon canvas in 1786. He reproduced several Negroes in the front ranks fighting valiantly, with visible results. Indeed, as Henry Wilson stated, "it is hardly too much to say that some of the most heroic deeds of the war of Independence were performed by black men."

The following incident is a case in point. When Major General Prescott commanded the British troops at Newport, Colonel Barton, with a black soldier named Prince, determined to capture him; and considering the fact that he was surrounded by his guard, with a large number of British soldiers quartered near, together with a fleet of ships, it was a remarkably successful stratagem. In company with "Black Prince," several other Negroes, and a detachment of the militia, Colonel Barton one dark night started in boats from a house about five miles above Newport. Muffling the oars, and avoiding the ships, they came on as noiselessly as possible, landing a short distance from the hotel, where he knew General Prescott had established his headquarters. It was arranged that Colonel Barton should take the lead, followed by Prince a short distance behind, while some of the other men brought up the rear.

When the Colonel drew near the hotel, the sentinel presented his gun and challenged him, but he continued to advance, throwing the sentinel off his guard by talking about rebel prisoners, and denouncing the rebels in general. Again the sentinel demanded the password; he replied that he did not have the password, but was loyal to his country. By this time he was near the sentinel, when, suddenly seizing his gun, he struck it to one side and wrenched it from his hand. Prince now seized the soldier in his vice-like grip, and having been bound and gagged he was handed over to the other men who had come up.

The Colonel and Prince now drew their weapons and rushed into the hotel office, where they met the landlord and demanded that he should show them General Prescott's room; he at first refused, but being threatened with instant death, he pointed to the room above. The Colonel and Prince now hurried up to this room, and finding it locked, the brave Negro burst in the door with his head, and seized General Prescott in bed. Seeing that resistance was useless and knowing that the slightest outcry meant death, he surrendered to his captors, was soon in the boat and conveyed within the American lines. He was afterwards exchanged for General Lee, an American officer of equal rank.

George W. Williams, the leading colored historian, estimates from official sources that there were not less than three thousand colored soldiers in the revolution, including Negro soldiers from every Northern colony, scattered throughout the white regiments; while Rhode Island raised a colored regiment commanded by Colonel Christopher Green, and Connecticut raised a black battalion of soldiers commanded in part by Colonel David Humphrey. But, as usual, Little Rhode Island was the most consistent of the thirteen colonies; she first made freemen of her black sons before permitting them to fight for freedom, and indeed it is not surprising that this regiment proved to have as gallant soldiers as any in the Revolution. The Negro troops turned the tide in the battle of Rhode Island, which was pronounced by Lafayette "the best fought battle of the war."

Arnold, in his history of the above named state,

thus referred to it: "It was in repelling these furious onsets that the newly raised black regiment under Colonel Green distinguished itself by deeds of valor. Posted behind a thicket in the valley, they three times drove back the Hessians who charged repeatedly down the hill to dislodge them."

One admirable trait that characterized this black regiment was devotion to their officers. This was nobly demonstrated in the attack made upon the American lines near Croton River, on the thirteenth of May, 1781. Colonel Green, their gallant commander, was cut down and mortally wounded; but the enemy's saber only reached him through the bodies of his faithful guard of blacks, who hovered over him to defend him and fought until every one of them was killed. Leonidas and the Spartans at Thermopylæ did no more. Truly did Tristam Burgess say in Congress in 1828, "No braver men met the enemy in battle."

We are indebted to William C. Nell's work on Colored Patriots of the American Revolution, for valuable information, including the following address, which was delivered in 1842, before the Congregational and Presbyterian Anti-Slavery Society, at Francestown, New Hampshire, by Dr. Harris, a Revolutionary veteran. It is of great interest, because it is an eye-witness describing what he had actually seen. Said he, after giving some of his own exploits: "There was a black regiment, yes, a regiment of Negroes, fighting for our liberty and independence—not a white man among them but the officers—stationed at what was called a flanking position, that is, upon a place which the enemy must pass in order to come round in our rear, to drive us from the fort. This pass was everything, both to the enemy and us. Had the colored soldiers given way before the enemy or been unfaithful, all would have been lost.

"Three times in succession were they attacked, with most desperate valor and fury, by well disciplined and veteran troops, and three times did they successfully repel the assault, and thus preserved our army from capture. They fought through the war. They were brave, hardy troops. They helped to gain our liberty and independence.

"Now, the war is over, our freedom is gained— what is to be done with these colored soldiers, who have shed their best blood in its defense? Must they be sent off out of the country, because they are black? Or must they be sent back into slavery, now they have risked their lives and shed their blood to secure the freedom of their masters? I ask, what became of these noble colored soldiers? Many of them, I fear, were taken back to the South, and doomed to the fetter and the chain. .

"And why is it that the colored inhabitants of our nation, born in this country, and entitled to all the rights of freedom, are held in slavery? Why, but because they are black! I have often thought that, should God see fit, by a miracle, to change their color, straighten their hair, and give their features and complexion the appearance of the whites, slavery would not continue a year. No, you would then go and abolish it with the sword, if it were not speedily done without. But is it a suitable cause for making men slaves because God has given them such color, such hair and such features as he saw fit?"

Simon Lee, the grandfather of William Wells Brown, on his mother's side, was a slave in Virginia, and served in the Revolution; although honorably discharged with the other Virginia troops, at the close of the war, he was sent back to his master, where he spent the remainder of his life in toiling on a tobacco plantation. Such is the injustice toward the colored American, that, after serving in his country's struggle for freedom he is doomed to fill the grave of a slave!

La Fayette, in his letter to Clarkson, said: "I would never have drawn my sword in the cause of America, if I could have conceived that thereby I was founding a land of slavery."

The following incident from Theodore Parker shows that other black veterans of the Revolution were remanded to slavery, and doubtless there were many such cases. A sea-captain of Massachusetts who commanded a small brig, which plied between Carolina and the Gulf States, said to Mr. Parker, "One day at Charleston a man came and brought to me an old Negro slave. He was very old and had fought in the Revolution, and had been much distinguished for bravery and other soldierly qualities. If he had not been a Negro, he would have become a captain at least, perhaps a colonel. But in his old age, his master found no use for him, and said he could not afford to keep him. He asked me to take the Revolutionary soldier and carry him South and sell him. I carried him to Mobile and tried to get as good and kind a master for him as I could, for I didn't like to sell a man who had fought for his country.

"I sold the old Revolutionary veteran for a hundred dollars to a citizen of Mobile, who raised poultry, and he set him to tend a hen coop." Mr. Parker remarked that he supposed the South Carolina master, "a true gentleman," drew the pension till the soldier died. Then turning to the sea captain, whom he knew to be an anti-slavery man, he asked: "How could you do such a thing?" "If I had not done it," he replied, "I never could have received another bale of cotton, nor hogshead of sugar, nor anything to carry from or to any Southern port."

Theodore Parker also stated that in his day workmen, while excavating for the foundations of the large dry goods stores of New York city, unearthed a large number of human skeletons. On investigation they proved to be the bones of colored American soldiers, who fell in the battle of Long Island in 1776. They were carted off to fill up a chasm, and thrown on the beach to make the foundations of warehouses, like any other rubbish of the city. Had they been white men they would have been buried anew, but as they were only Negroes who had died for their own and their masters' country, this was their fate.

Hon. Calvin Goddard, of Connecticut, states that he was instrumental in securing, under Act of 1818, the pensions of nineteen colored soldiers. "I cannot," he says, "refrain from mentioning one black man, Primus Babcock, who proudly presented to me an honorable discharge from service during the war, dated at the close of it, wholly in the handwriting of George Washington. Nor can I forget the expression of his feelings when informed, after his discharge had been sent to the War Department, that it could not be returned. At his request it was written for, as he seemed inclined to spurn the pension and reclaim the discharge."

There is a pathetic anecdote told of Baron Steuben, at the time the American army disbanded. "A black soldier with his wounds unhealed, utterly destitute, stood on the wharf just as a vessel bound for his distant home was getting under way. The poor fellow gazed at the vessel with tears in his eyes, and gave himself up to utter despair. The warm-hearted foreigner noticed his emotions, and inquiring into the cause of it, took his last dollar from his purse and gave it to him, while tears of sympathy trickled down his cheeks. Overwhelmed with gratitude, the poor wounded soldier hailed the ship and was received on board. As it moved out of the wharf he cried back to his noble friend on shore, 'God Almighty bless you, Master Baron.'"

We have already stated that Connecticut raised a battalion of colored soldiers, who were among the bravest in the American army. Some of them even immortalized their names as heroes "who were not born to die," as the following letter from Parker Pillsbury of New Hampshire, to William C. Nell, clearly indicates: "The names of the two brave men of color who fell with Ledyard at the storming of Fort Griswold, were Lambo Latham and Jordan Freeman. All the names of the slain at that time, are inscribed on a marble tablet, wrought into the monument—the names of the

CHAS. CHESNUT,
Of Cleveland, Ohio, Author of "The Conjure Woman," "Life of Frederick Douglass," and Volume of Short Stories.

colored soldiers last, and not only last, but a blank space is left between them and the whites; in genuine keeping with the "Negro Pew distinction—setting them not only below all the others, but by themselves, even after that. And it is difficult to say why. They were not last in the fight.

"When Major Montgomery, one of the leaders in the expedition against the Americans, was lifted upon the walls of the fort by his soldiers, flourishing his sword and calling on them to follow him, Jordan Freeman received him on the point of a pike, and pinned him dead to the earth (see Historical Collections of Connecticut); and the name of Jordan Freeman stands away down last on the list of heroes—perhaps the greatest hero of them all." But what of the other black hero who was with him? We will let a nephew of his, William Anderson, of New London, Connecticut, tell the story.

"September 6th, 1781, New London was taken by the British, under the command of that arch traitor, Benedict Arnold. The small band composing the garrison retreated to the fort opposite, in the town of Groton, and there resolved either to gain a victory or die for their country. The latter pledge was faithfully redeemed and by none more gallantly than the two colored men; and if the survivors of that day's carnage tell truly, they fought like tigers and were butchered after the gates were burst open. One of these men was the brother of my grandmother, by the name of Lambert, but called Lambo, since chiseled on the marble monument by the American classic appellation of

'Sambo.' The name of the other black man was Jordan Freeman.

"Lambert was living with a gentleman in Groton by the name of Latham; so of course he was called Lambert Latham. Mr. Latham and Lambert, on the day of the massacre, were working in a field at a distance from the house. On hearing the alarm upon the approach of the enemy, Mr. Latham started for home, leaving Lambert to drive the oxen up to the house. On arriving at the house, Lambert was told that Mr. Latham had gone up to the fort. Unyoking the oxen from the wagon and making all secure, he started for the point of defense, where he arrived before the British began the attack.

"The assault on the part of the British was a deadly one, and manifestly resisted by the Americans, even to the clubbing of their muskets after their ammunition was expended; but finally the little garrison of brave defenders was reduced to a handful, and could hold out no longer.

"On the entrance of the enemy, the British officer inquired, 'Who commands this fort?' The gallant Ledyard replied, 'I once did; you do now,' —at the same time handing him his sword, which was seized, and immediately run through his body to the hilt by the officer. This was the commencement of an unparalleled slaughter.

"Lambert, being near Colonel Ledyard when he was slain, retaliated upon the officer by thrusting his bayonet through his body. Lambert in return received from the enemy thirty-three bayonet wounds, and thus fell, nobly avenging the death of his commander. These facts were given me on

the spot, at the time of the laying of the corner-
stone, by two veterans who were present at the
battle."

We learn from Kent's Commentary that the
Legislature of New York passed an Act during
the Revolutionary War granting freedom to all
slaves who should serve in the army for three
years, or until regularly discharged.

The Hartford *Review* for September, 1839,
gives the following account of a colored man by
the name of Hamet, living at that time in Middle-
town, Connecticut, who was formerly owned by
Washington:—"Hamet is, according to his own
account, nearly one hundred years old. He draws
a pension for his services in the Revolutionary war,
and manufactures toy drums for his support. He
has a white wife and one child   His hair is white
with age and hangs matted together in masses over
his shoulders.   He retains a perfect recollection
of his Massa and Missus Washington, and has
several mementoes of them.   Among these there
is a lock of the General's hair, and his service
sword.   He converses in three or four different
languages,—the French, Spanish and German, besides his native African tongue."

Another black veteran, Oliver Cromwell, served
six years and nine months under Washington's
immediate command, and received an honorable
discharge in Washington's own handwriting, of
which he was very proud.   He received a pension
of ninety-six dollars annually. Was in the battles
of Trenton, Princeton, Brandywine, Monmouth
and Yorktown, at which place he claims to have
seen the last man killed.   He enlisted in a company

commanded by Captain Lowery, attached to the second New Jersey Regiment, under the command of Colonel Israel Shreve. He brought up seven sons and seven daughters, who reached the age of maturity. He was a man of strong natural ability —never using tobacco or liquor in any form. He was more than a hundred years of age when he died at his native town, Columbus, New Jersey, January 24, 1853.

Another Revolutionary hero, Charles Bowles, was born in 1761, and at the age of twelve was placed in the family of a Tory. But he was too patriotic to be contented with his home, and two years later found him in the American army a servant to an officer. When sixteen years of age he became a regular soldier, serving faithfully to the end of the war. He then went to New Hampshire and engaged in farming. He obtained a pension, became a Baptist preacher of some prominence, and died in 1843, at the age of eighty-two.

Rev. Henry F. Harrington wrote an article on General Washington and Primus Hall, body servant to Colonel Pickering, of Massachusetts, which was published in the June issue of Godey's Lady's Book, 1849.

"On one occasion, the General was engaged in earnest conversation with Colonel Pickering in his tent, until after the night had fairly set in. Headquarters were at a considerable distance, and Washington signified his preference to stay with the Colonel over night, provided he had a spare blanket and straw. 'O, yes,' said Primus, who was appealed to; 'plenty of straw and blankets – plenty.'

"Upon this assurance, Washington continued his conference with the Colonel until it was time to retire to rest. Two humble beds were spread, side by side, in the tent, and the officers laid themselves down, while Primus seemed to be busy with duties that required his attention before he himself could sleep. He worked or appeared to work, until the breathing of the prostrate gentlemen satisfied him that they were sleeping; and then seating himself upon a box or stool, he leaned his head on his hands to obtain such repose as so inconvenient a position would allow. In the middle of the night Washington awoke. He looked about and descried the Negro as he sat. He gazed at him awhile, and then spoke. 'Primus,' said he, calling; 'Primus!' Primus started up and rubbed his eyes. 'What, General?' said he.

"Washington rose up in his bed. 'Primus,' said he, 'what did you mean by saying that you had blankets and straw enough? Here you have given up your blanket and straw to me, that I may sleep comfortably, while you are obliged to sit through the night.' 'It's nothing, General,' said Primus. 'It's nothing. I am well enough. Don't trouble yourself about me, General, but go to sleep again. No matter about me, I sleep very good.'

"'But it is matter—it is matter,' said Washington, earnestly. 'I cannot do it, Primus. If either is to sit up, I will. But I think there is no need of either sitting up. The blanket is wide enough for two. Come and lie down here with me.' 'Oh, no!' said Primus, starting, and protesting against the proposition. 'No; let me sit here. I'll do very well on the stool.' 'I say, come and lie down here!' said Washington authoritatively. 'There is room for both, and I insist upon it!' He threw open the blanket as he spoke, and moved to one side of the straw. Primus professed to have been exceedingly shocked at the idea of lying under the same covering with the commander-in-chief, but his tone was so resolute and determined that he could not hesitate. He prepared himself, therefore, and laid himself down by Washington; and on the same straw, and under the same blanket, the General and the Negro servant slept until morning."

Seymour Burr lived in Connecticut; he was a slave to a brother of Colonel Aaron Burr, from whom he received his name. His master treated him kindly, but the slave sighed for freedom and was resolved, if possible, to obtain it. Persuading a number of other slaves to go with him, they seized a boat, intending to join the British army, that by so doing they might become freemen. Nevertheless their owners pursued and overtook them, and being heavily armed the slaves surren-- dered.

Mr. Burr did not punish Seymour, but asked him why he had left such a kind master. The Negro replied that he wanted his liberty. The master consented that the Negro should join the American army, on condition that the master should receive the bounty money and the slave be free at the close of the war. Accordingly he en- listed in the seventh regiment, commanded by Colonel Brooks of Medford.

He was with his company in the siege of Fort

Catskill, where they endured great suffering from cold and starvation, until at last relieved by the arrival of General Washington, who was overjoyed on finding them unexpectedly alive, and holding the fort.

He served faithfully until the close of the war, receiving a pension. He afterwards married an Indian woman and established a home at Canton, Massachusetts. His wife survived him, dying in 1852, having lived more than five score years.

Jeremy Jonah (colored) also served valiantly in the same Regiment, afterwards obtaining a pension. He lived near Seymour Burr, and the two old comrades often made a night of it, after the manner of veterans, fighting their battles over again.

On August 16, 1777, the "Green Mountain Boys," aided by troops from New Hampshire and a few from Massachusetts, commanded by General Stark, captured the left wing of the British army near Bennington. When the prisoners, to the number of between seven and eight hundred, were collected to be tied on either side of a rope, it was found to be too short. The General called for more, but there was none at hand. In this emergency the patriotic wife of Hon. Moses Robinson stepped forward and said: "General, I will take down the last bedstead in the house and present the rope to you on one condition. When the prisoners are all tied to the rope, you shall permit my Negro man to harness up my old mare and hitch the rope to the whiffletree, mount the mare, and conduct the British and Tory prisoners out of town." The General willingly accepted Mrs.

Robinson's proposition. The Negro mounted the mare, grinning from ear to ear, and thus conducted the left wing of the British army into Massachusetts, on their road to Boston.

The following instance of Negro wit is often told. After Cornwallis surrendered at Yorktown, an acquaintance of his, a colored soldier, stepped up to him quite elated, and remarked: "You used to be called Cornwallis, but it is Cornwallis no longer; it must now be Cobwallis, for General Washington has shelled off all the corn."

The gallant historian is proud to record the heroic deed of Molly Pitcher, whose husband was killed in the battle of Monmouth, and she took his place at the cannon, until the end of that battle. But here is the record of a black heroine who faithfully discharged all the duties of a soldier for nearly a year and a half.

The following extract is a copy of one of the Resolutions of the General Court of Massachusetts during the session of 1791-2:—"XXIII. Resolution on the petition of Deborah Gannett, granting her £34 for services rendered in the Continental army.

"On the petition of Deborah Gannett, praying for compensation for services performed in the late army of the United States. Whereas, it appears to this Court that the said Deborah Gannett enlisted under the name of Robert Shurtliff in Captain Webb's company in the 4th Massachusetts Regiment, on May 20th, 1782, and did actually perform the duty of a soldier, in the late army of the United States, to the 23rd day of October, 1783, for which she has received no compensation; and whereas it further appears that the said Deborah Gannett exhibited an extraordinary instance of female heroism, by discharging the duties of a faithful, gallant soldier, and at the same time preserving the virtue and chastity of her sex unsuspected and unblemished, and was discharged from the service with a fair and honorable character · therefore, Resolved, That the treasurer of this commonwealth be, and hereby is, directed to issue his note to the said Deborah for the sum of thirty-four pounds, bearing interest from October 23, 1788."

Prince Richards was a pensioned Revolutionary veteran, of East Bridgewater. When a slave he learned to write with a charred stick, thus showing a *burning* desire for learning, even against the command of his master, and perhaps, the law of the state.

At the close of the war, John Hancock presented the colored company called "The Bucks" with a beautiful and appropriate banner, bearing his initials, as a token of his appreciation of their courage and patriotism during the struggle. "The Bucks," under command of Colonel Middleton, marched through Boston, halting in front of the Hancock mansion on Beach Street, where the Governor and his son united in presenting the banner.

One of the most brilliant exploits of the Revolution was the capture of Stony Point by Mad Anthony Wayne. But it must not be forgotten that the countersign and password, "The Fort is Ours," was obtained by the shrewdness of a patriotic Negro who was in the habit of selling strawberries to the British. This same Negro guided the troops through the inky darkness, to the causeway over the marsh, around the foot of the hill. Then going in advance up the hill, he gave the countersign to the sentinel and engaged him in a friendly conversation, always keeping his back down the hill, until he was suddenly seized from behind and gagged; the rest was easy.

The historian will tell us that Washington planned, and Wayne executed this glorious exploit; but we maintain that but for this nameless black hero, the impregnable Stony Point could not have been taken.

We also read of the brig on which Jack Grove (colored) was steward; while sailing from the West Indies to Portland in 1812, it was captured by a French vessel, whose commander placed a guard on board. Jack urged his commander to make an effort to retake the ship, but the captain saw no hope. Again he urged him, saying: "Captain McLellan, I can take her myself if you will only let me go ahead " But the captain was rather cowardly and checked him, warning him not to hint such a thing, as there was danger in it. But Jack, disappointed and disgusted with him, though not daunted, rallied the men on his own hook. Captain McLellan and the rest, inspired by his example of courage and leadership, joined them, and the attempt resulted in victory. They weighed anchor and took the vessel into Portland. The owner of the brig offered Jack fifty hogsheads of molasses for his brave deed; but Jack demanded one half of the brig, which being denied, he employed two Boston lawyers and brought suit. We were unable to learn how the case terminated.

The artist has vied with the historian in proclaiming the fact that the black men were among the bravest of the brave, with Perry in the squadron fight of Lake Erie, and Jackson at New Orleans. What student of history has not read Jackson's eloquent tribute to his brave colored fellow soldiers, after that glorious victory which they helped him to gain?

In the Chicago Tribune of February 26, 1894, Simon Young said in reply to the proposition of the Knights of Labor to deport the Negroes to Africa: "We are part and parcel of this country. Why, only to-day we buried from No. 3331 Dearborn Street old Captain Jackson, a Mexican war veteran, whose father fought in the war of 1812, and his grandfather worked a musket in the Revolutionary set-to. Our blood and brawn and brain helped to make this country. This is our home, and we're going to stay at home." Rev. Peter Williams of New York said on one occasion: "We are natives of this land; we ask only to be treated as well as foreigners. Not a few of our fathers suffered and bled to purchase its independence; we ask only to be treated as well as those who fought against it. We have toiled to cultivate it, and raise it to its present prosperous condition; we ask only to share equal privileges with those who come from distant lands to enjoy the fruits of our labor."

Let us smother all the wrongs we have endured. Let us forget the past. If we are brethren let us yield ourselves to charity, and let us concede the fact that many times have our dusky brothers shown their power, their energy, their skill, in behalf of their friends, their masters, their country! Can we be so thoughtless—yea, so heartless as to begrudge them a place, a home in this broad land of ours for which they have fought, bled, and many of them died to save?

CHAPTER IX.

SLAVERY AND THE CONSTITUTION AND
DECLARATION OF INDE-
PENDENCE.

The noble heroes and patriots who survived
the Revolutionary struggle, in which one of the
main issues was "equal right to all and exclusive
privileges to none," must have been impressed
with the inconsistency of holding their fellow men
in cruel bondage. Certain it is Vermont separated
from New York in 1777, and in framing her state
constitution she forever prohibited slavery. However, Pennsylvania, through the influence of the
Quakers, was the first of the original thirteen colonies to abolish the system, which she did by adopt-
ing a measure of gradual emancipation in 1780.
A little later in the same year Massachusetts abolished slavery by her state constitution.

In 1784 Jefferson proposed an ordinance to con
gress, prohibiting slavery in all the western countr,
above the parallel of 31 north latitude, to go into

DR. A. R. ABBOTT,
Prominent Physician of Toronto, Ont., and One of the Eight
Colored Surgeons Commissioned as Surgeon in
the United States Army by President Lincoln.

effect after the year 1800. To his infinite regret and lasting sorrow, this was lost by one vote. This great statesman afterwards wrote concerning it: "The voice of a single individual would have prevented this abominable crime. Heaven will not always be silent; the friends to the rights of human nature will in the end prevail."

When the constitution was adopted, the leading question considered was, how to obtain a harmonious union of all the colonies; how to fuse these distinct governments, with different interests, into one strong government. Weakened as they were by the long and bloody war with the Mother Country; bankrupt and almost discouraged, they were willing for harmony and unity on almost any terms. Accordingly, we find the framers of the constitution compromising and using ambiguous language in regard to slavery right in the constitution itself.

The words slave, slavery, or Negro, are systematically avoided, and they are spoken of as "persons bound to service," and "three-fifths of all other persons." But it nowhere says how bound, and an honest constitutional judge construing this clause to harmonize with the Declaration of Independence (which preceded and was in a sense the basis of the constitution), would certainly have decided that "bound to service" meant in equity, "bound by contract to service," not forced under the lash, without any contract, and for the entire benefit of the so-called master class.

The framers of the constitution differed widely as to whether the Negroes should be regarded as persons or property? It was finally settled that they were neither absolutely the one nor the other, but partook of both qualities; and it was provided that five slaves should count as three freemen, in the apportionment for representatives and for direct taxation. As an expounder of the compromise on this basis said, the slave was considered "as divested of two-fifths of the man." This is why the constitution was claimed by both sides in the "irrepressible conflict." This instrument was necessarily compromising as touching slavery, but we should be very charitable in reviewing it, when we consider that an unconditional pro-slavery, or anti-slavery constitution, would not have been adopted by the members of the constitution, nor ratified by the different states. The leadership of Washington and the wisdom of Franklin were strained to their utmost before this question was finally settled by compromise, in the constitutional convention.

Even then, as might have been expected, slavery would not remain settled, for while not strictly in the constitution, it was not expunged from it, and proved to be a veritable "Old Man of the Sea," riding on the back of the constitution, seeking to strangle it, until, drunken with the wine of its own violence, it was shaken off and crushed in the war of the Rebellion.

Theodore Parker illustrates slavery and the constitution as follows: "There is an old story told by Hebrew rabbis, that before the flood there was an enormous giant called Gog. After the flood had got into the full tide of successful experiment, and every man was drowned except those taken into the ark, Gog came striding along after Noah, feeling his way with a cane, as long as a mast of the "Great Eastern." The water had only come up to his girdle. It was then over the hill-tops and still rising—raining night and day. The giant hailed the Patriarch. Noah put his head out of the window, and said, 'Who is there?' 'It is I,' said Gog. 'Take us in; it is wet outside!' 'No,' said Noah; 'you're to big; no room. Besides, you've a bad character. You may get on top if you like,' and he closed the window. 'Go to thunder,' said Gog; 'I will ride after all.' And he strode after him, wading through the waters; and mounting on top of the ark, with one leg over the larboard and the other over the starboard side, he steered it just as he pleased and made it rough weather inside.

"Now in making the constitution, we did not care to take in Slavery in express terms. It looked ugly. We allowed it to get on top astride, and now it steers us just where it pleases." Hence the question, Could slavery find shelter behind the constitution of the United States? received almost as many different answers as there were men attempting it. To this great question the abolitionists, led by Garrison, replied, "Yes, therefore away with the constitution." "Yes," replied the anti-abolitionists, "therefore let slavery alone." "No," said the anti-slavery Whigs, "for the constitution is not a pro-slavery instrument." "No," said Gerrit Smith, "for slavery, in the nature of the case, cannot find a shelter behind anything that bears the name of law; the constitution that offered shelter to slavery would have no validity. The question whether or no slavery finds shelter behind the constitution, is wanting in pertinency; there is no such question."

This was substantially the view of Frederick Douglass, who defended it against all gainsayers, with great boldness and power.

Whatever the constitution might be, no one could question the fact that the Declaration of Independence, the Magna Charta of American Liberty, was anti-slavery, when it published to the world the following glorious principles: "We hold these truths to be self-evident, that all men are created *equal*, that they are endowed by their Creator with certain inalienable Rights, that among these are *Life, Liberty* and the pursuit of *Happiness*. That to secure these rights, governments are instituted among men, deriving their just powers from the consent of the governed."

Remember the equality and liberty were not limited to the white, black or red men, for all were in the colonies at that time, but it emphatically says all men; it includes all races, and excludes none. The pursuit of happiness was also guaranteed unto all men, by this instrument, but was there any happiness for the poor souls driven like galley-slaves, and treated like beasts of burden?

Moreover, we read that "Governments are instituted among men, deriving their powers from the consent of the governed." When did the Negro ever give his consent, or, indeed, when was he ever consulted as to how he should be governed from the time he was kidnaped by piratical man-stealers in Africa, until he escaped their clutches at death?

At its conclusion we find this passage: "And for the support of this Declaration, with a firm reliance on the protection of Divine Providence, we mutually pledge to each other our Lives, our Fortunes, and our sacred Honor." In view of the treatment the Negro received, mainly because he was black, this reliance on the "protection of Divine Providence" appears sacrilegious, and this pledge of "sacred honor," a farce.

Can it be that this palladium of Liberty, penned by the immortal Jefferson, was superseded by the constitution and thrown aside as a cast-off garment? It certainly appears so. For if any regard had been paid to this Declaration of Independence, slavery would not have cursed the nation a single year. For it was an unmitigated curse, its advocates being judges. Henry Clay himself said, "Slavery is a curse to the master and a wrong to the slave." Its cloven foot was shown even in drafting this important instrument. It may not be known to all our readers that part of the original document drawn up by the committee consisting of Jefferson, Adams, Livingston, Sherman and Franklin, was rejected and stricken out in deference to slavery, but such is an undoubted historical fact.

The first draft of the Declaration of Independence can be seen in the American Philosophical Society of Philadelphia, an institution founded by Franklin. It contains this forcible language: "He," (King George III.), "has waged cruel war against human nature itself, violating its most sacred rights of life and liberty in the persons of a distant people, who never offended him, captivating and carrying them into slavery in another hemisphere, or to incur a miserable death in their transportation thither. This piratical warfare, the opprobrium of infidel powers, is the warfare of the Christian King of Great Britain. Determined to keep open market where men should be bought and sold, he has prostituted his negative for suppressing every legislative attempt to prohibit or to restrain this execrable commerce."

Mr. William Chambers, the English traveler and author, considers this original draft of our Declaration the greatest archæological curiosity in America.

Thus a union embracing the Southern colonies could only be obtained by withdrawing this scathing rebuke, and prostituting liberty to slavery. In fact, we are forced to the conclusion that the Declaration of Independence, contrary to the design of those who drafted it, never had the validity of law. Though announcing the doctrine of human equality and inalienable rights, it proved to be, as far as effectiveness was concerned, only a respectable piece of buncombe, simply words. Certain it was, when the surrender at Yorktown ended our allegiance to the mother country, we had simply exchanged masters. This country was no longer owned and governed by King George and his Parliament, but from the day of the surrender at Yorktown, 1781, to the day of a still greater surrender at Appomattox in 1865, a period of nearly eighty-five years, this country was ruled with a rod of iron by a domineering minority, in the form of an aristocracy of Southern slave holders, aided by Northern sympathizers. Hence the surrender at Appomattox secured liberty to the white man at the North as well as the black slave at the South.

Since then the Declaration has meant what its language would imply, and this glorious old expunged paragraph should be restored. At the time of the adoption of the Federal Constitution in 1787, it was generally believed that slavery would die out in all the states. A man would not have been laughed to scorn had he predicted that Maryland, Delaware and Virginia would be free states in his lifetime. Seven states had already abolished slavery, or were preparing to do so. And it must be borne in mind that the constitution abolished the African slave trade after the year 1808, though why this clause was never enforced is not apparent. Certain it is, public sentiment was gaining ground against slavery even in Georgia, as is shown by the fact that one of her representatives stated on the floor of the House, without contradiction, "that there was not a man in Georgia who did not wish there were no slaves, and everybody believed they were a curse to the country."

Several influences contributed to mould public opinion against slavery at this time. First in order of importance, as we have already seen, was the Declaration of Independence. Second, the bravery of the colored soldiers in the war of Independence. Having aided his master in breaking the yoke of oppression, it was inconsistent for the black man to continue a servant in

"The land of the free and the home of the brave."

Third, the opposition of abolition societies, and religious bodies, particularly the Quakers, who were most aggressive; the Methodists, who resolved in general conference that "slave-keeping was hurtful to society, and contrary to the laws of God, man and nature;" and the Baptists especially in Rhode Island. Fourth, the influence and example of such fathers of the Republic as Washington, Jefferson, Adams, Franklin, Hamilton and Madison. Fifth, the fact that it had been demonstrated that slavery did not pay.

Washington and Jefferson both opposed the idea of buying or selling Negroes off the plantations to which they belonged, and both proved by their personal experience that a large number of Negroes on a Virginia plantation was an economical failure. Supporting his numerous slaves brought Jefferson to poverty in his old age. Washington, in a private letter written while President, expresses an opinion that slavery must soon be abolished in Virginia and Maryland, and as is well known, manumitted his own slaves by his last will.

Neither Jefferson nor Adams had any part in framing the constitution, as they were both absent at foreign courts. They held identically the same views on the slavery question, for in a letter written about this time Jefferson expressed a strong desire that the slave trade, and slavery itself, might be abolished; while John Adams never owned a slave during his life, because of his abhorrence to slavery.

Franklin, as president of the Pennsylvania abolition society, earnestly besought Congress to give immediate attention to the subject of slavery. He further petitioned, "that you will be pleased to countenance the restoration of liberty to those unhappy men, who are degraded into perpetual bondage; and that you will discourage every species of traffic in persons of our fellowmen."

Hamilton, while secretary of the New York abolition society, received a request from La Fayette, proposing himself as a fellow member of his society. And Madison in the constitutional convention urged the members to strike out the section delaying the prohibition of the slave trade until the year 1808, saying: "Twenty years will produce all the mischief that can be apprehended from the liberty to import slaves. So long a term will be more dishonorable to the American character than to say nothing about it in the Constitution."

Of course such statesmen and patriots as these would create a strong public sentiment against slavery, which was fast spreading over the entire nation. But an event occurred in 1793 which turned the tide in favor of slavery, and benefited the planter more than the Fugitive Slave law.

"What," asked Webster, "created the new feeling in favor of slavery in the South, so that it became a cherished institution, no evil, no scourge, but great religious, social and moral blessing?"

To answer the question in a sentence we would say, the invention of the cotton-gin. This was due to the mechanical skill of Eli Whitney of Massachusetts. Young Whitney, while engaged in school-teaching, was making his home at the hospitable mansion of Mrs. General Nathaniel Green, on her Georgia plantation, where he perfected his invention with the aid of his kind partner, Mrs. Green.

Prior to this invention it was the work of

a man for one whole day to separate a pound of cotton fiber from the seed; but by the use of this machine one man could do the work of fifty or more.

Undoubtedly the wealth of the South was augmented by this invention more than any other, or perhaps all others combined. Instead of being grateful to Whitney for conferring untold wealth upon them, some neighboring planters broke into the house where it was kept and stole his invention; so that much of his life was embittered by tedious and expensive lawsuits for the recovery of his rights. Whitney, however, invented a gun after this from which he realized a fortune. The cotton-gin, by making slave labor profitable, tended to rivet the chains more firmly on these unfortunate people. In the same year of this invention, a duty of three cents a pound was placed on cotton, which stimulated its production.

The slave territory was extended by the purchase of Louisiana in 1803, of Florida in 1819, and the annexation of Texas in 1845. Slavery had been quickened in the border states, Maryland, Virginia and Kentucky, which had been in fair way to abolish it altogether as unprofitable in the raising of grain, tobacco and live stock Sad to relate, some of the most conscientious Christian people of these states, and the District of Columbia, engaged in the disreputable business of raising slaves for the Southern market, the same as they did mules or cattle, and kept this up as one of the main sources of weath until slavery was overthrown.

The first Fugitive Slave law was passed in 1793,

the same year of Whitney's cotton-gin. It grew out of the fact that a free Negro had been kidnaped in Pennsylvania, by three white ruffians, and carried to Virginia. When the Governor of Pennsylvania could not get him from the Governor of Virginia, he called the attention of President Washington to it, who in turn brought it before Congress, and urged them to take some action in the matter. The result was the passage of this first Fugitive Slave Bill. But the record does not show what became of the poor kidnaped free Negro.

Such laws were not designed to give the Negro any protection, but were all in sympathy with the supposed master.

It may be said that from this time on the aggressive power was ever ready to "lengthen her cords, and strengthen her stakes," and extend her boundaries, by fair means if she could, foul if she must; and the latter was usually adopted. Her motto seems to have been "rule or ruin."

Everything was forced to bow submissive to the Peculiar Institution. Her usual threat which she hung suspended over the North like Damocle's sword, was, "Do this or we will secede!" Even the matchless Daniel Webster had proven recreant to his early principles and bowed the knee to this Baal, in his eagerness for a Presidential nomination; while his no less distinguished contemporary, Henry Clay, living midway between the two sections, was ever ready to step in between the belligerents with a cunningly devised compromise, as one-sided as that of the two boys who found a knife jointly, and decided that the smaller boy should own, and the larger should carry and use it.

Even in the North there were many open sympathizers with slavery, while others were disposed to apologize for it; but those in the main were either concerned in manufacturing cotton, or ignorant of the heartless cruelty of the institution.

The national capital was located on slave territory, and her slave-pen became a great market, where human cattle were daily disposed of to the highest bidder, and was one of the most infamous in the nation. The story is told of a woman who escaped from it, and was pursued by four men across the long bridge. She was fast gaining on them, when they shouted to others on the Virginia side, who ran to that end of the bridge to intercept her. Seeing this, she uttered a wild cry of despair and threw herself into the river, preferring death to falling into the heartless hands of her pursuers Another woman and two children fled for protection to the steps of the capitol building, and while the emblem of liberty floated from its dome, she was forced to the slave-pen.

Perhaps the most baneful feature of slavery, from a moral standpoint, was the unbridled license it gave to amalgamation. I don't mean theoretically—only the despised abolitionists were accused of that—but real practical amalgamation, such as men in power, and the most prominent statesmen were notoriously guilty of. Well might Thomas Jefferson say: "The best blood of Virginia runs in the veins of her slaves." Jane Grey Swisshelm, in her "Half a Century," says: "One of President Tyler's daughters ran away with the man she loved, in order that they might be married, but for this they must reach foreign soil. A young lady of the White House could not marry the man of her choice in the United States. The lovers were captured, and she was brought to His Excellency, her father, who sold her to a slave trader. From that slave-pen she was taken to New Orleans, by a man who expected to get twenty-five hundred dollars for her on account of her great beauty."

The same author gives some evidence that Harrison and Taylor both preceded Lincoln as victims of Southern plots. As it is rather startling, or plausible, to say the least of it, we will quote it in full. Said she of her visit to Washington during Taylor's administration, "Mr Taylor, the Whig President, had pronounced the Fugitive Slave Bill an insult to the North, and stated his determination to veto it. Fillmore, the Vice-President, was in favor of it. So Freedom looked to a man owning three hundred slaves, while slavery relied on a Northern man with Southern principles. President Taylor was hated by the South, was denounced as a traitor to his section, while Southern men and women fawned upon and flattered Fillmore. . . . . When it became known that the Fugitive Slave Bill could pass Congress, but could not command a two-thirds vote to carry it over the assured veto of President Taylor, he ate a plate of strawberries, just as President Harrison had done when he stood in the way of Southern policy, and like his great predecessor, Taylor died opportunely, when Mr. Fillmore became president and signed the bill."

She visited Charles Sumner while he was in the Alleghany Mountains, recovering from the Brooks assault. Referring to it, she said: "In talking with Mr. Sumner during that visit, I learned that the same doctor attended both President Harrison and President Taylor in their last illness, and used his professional authority to prevent their friends seeing them until the fatal termination of their illness was certain. Also, that it was that same doctor who was within call when Brooks made his assault on Sumner; took charge of the case, and made an official statement that the injury was very slight, gave it a superficial dressing and sought to exclude every one from the room of his patient. Said Sumner: 'I shuddered when I recovered consciousness, and found this man beside me.' He dismissed him promptly, and did not hesitate to say that he believed he would not have recovered under his treatment. When the South seceded, this useful man left Washington and joined the Confederacy."

This is certainly a very strong chain of circumstantial evidence that Lincoln and Garfield were not our only martyred Presidents.

The following is from a letter written by the celebrated Irish orator and statesman, Daniel O'Connell. It was written at Dublin, October 11th, 1843, to his fellow countrymen in America, concerning slavery, which they were disposed at that time to endorse or apologize for: "You say the Negroes are naturally an inferior race. That is a totally gratuitous assertion on your part. In America you can have no opportunity of seeing the Negro educated. On the contrary, in most of

your states it is a crime—sacred Heaven!—a crime
to educate even a free Negro! How, then, can you
judge of the Negro race, when you see them despised and condemned by educated classes—reviled
and looked down upon as inferior? The Negro
race has naturally some of the finest qualities.
They are naturally gentle, generous, humane, and
very grateful for kindness. They are brave and
as fearless as any other of the race of human beings; but the blessings of education are kept from
them, and they are judged of, not as they would
be with proper cultivation, but as they are rendered by cruel and debasing oppression.

"It is as old as the days of Homer, who truly
asserts that 'the day which sees a man a slave takes
away half his worth.' Slavery actually brutalizes
human beings. It was about sixty years ago when
one of the Sheiks, not far south of Fez, in Morocco,
who was in the habit of accumulating white slaves,
upon being strongly remonstrated with by a
European Power, gave for his reply that, by his
own experience he found it quite manifest that
white men were of an inferior race, intended by
nature for slaves; and he produced his own brutalized white slaves to illustrate the truth of his
assertion. And a case of an American with a
historic name—John Adams—is quite familiar.
Some twenty-five years ago—not more—John
Adams was the sole survivor of an American crew
wrecked on the African coast. He was taken
into the interior as a slave of an Arab chief. He
was only for three years a slave, and the English
and American consuls having been informed of a
white man's slavery, claimed him and obtained

his liberation. In the short space of three years
he had become completely brutalized; he had
completely forgotten the English language, without having acquired the native tongue. He spoke
a kind of gabble, as unintellectual as the dialects
of most of your Negro slaves; and many months
elapsed before he recovered his former habits
and ideas.

"We cannot bring ourselves to believe that you
breathed your natal air in Ireland—Ireland, the
first of all the nations on the earth that abolished
the dealing in slaves. The slave trade of that
day was curious enough, a slave trade in British
youths—Ireland, that never was stained with Negro
slave trading—Ireland, that never committed
offense against the men of color—Ireland, that
never fitted out a single vessel for the traffic in
blood on the African coast.

"We ask you to exert yourselves in every
possible way to put an end to the internal
slave trade of the states. The breeding of
slaves for sale is probably the most immoral
and debasing practice ever known in the world.
It is a crime of the most heinous kind, and
if there were no other crime committed by
the Americans, this alone would place the advocates, supporters and practicers of American
slavery in the lowest grade of criminals It is no
excuse to allege that the Congress is restricted
from emancipating slaves by one general law.
Each particular slave state has that power within
its own precincts; and there is every reason to be
convinced that Maryland and Virginia would have
followed the example of New York, and long ago

abolished slavery, but for the diabolical practice of 'raising,' as you call it, slaves for the Southern market of pestilence and death.

"Irishmen! sons of Irishmen! descendants of the kind of heart and affectionate disposition, think, oh! think only with pity and compassion on your colored fellow creatures in America. Offer them the hand of kindly help. Soothe their sorrows. Scathe their oppressor. Join with your countrymen at home in one cry of horror against the oppressor; in one cry of sympathy with the enslaved and oppressed,

> 'Till prone in the dust slavery shall be hurl'd,
> Its name and nature blotted from the world.'

"Irishmen, I call upon you to join in crushing slavery, and in giving liberty to every man and every caste, creed, or color.

"D. O'C."

These soul-stirring sentiments are quite different to those of another Irishman, who was in the act of marrying a Planter's widow. When the minister asked, "Do you take this woman to be your lawfully wedded wife?" he replied, "Yis, your riverance, and the Naygurs too."

Henry Wilson, in his "Rise and Fall of the Slave Power," informs us that when the news of the French Revolution of 1848, in which the King was deposed and driven into exile, reached Washington, it was the occasion of great rejoicing. President Polk sent a message to Congress in which he announced the event, and stated that "the world has seldom witnessed a more interesting and sublime spectacle than the peaceful rising of the French people, resolved to secure for themselves enlarged liberty."

On the same day a series of resolutions were introduced into the House expressing satisfaction that "the sentiment of self-government is commending itself to the honorable consideration of the more intelligent of nations;" and announcing the hope that "down-trodden humanity may succeed in breaking down all forms of tyranny and oppression;" and tendering their "warmest sympathies to the people of France and Italy in their present struggle."

The following amendment was offered by Mr. Ashmun of Massachusetts, that "we especially see an encouraging earnest of their success in the decree which pledges the government of France to early measures for the immediate emancipation of all slaves in the colonies." The following amendment to the amendment was offered by Mr. Schenck of Ohio, "recognizing, as we do, that there shall be neither slavery nor involuntary servitude."

This was followed by a speech from Mr. Hillard of Alabama, in which he said, "I solemnly believe that the time has come when kingcraft has lost its hold upon the human mind. The world is waking from its deep slumber, and mankind begin to see that the right to govern belongs, not to crowned kings, but to the great masses."

He was not ready to recognize the doctrine of human equality *per se*. He referred to Mr. Ashmun's amendment as "a matter which does not belong to it," and defiantly asserted that all over the South there was a determination on the part of the masters to maintain the claim on their slaves, "with a courage and firmness which nothing can intimidate or shame." The same inconsistency was displayed by Mr. Haskell of Tennessee, who stated that the kingdoms of Europe "were upheaving beneath the throb of liberty which was animating the bosoms of the people, and that it was from this country that they had caught the flame;" he then declared that he was "sick and tired of this continual thrusting in this subject of slavery," which tended "to stop the progress of freedom, to injure this government itself, and put out this light toward which with hope were turned the eyes of the down-trodden world."

The handful of anti-slavery members made gallant fight defending their principles, and pointing out the gross inconsistency of singing pæans over the triumph of liberty in France, and at the same instant expressing a determination to perpetuate a more cruel and despotic tyranny in this Republic.

Mr. Giddings, seeing this inconsistency, said: "Look from that window, and you will see a slave-pen, whose gloomy walls in mute but eloquent terms proclaim the hypocrisy of the deed." After reminding the House that all this is sustained by laws passed by Congress, he continued, "Will not the French cast back all such pretended sympathy with abhorrence? Will they not look with disgust on such deception and hypocrisy when they see a nation of slave dealers tendering their sympathy to a free people?"

About this time seventy-seven slaves of Washington attempted to gain for themselves that freedom they had just heard so highly eulogized for others. They doubtless reasoned that if freedom was a glorious boon for the French peasant—and had not the Southern statesmen said so?—it could not be wrong for them to desire it.

An old gentleman in Kentucky advised his neighbor's sons to enlist for the Mexican war; but was terribly worried when two of his own sons took his advice. So in this case, liberty was a glorious thing for their neighbors across the ocean, but not to be even thought of in this (so-called) land of the free. So the schooner Pearl, in which these slaves embarked for freedom, was overtaken at the mouth of the Potomac, and forced to return to Washington with its unfortunate passengers. Having been committed to jail, they fell into the hands of the merciless slave dealers and received the dreaded doom of being sent South.

Among these poor victims of man's cruelty and lust, was the beautiful quadroon, Emily Russell, a sweet, amiable, gentle Christian girl. She, with the others, was suffered to be bought by the cruel Baltimore slave dealers, who fixed her ransom at eighteen hundred dollars on the shameful plea that she was the most beautiful woman in all that country. She was consigned to the South. But the sun of her life was about to set below the horizon, and death came to her relief in all the vigor and freshness of girlhood, saving her from what probably would have been a life of misery, and causing her mother to exclaim: "The Lord be thanked. He has heard my prayers at last."

Though ignorant, helpless, crushed in spirit, weighed down with hardship and cruel bereavement, they were still human, and as true and affectionate hearts beat within their breasts as any that throbbed beneath lighter skins.

CHAPTER X.

SLAVERY UNMASKED.

We would gladly pass by this chapter in silence, for it must be painful alike to writer and reader.

But as the surgeon must harden his heart while he probes the wound, that he may apply a healing lotion; so the historian must record the facts however heart-rending, that he may perchance suggest a remedy.

As has been stated, slaves were found to be profitable for labor, only in the Southern states, where the semi-tropical crops, rice, indigo, sugar and cotton were produced. This includes those states from Maryland, Virginia, Kentucky and Missouri, southward. Then the question might be asked, Why did not these four states either manumit their slaves or sell them to the Southern planters, and thereby stop an unprofitable business, and restrict the slave territory? Simply "because the love of money is the root of all evil." For while slaves were not profitable in the border states for labor, they were profitable for propagating the race, increasing the numbers; and to have sold off all the slaves of those states would have been to kill the goose that laid the golden egg.

When it was found that the raising of grain, live stock, and so forth, by slave labor was unprofitable, many slaves were sent South, where they brought a high price; but enough were reserved for cultivating the farms and to increase the numbers, so as to again flood the market. For, horrible to relate, in the four border states and the District of Columbia, the slaves themselves became one of the large products of export. According to "Wilson's Rise and Fall of the Slave Power in America," "this traffic had become so enormous that in 1836 it was estimated that the number sold from the single state of Virginia was forty thousand, yielding a return of twenty-four millions of dollars. It was in fact the great business, licensed and protected by laws, advertised in the papers and recognized as one of the branches of legitimate production and trade." But of course there were humane men even in the South, whose hearts were grieved at the cruel traffic conducted around them. They denounced in vehement and scathing language a barbarous custom which tore the infant from its mother's yearning breast, that the one might be sold and the other left; scattering families, severing husbands and wives never to meet again, until they met at the bar of a just God as common accusers of an inhuman master. There are times when ties of blood hold us but loosely; still a day comes when nature asserts itself, and no acquired affection has the power over us that is wielded by the love we are born to; and we can but appreciate the melancholy scene the song-writer describes: —

"I am thinking to-day of dem years dat's passed away,
  When dey tied me up in bondage long ago;
In old Virginny state, it was there we separate,
  And it fill my heart with misery and woe.
Dey took away my boy, he was his mother's joy,
  From a baby in de cradle we him raise;
Oh! dey put us far apart and dey broke de old man's heart
  In dem agonizing,cruel slavery days."

Even one of the governors of South Carolina, in a message to the Legislature, denounced "this remorseless and merciless traffic, the ceaseless dragging along the streets and highways of a crowd of suffering victims to minister to insatiable avarice."

A Presbyterian synod of Kentucky refers to the slave caufle often seen there as proclaiming "the iniquity of our system." It adds, "There is not a village that does not behold the sad procession of manacled victims."

A Southern editor wrote of such a procession he saw passing through his city, "with heavy, galling chains riveted on their person, half naked, half starved," traveling to the plantations of the South, where "their miserable condition will be second only to the wretched creatures in hell."

The pathetic scene as described by the following verse was often enacted.

"One night I went to see her, but she's gone, the neighbors say,
  The white man bound her with his chain;
They have taken her to Georgia for to wear her life away,
  As she toils in the cotton and the cane."

A Baltimore journal of this period said: "Dealing in slaves has become a large business; establishments are made in several places in Maryland

DR. J. FRANK McKINLEY,
Graduate of the Medical Department of the University of
Michigan; noted physician.

and Virginia, at which they are sold like cattle. These places of deposit are strongly built, and well supplied with iron thumb-screws and gags, and ornamented with cow-skins, oftentimes bloody."

One of Virginia's most gifted sons of his day, Thomas Jefferson Randolph, said in the Legislature of that state, in 1832, that "the state was one grand menagerie, where men are reared for the market like oxen for the shambles." He even considered the domestic slave trade much worse than foreign; for in the latter, said he, "only strangers in aspect, language and manner" are taken; while in the former the master class sells those he has "known from infancy, into a strange country, among a strange people, subject to cruel taskmasters." Evidently an extensive traffic was carried on in slaves all through the South, as the papers of that period were filled with such advertisements as "Cash for Negroes," "Negroes for sale," and "Negroes wanted."

By actual count, four thousand and one hundred Negroes were advertised for sale in sixty-four newspapers of the eight slave states in the last two weeks of November, 1852. We have quoted thus from Southern authority; so also is the following curious advertisement which appeared in the *New York Independent* of March 1850, copied from the *Religious Herald*, a Baptist paper of Richmond, Virginia: "Who wants thirty-five thousand dollars in property? I am desirous to spend the balance of my life as a missionary, if the Lord permit, and therefore offer for sale my farm, the vineyard adjacent to Williamsburg. . . . . and also about forty servants, mostly young and likely, and rapidly increasing in number and value." Truly consistency is a jewel, but this good man (?) evidently was a stranger to it.

Perhaps the most demoralizing phase of the slave trade was the fact that fathers would often sell for the Southern market their own children without the slightest compunctions of conscience. But how were these poor creatures treated when once they arrived at their destination on the Southern plantations, weary and foot-sore, galled by their heavy chains? All that these poor victims of unrequited toil could expect to get out of this life was food and clothing, and a place to shelter them, and did they always get that? The Secretary of the Treasury obtained a report from forty-six sugar plantations of Louisiana; according to this, the cost of feeding and clothing an able-bodied slave was thirty dollars per year. Olmstead, who has traveled extensively through the South, estimates that ten dollars would be necessary for clothing, which would leave only twenty dollars for food, or five and one-half cents per day. He then asks, "Does the food of a first-rate laborer anywhere in the free world cost less?" Corn-meal was the invariable article of food, though sometimes at rare intervals, bacon, molasses or rice was provided.

A Louisiana cotton planter furnished De Bow, author of "De Bow's Resources of the South and West," an itemized estimate of the expense of a cotton crop. In this the cost of feeding a hundred slaves, furnishing the overseer's table, and the hospital, was estimated at seven hundred and fifty dollars for the year. This was seven dollars and a half for each slave, or less than three cents per day. From the same planter De Bow also learned that the cost of furnishing shoes, clothes, and beds for one hundred slaves, also sacks to gather cotton, did not exceed seven hundred and fifty dollars per annum. This statement accounts for the fact that all the slaves on the cotton and sugar plantations invariably looked ragged and dirty. The supply of food for slaves was fixed by the Legislature of several Southern states. Louisiana required that meat should be furnished, but this law became obsolete. North Carolina fixed the daily allowance of corn. And yet to-day Southern statesmen are fond of assuring us that they have always "opposed all sumptuary laws." It might be added that they prohibited any one selling or giving whisky to their Negroes. But since the war they have bitterly opposed Prohibition as a sumptuary law.

In the cotton, sugar and rice districts the slaves were systematically overworked. In South Carolina the legal limit of a day's work on a cotton plantation was fixed at fifteen hours. But during the picking season the slaves labored sixteen hours under the driver's lash; while on the sugar plantations of Lousiana, during the grinding season, eighteen were exacted, often with no Sunday's rest. Think of it, you free laborers, who very properly draw the line at about half of this time, with good wages and Sunday rest.

Patrick Henry said of the overseer of his day, "They are the most abject, degraded, and unprincipled race." Time and new conditions did not improve them, for the historian Rhodes says of them, "They were generally ignorant, frequently intemperate, always despotic and brutal. Their value was rated according to the size of the cotton crop they made, and with that end in view they spared not the slaves, who always worked under the lash." Even Chancellor Harper, who wrote a strong defense of slavery, says: "It is true that the slave is driven to labor by stripes."

The fact is demonstrated that the Negroes were often overtasked to their permanent injury, from the complaint made by Southern agricultural journals of the bad policy of thus wasting human property. But nothing was said about the inhumanity of thus killing slaves by abuse.

A stout Negro driver, chosen because of his unusual cruelty, followed each gang of working slaves, urging them on with loud voice and the cracking of his long whip.

A tradesman in Alabama told Olmstead that if the overseers raise "plenty of cotton, the owners never ask how many niggers they kill." Olmstead also learned that "a determined and perfectly relentless overseer could get almost any wages he demanded, for when it became known that such a man had made more bales to the slave than his competitors, every planter would try to get him."

The name Alabama means, "Here we rest," but this certainly did not apply to the poor colored people.

"If you don't work faster, or if you don't work better, I will have you flogged," was often heard, and seldom an idle threat.

In Olmstead's "Cotton Kingdom," he quotes from an overseer who said: "Why, sir, I wouldn't mind killing a nigger more than I would a dog." Fannie

Kemble is responsible for the statement, that the sugar planters of Louisiana unhesitatingly avowed that they found it upon the whole their most profitable plan to work off (kill with labor) their whole number of slaves about once in seven years and renew the whole stock. They proceeded to adopt this plan, as we have seen, by working during the grinding season eighteen hours per day, and seven days for a week, contrary to the laws of God, man and nature.

Again quoting from Rhodes: "No one can wonder that it was a painful sight to see slaves at work in the cotton field. Their besotted and generally repulsive expression, their brute-like countenances, on which were painted stupidity, indolence, duplicity, and sensuality; their listlessness; their dogged action; the stupid, plodding, machine-like manner, in which they labored, made a sorrowful picture of man's inhumanity to man." General Sherman, while living in Louisiana, observed that "the field slaves were treated like animals."

Frederick Douglass, speaking of one period in his life, said: "My natural elasticity was crushed; my intellect languished; the disposition to read departed; the cheerful spark that lingered about my eye died out; the dark night of slavery closed in upon me, and behold a man transformed to a brute."

As is generally known, cotton was the main crop raised by slave labor, and the great hope of the Southern Confederacy. Their leaders believed two errors, and from these drew a false conclusion. First, they said, cotton cannot be grown without slave labor; and second, England cannot exist

without Southern cotton, *ergo*, England must
come to "the gigantic relief" of the Southern Confederacy.

According to De Bow's estimate in 1850 of the
three million one hundred and seventy-seven
thousand slaves in the South, one million eight
hundred thousand were employed in cotton culture. The motto of the planter seemed to be,
"Let us buy more Negroes to raise more cotton, to
buy more Negroes to raise mcre cotton," and so
on *ad infinitum*. The same year there were only
three hundred and forty-seven thousand, five hundred and twenty-five slave holders, who with their
families numbered about two millions. The entire
white population of the South was six million one
hundred and twenty-five thousand; consequently
less than one third of the white people of the slave
states could have been in any way benefited by
this "peculiar institution," and more than seven
millions bond and free either labored for them, or
were controlled by this aristocracy.

The curse of slavery fell hardest upon the wom-
en, those who were least able to bear it, as the
following quotations from Fanny Kemble's Journal of a Residence on a Georgia Plantation will
show. Said she: "On my husband's first visit to
his estate he found that the men and the women
who labored in the fields had the same tasks to
perform. This was a noble admission of female
equality, was it not? And thus it had been on the
estate for many years past. He, of course, altered
the distribution of the work, diminishing the quantity done by the women." Fanny Kemble had a
woman's sympathy for the slave women of her hus-

band's plantation, and did all in her power to alleviate their condition. She noted with burning shame the general lewdness and gross immorality prevalent among the slaves.

The increasing of families was indirectly encouraged without the slightest restriction. A woman seemed to think that "the more she added to her master's property by bringing new slaves into the world, the more claim she would have upon his consideration and good will. This was perfectly evident to me from the meritorious air with which the women always made haste to inform me of the number of children they had, and the frequent occasions on which the older slaves would direct my attention to their children, exclaiming, 'Look, missis! plenty little niggers for you and little missis!'"

Sad to relate, this idea seems to have been instilled into the slaves almost from childhood, as the following from the same author shows: "On my return home I was met by a child (as she seemed to me) carrying a baby, in whose behalf she begged me for some clothes. On making some inquiry I was amazed to find that the child was her own; she said she was married and fourteen years old; she looked much younger even than that, poor creature. Her mother, who came up while I was talking to her, said she did not herself know the girl's age; how horribly brutish it all did seem, to be sure!"

A short time after this several slave women called on her at the great house; and this is what she says of two of them: "Among others, a poor woman called Mile, who could hardly stand for pain and swelling in her limbs; she had brought

fifteen children into the world, nine of them having died; for the last three years she had become
almost a cripple with chronic rheumatism, yet she
is driven every day to work in the field.   She held
my hands, and stroked them in the most appeal-
ing ways, while she exclaimed, 'Oh, my missis!
my missis! me neber sleep till day for de pain,' and
with the day her labor must again be resumed.   I
gave her flannel and sal volatile to rub her poor
swelled limbs with; rest I could not give her—rest
from her labor and her pain—this mother of fifteen
children.

"Another of my visitors had a still more dismal
story to tell; her name was Die; she had had sixteen children, fourteen of whom were dead.   They
had strained her arms up to be lashed   I asked
her what she meant by having her arms tied up.
She said their hands were first tied together, sometimes by the wrists and sometimes, which was
worse, by the thumbs, and they were then drawn
up to a tree or post, so almost to swing them off
the ground, and then their clothes rolled round
their waist, and a man with a cowhide stands and
stripes them.   I give you the woman's words.
She did not speak of this as anything strange, unusual, or especially horrid and abominable."

One more extract concerning the manner in
which her husband's slaves were fed.   Said she to
the lady friend for whom she wrote the journal:
"How do you think Berkshire County farmers
would relish laboring hard all day upon two meals
of Indian corn or hominy?   Such is the regulation
on the plantation, however, and I beg you to bear
in mind that the Negroes on this estate are gener-

ally considered well off. They go to the field at daybreak, carrying with them their allowance of food for the day, which toward noon, and not till then, they eat; cooking it over a fire which they kindle as best they can, where they are working. Their second meal in the day is at night, after their labor is over, having worked, at the very least, six hours without intermission of rest or refreshment since their noonday meal, properly so-called, for it was meal and nothing else." She also stated that their houses were miserable little squalid hovels, swarming with vermin, crowded to suffocation, and so poorly ventilated that in that hot climate it was almost impossible to get a breath of fresh air. The same was in a measure true of the so-called slave hospitals.

Jane Grey Swisshelm, sometimes called the "Fanny Kemble of America," in her book entitled "Half a Century," speaking of the time she lived in Louisville, Kentucky, almost fifty years ago, said: "While I lived on that dark and bloody ground, a Negro was beaten to death in an open shed, on the corner of two public streets, where the sound of the blows, the curses of his two tormentors, and his shrieks and unavailing prayers for mercy were continued for a whole forenoon, and sent the complaining air shuddering to the ears of thousands, not one of whom offered any help.

"Passing a crowded church on a Sabbath afternoon, I stepped in, when the preacher was descanting on the power of religion, and, in illustration, he told of two wicked young men in that state, who were drinking and gambling on Sunday morning, when one said: 'I can lick the religion out of any nigger.'

"The other would bet one hundred dollars that he had a nigger out of whom the religion could not be licked. The bet was taken and they adjourned to a yard. This unique nigger was summoned, and proved to be a poor old man. His master informed him he had a bet on him, and the other party commanded him to 'curse Jesus,' on pain of being flogged until he did. The old saint dropped on his knees before his master, and pleaded for mercy, saying: 'Massa! Massa! I cannot curse Jesus! Jesus die for me! He die for you, Massa. I no curse him; I no curse Jesus!'

"The master began to repent. In babyhood he had ridden on those old bowed shoulders, then stalwart and firm, and he proposed to withdraw the bet, but the other wanted sport and would win the money. Oh! the horrible details that the preacher gave of that day's sport, of the lashings, and faintings, and revivals, with washes of strong brine, the prayers for mercy, and the recurring moan, 'I no curse Jesus, Massa! I no curse Jesus. Jesus die for me, Massa; I die for Jesus!'

"As the sun went down Jesus took him, and his merciless master had sold a worthless nigger for one hundred dollars. But the only point which the preacher made was that one in favor of religion: When it could so support a Nigger, what might it not do for one of the superior race?"

A female member of the Fourth St. Methodist Church was threatened with discipline, for nailing her cook to the fence by the ear with a ten-penny nail. The preacher in charge witnessed the punishment from a back window of his residence. Hundreds of others witnessed it, called by the shrieks of the victim; and his reverence protested on the ground that "such scenes were calculated to injure the church."

The following is an extract from a letter written by Rev. John H. Aughey, a brilliant young Presbyterian minister, who fled from the South to save his life shortly after penning these lines, having been an eye-witness to many of the scenes.

"Kosciusko, Atlanta Co., Mississippi, December 25, 1861.

"Mr. William Jackman.

"Dear Sir:—Your last kind and truly welcome letter came to hand in due course of mail. . . .

"In your letter you desired me from my standpoint to give you my observations of the workings of the peculiar institution, and an expression of my views as to its consistency with the eternal principle of rectitude and justice. In reply I will give you a plain narrative of facts. On my advent to the South, I was at first struck with the fact that the busy hum of labor had in some measure ceased. What labor I did observe prcgressing was done with little skill and mainly by Negroes. I called upon the Rev. Dr. R. J. Breckenridge, to whom I had a letter of introduction, who treated me with the greatest kindness, inviting me to make his home my home when I visited that section of the country. On leaving his house, he gave me some directions as to the road I must travel to reach a certain point. 'You will pass,' said he, 'a blacksmith's shop, where a one-

eyed man is at work—my property.' The phrase,
'my property,' I had never before heard applied
to a human being, and it grated harshly upon my
ears. But it grated much more harshly a week
after this to hear the groans of two such chattels,
as they underwent a severe flagellation, while
chained to the whipping-post, because they had,
by half an hour, overstayed their time with their
families on the adjoining plantation. The next
peculiar abomination of the peculiar institution
which I observed was the licentiousness engendered
by it. Mr. D. F— of Madison County, Kentucky,
had a white family of children, and a black, or
rather mulatto family. As his white daughters
married he gave each a mulatto half-sister, as a
waiting-girl or body-servant.

"Mr. B— of Marshall County, Mississippi, lived
with his white wife till he had grandchildren, some
of whom came to school to me, when he repudi-
ated his white wife, and attached himself to a very
homely African, who superintends his household,
and rules his other slaves with rigor. Mr. S— of
Tishomingo County, Mississippi, took a Negro for a
wife, and had a large family of mulatto children.
He once brought this woman to church at Rienzi,
to the great indignation of the white ladies, who
removed to a respectable distance from her. I
preached recently to a large congregation of slaves,
one-third of which were as white as myself. Some
of them had red hair and blue eyes. If there are
any marked characteristics of their masters' families, the mulatto slaves are possessed of these characteristics.

"I never knew a pious overseer—never! There

may be many, but I never saw one. Overseers, as
a class, are worse than the slaveholders themselves.
They are cruel, brutal, licentious, dissipated and
profane. They always carry a loaded whip, a
revolver and a bowie-knife. These men have the
control of women, whom they often whip to death.
Mr. P—, who resided near Holly Springs, had a
Negro woman whipped to death while I was at his
house during a session of Presbytery. Mr. C—
of Waterford, Mississippi, had a woman whipped
to death by his overseer. But such cruel scourg-
ings are of daily occurrence.

"Colonel H—, a member of my church, told me
yesterday that he ordered a boy, who he supposed
was feigning sickness, to the whipping-post, but
that he had not advanced ten steps towards it
when he fell dead!—and the servant was free from
his master. During our conversation, a girl passed.
'There is a girl,' said he, 'who does not look very
white in the face owing to exposure, but when I
strip her to whip her I find she has a skin as fair
as my wife.'

"Mrs. T— recently whipped a boy to death within
half a mile of my residence. A jury of inquest
returned a verdict that he came to his death by
cruelty, but nothing more was done. Mrs. M—
and her daughter, of Holly Springs, abused a girl
repeatedly. She showed her bruises to some of
my congregation, and they believed them fatal.
She soon after died. Mrs. S—, a member of my
church, has several maimed Negroes from abuse on
the part of the overseer. I am residing on the banks
of the Yock-a-nookany, which means 'meander-
ing' in the Indian tongue. In this vicinity there

are large plantations, cultivated by hundreds of Negroes. The white population is sparse Every night the Negroes are brought to a judgment-seat. The overseer presides. If they have not labored to suit him, or if their task is unfulfilled, they are chained to a post and severely whipped. The victims are invariably stripped, to what extent is at the option of the overseer.

"Mr. C— of Waterford, Mississippi, punished his Negroes by slitting the soles of their feet with his bowie-knife! One man he put into a cotton-press and turned the screw till life was extinct. He stated that he only intended to alarm the man, but carried the joke too far. I have heard women thus plead, in piteous accents, when chained to the whipping-post and stripped: 'O my God, master! don't whip me! I was sick! Indeed I was sick! I had a chill and the fever is on me now! I haven't tasted a morsel to-day! You know I works when I is well! O, for God's sake don't whip a poor sick nigger! My poor chile's sick too! Missis thinks its dyin'! O master, for the love of God, don't cut a poor distressed woman wid your whip! I'll try to do better, ef you'll only let me off this once!'

"These piteous plaints only roused the ire of their cruel task-masters, who sometimes knocked them down in the midst of their pleadings. One beautiful Sabbath morning, I stood on the levee at Baton Rouge, Louisiana, and counted twenty-seven sugar houses in full blast. I found the Negroes were compelled to labor eighteen hours per day, and were not permitted to rest on the Sabbath during the rolling season. The Negroes of most plantations have a truck patch, which they cultivate on the Sabbath. I have pointed out the sin of thus laboring on Sunday, but they plead necessity; their children, they stated, must suffer from hunger if they did not cultivate their truck patch, and their masters would not give them time on any other day.

"Negroes, by law, are prohibited from learning to read. This law was not strictly enforced in Tennessee and some other states till within a few years past. I had charge of a Sabbath school for the instruction of the blacks in Memphis, Tennessee, in 1853. This school was put down by the strong arm of the law in a short time after my connection with it ceased. In Mississippi a man who taught slaves to read or write would be sent to the penitentiary instanter. The popular plea for this wickedness is that if they were taught to read they would read the abolition documents; and if they were taught to write, they would write themselves passes, and pass northward to Canada. Such advertisements as the following often greet the eye: 'Kansas War.—The undersind taks this metod of makkin it noan that he has got a pack of the best nigger hounds in the South. My hounds is well trand, and I has had much experience a huntin niggers, havin follered it for the last fifteen years. I will go anywhar that I'm sent for, and will ketch niggers at the follerin raits. My raits fur ketchin runaway niggers $10 per hed, ef they's found in the beat whar thar master lives, $15 if they's found in the county and $50 if they's tuck out on the county. N. B.—Pay is due when the nigger is tuck. Planters ort to send fur me as soon as thar niggers runs away. while thar track is fresh.'

DR. JOHN R. FRANCIS,
Graduate of the Medical Department of the University of
Michigan, and One of the Best Known
Physicians in Washington, D. C.

"Every night the woods resound with the deep-mouthed baying of the bloodhounds. The slaves are said by some to love their masters; but it requires the terrors of bloodhounds and the fugitive slave law to keep them in bondage. You in the North are compelled to act the part of the bloodhounds here, and catch the fugitives for the planters of the South. Free Negroes are sold into bondage for the most trivial offenses; slaveholders declare that the presence of free persons of color exerts pernicious influence upon their slaves. They therefore are very desirous of getting rid of these persons, either by banishing from the state or enslaving them. The Legislature of Mississippi and other states passed laws for their expulsion. The Governor of Missouri vetoed the law in that state, on the grounds that it was unconstitutional. The question is often asked, Is slavery sinful in itself? My observation has been extensive, embracing eight slave states, and I have never yet seen any example of slavery that did not seem sinful. If slavery is not sinful in itself, I must have always seen it out of itself. I have observed its workings during eleven years among a professedly Christian people, and pronounce it an unmitigated curse.

"JOHN H. AUGHEY.

"To Mr. William Jackman,
        "Amsterdam,
                "Jefferson County, Ohio."

CHAPTER XI.

UNDERGROUND RAILROADS.

The necessity for this so-called "Railroad" grew out of the passage of the Fugitive Slave Law of 1850, which established courts and commissioners unknown to the constitution, and was certainly the most inhuman law passed by a civilized country in the nineteenth century.

The most common act of benevolence to a fugitive slave had to be kept a profound secret. The penalty for giving or selling a meal to one of the passengers on this Road, or helping them on their way, was imprisonment and one thousand dollars fine; while those who aided and encouraged slaves to escape, were subject to a long term in the penitentiary.

Naturally when the better element of the people found that this infamous law, passed at the dictation of the slave power, was diametrically opposed to the golden rule, and the example of Him who "went about doing good," they believed with the apostles that they "ought to obey God rather

than men," and rightly spurned this law by hero-
ically helping the poor bondmen to the free states
and Canada, the Mecca of the fleeing slaves. The
result was a spontaneous uprising and banding together of determined men and women from Maine
to Kansas, with many stations and starting points
through the South, which on account of its rapid
transit, unity of action and secret operation, was
called the Underground Railroad. There is said
to have been four main trunk lines across the
state of New York, and several through Ohio and
southern Michigan. But how was it operated?
Like other railroads, it had its officers, engineers,
conductors, ticket agents, train dispatchers, stations, hotels and lunch counters. Its business
was conducted with great harmony, profound se-
crecy and perfect fidelity.

Unlike other railroads, when it ceased to exist,
it divided its immense profits among its passengers,
who invested it in large tracts of land in Canada,
in building dwellings, barns, churches, schoolhouses, factories of all kinds, and in stocking, improving and cultivating farms.

The poor slaves, groaning under cruel bondage,
and sighing for freedom, often heard of this Road
in various ways; sometimes a Northern traveler
would show them how to find the north star and
hint that in that direction lay liberty, and that he
would find friends to help him on his way. Frequently a slave who had escaped would get a
friend to write back to a benevolent neighbor,
and tell him all about it, who, in turn, would inform the Negroes of his neighborhood. But more
often they found out about this Road by a per-

GEO. W. WILLIAMS.

fectly organized system of communication and co-operation, established even in the South.

There have always been scattered throughout the South people who hated slavery, and had compassion on the poor victims of this American despotism. Such individuals have known, or made it a point to find out and communicate with others of "like faith and order," northward of them at convenient stages, who had acquaintances in the free states, and could be depended upon to help the fugitive on his way to freedom.

Thus lines were formed from the South to the very borders of Canada, and while they may have been more or less zigzag, they always trended northward and the fleeing black man found them safe and reliable. If he succeeded in escaping his pursuers until he reached the second or third station, he was seldom overtaken.

Samuel J. May estimates that more than twenty thousand found homes in Canada, while hundreds ventured to remain in the free states. The business was managed with such prudence and cautiousness that few of those engaged in it realized the penalties provided. Yet some of the noblest of earth suffered martyrdom, as victims of the cruel fugitive slave law.

Rev. John Rankin, of Ohio, was fined one thousand dollars, besides serving a term in prison. Rev. C. T. Torry died in a Virginia prison.

W. L. Chaplin, of Massachusetts, became editor of the Albany Patriot in 1844. In 1850, while in Washington as correspondent for his own paper, he was induced to aid two young men, slaves of Robert Toombs and Alexander H. Stephens of

Georgia, to escape. Surprised in the act, he was arrested and imprisoned, charged with abducting slaves. Having been a prisoner five months, he was released on the enormous bail of twenty-five thousand dollars. Knowing that if convicted he would certainly be sent to the penitentiary for a long term of years or perhaps for life, his friends decided that the bail must be forfeited and paid. His own little property was sacrificed, and this large amount was finally raised, mainly through the princely beneficence of that grand philanthropist, Gerrit Smith.

Calvin Fairbank spent seventeen years and four months in the Kentucky penitentiary at Frankfort for the glorious crime of "Nigger Stealing." During this time, he is said to have received thirty-five thousand stripes on his bared body.

About the year 1840 Captain Jonathan Walker of Massachusetts took a contract to build a section of a proposed railroad in Florida, employing a number of Negroes in its construction. Being a Christian and kind-hearted man he treated his men with kindness, permitting them to eat at the same table with himself, and bow the knee to a common heavenly Father around a common altar. As a natural consequence, he gained the respect and love of his men, who in 1844 persuaded him to aid them in an attempt to escape in an open boat to an island not far distant, belonging to England.

All went well until the captain was taken violently sick, and the fugitives, having no knowledge of navigation, were at the mercy of wind and wave, until picked up by the crew of a wrecking sloop and conveyed to Key West, where he was imprisoned, until sent to Pensacola. Arriving here, he was chained to the floor of a cell, where two days before a man had committed suicide, the floor being still covered with blood.

In his trial in the United States court, he was sentenced "to be branded on the right hand with the capital letters, 'S. S.'; to stand in the pillory one hour; to pay as many fines as there were slaves 'stolen;' to suffer as many terms imprisonment; to pay the costs, and to stand committed until the fines were paid."

The execution of these sentences began at once. The initials of the words "Slave Stealer" were branded upon his hand, by a brutal United States marshal. He stood an hour in the pillory, during which, while utterly helpless, he was pelted with rotten eggs by a cowardly, renegade "Northern man with Southern principles."

He was now sent to prison, where he remained eleven months with a heavy chain on his leg, which was never removed even for changing his clothing. Money was raised by his friends to pay his fines and he was liberated in 1845.

The effort thus made to stigmatize and heap odium upon this noble hero and philanthropist, recoiled on the national Government, whose craven cowardice and heartless ignominy was alone responsible for it. Whittier enshrined this event in a grand patriotic poem, and completely turned the tables, making "S. S." a badge of honor indicative of the "heroic spirit of an earlier, better day."

"Then lift that manly right hand, bold plowman of the wave,
Its branded palm shall prophesy Salvation to the Slave;
Hold up its fire-wrought language, that whoso reads may feel
His heart swell strong within him, his sinews change to steel.

Hold it up before our sunshine, up against our Northern air.
Ho! men of Massachusetts, for the love of God look there!
Take it henceforth for your standard, like the Bruce's heart of
        yore;
In the dark strife closing round ye, let that hand be seen before."

According to Henry Wilson, Thomas Garrett, a Quaker of Delaware, was the most prominent and successful agent of the Underground Railroad, continuing the good work for more than fifty years; he assisted nearly three thousand slaves to escape from bondage.   During this long time he kept open house for the poor fugitives, and was considered the good Samaritan of the Delaware.   In 1848 James Bayard, afterwards United States senator, headed a prosecution against him before Judge Taney, for abducting two slave children. Of course he was convicted—they invariably were, and fined so heavily as to sweep all his property away, rendering him almost penniless at the age of sixty.   When the auctioneer had knocked off his last piece of property to pay the fines, he remarked that he hoped he would "never be guilty of doing the like again."   To which the good Quaker replied, "Friend, I haven't a dollar in the world, but if thee knows a fugitive who needs a breakfast, send him to me."   Never was a grander sentence uttered, and we doubt not the angel in heaven recorded it with a smile of approval.

It is gratifying to read that he outlived the cruel system which converted his neighbors into persecutors; that, like Job of old, he was more prosperous in the latter part of his life than ever before, living to a ripe old age in peace and tranquility.   And when he passed away, the whole community realized that they had sustained the irreparable loss of one of God's noblemen. He chose for his pallbearers, representatives of the race for whom he had spent his life.

Levi Coffin of Cincinnati, another Quaker, was familiarly called the President of this Road; he was a man of high social position and sterling worth. It is estimated that he has been instrumental in aiding between two and three thousand slaves to escape.

It must not be forgotten that those who managed this Road were, for the most part, philanthropists and noble Christian men and women; while on the other hand the slave hunters and overseers were, with an occasional exception, as cruel and remorseless as their own bloodhounds.

The managers availed themselves of a great variety of facilities for traveling; lumber-wagons, carriages, stage-coaches, canal, ferry and steamboats, also ships and railroads, were all used when needed.

Sometimes in the Southern cities such precautions were taken as to render it next to impossible for a slave to escape detection. Even then he did not despair, but would risk his life for a prospect of liberty, by getting his friends to box him up and send him to a Northern city as express or freight.

William Still, colored, has written the best history of the Underground Road we have seen. In it he mentions several who were boxed up and so escaped in spite of extra vigilance. William Box Peel Jones arrived at Philadelphia from Baltimore in 1859. He belonged to one Robert Carr, a gro-

cer and commission merchant, who had sold a
number of slaves, one at a time, and William
preferred the box to the auction block. He was a
little unfortunate in the choice of a box, there not
being sufficient room to straighten out his legs;
the cramped position causing such intense pain he
was almost forced to scream out. At last he
fainted away, but when he revived the pain was
less intense. Arriving in Philadelphia Sunday
morning, just seventeen hours from starting, he
was met by the same friend who had boxed him
up, he having come through on the cars. Although
it was Sunday morning, this friend managed to get
his piece of freight from the vessel. His joy was
very great on being released, and as soon as he
had recovered sufficient strength and use of his
limbs he was on his way to Canada, the friend returning to Baltimore.

Henry Box Brown was boxed up in Richmond,
Virginia, by his friend James A. Smith. The exact size of the box was two feet eight inches deep,
two feet wide, and three feet long. Having been
supplied with a large gimlet, a bladder of water,
and a few biscuits, he got inside, was nailed up,
and five hickory hoops were put around the box.
It was now marked, "Wm. H. Johnson, Arch
Street, Philadelphia. This side up with care,"
and sent by Adams Express. Sometimes the
notice, "This side up with care," did not avail; for
miles he was on his head. At last, after twenty-
six long weary hours, the box and contents arrived
at its destination.

In the afternoon of the same day Mr. McKim,
a member of the vigilance committee in Philadel-

phia, received the following telegram: "Your case of goods is shipped and will arrive to-morrow morning early." The box was brought at once to the anti-slavery office, where William Still, Prof. C. D. Cleveland and Lewis Thompson were invited to be present at the "opening." When all was ready Mr. McKim rapped quietly on the lid of the box and called out, "All right!" Instantly came the answer, "All right, sir!" Soon the hickory hoops were cut, the top of the box removed, when he arose, ringing wet with perspiration, and said, "How do you do, gentlemen?"

After resting a few moments he remarked that before leaving Richmond he had selected for his arrival hymn, if he lived, the Psalm beginning, "I waited patiently for the Lord, and He heard my prayer." Most feelingly did he sing the hymn, to the delight of his small audience.

After spending some time resting and straightening his limbs at the hospitable home of James and Lucretia Mott, and remaining two days with Wm. Still, he left for Boston. Mr. Samuel A. Smith, the shoe dealer, who boxed him up in Richmond, did the same thing for two others, but was detected and spent seven years in the Virginia penitentiary, a martyr to the cause of freedom.

The following advertisement appeared in the Baltimore Sun: "One hundred and fifty dollars reward. Ran away from the subscriber Sunday night, twenty-seventh inst., my Negro girl Lear Green, about eighteen years of age, black complexion, round features, good-looking and ordinary size; she had on and with her when she left a tan-colored silk bonnet, a plaid silk dress, a light muslin de laine, also one watered silk cape, and one tan-colored cape. I have reason to be confident that she was persuaded off by a Negro man named William Adams; black, quick-spoken, five feet ten inches high, a large scar on one side of his face, running down in a ridge by the corner of his mouth, about four inches long, barber by trade, but works mostly about taverns, opening oysters, etc. He has been missing about a week; he had been heard to say he was going to marry the above girl and ship to New York, where, it is said, his mother resides. The above reward will be paid if the said girl is taken out of the state of Maryland and returned to me; or fifty dollars if taken in the state of Maryland. James Noble, No. 153 Broadway, Baltimore."

Lear Green, so particulary described in this advertisement, deserved to be ranked among the heroines of this century. She is said to have been a "dark brown color," instead of "black," (fear of complimenting a slave often led to a false description) and possessed a countenance of peculiar modesty and grace. Her young mistress was very exacting and overbearing towards her; so she resolved to take the advice of her lover, William Adams, and thereby gain her freedom and a husband at the same time. All the avenues of travel at this time were so closely guarded there seemed but one chance to escape, the trial of which required heroic courage. But it was decided to make this attempt, for what will a woman not encounter or what obstacles will she not overcome for the double motive of love and a prospect of liberty?

An old sailor's chest was procured; a quilt, a

pillow and a few articles of clothing, with a small quantity of food and a bottle of water, were put into it, and Lear getting inside, the top was closed and strong ropes tied around it, leaving a small crevice between the edge of the chest and the top. The chest with its contents was soon stored away among ordinary freight on one of the Ericson line of steamers.

The mother of her intended, a free woman, agreed to come as a passenger on the same boat and look after this precious piece of freight.

The rules of the company assigned colored passengers to the deck, which was the very place this woman wanted, so as to be as near the chest as possible. During the night, when all was still, she could not refrain from opening the lid a little to see if her charge lived, and give her a breath of fresh air.

At the end of eighteen hours they landed at Philadelphia. Soon the chest and living freight were taken to the home of friends of the mother, on Barley Street. Later the chest and its late occupant were removed to the residence of William Still, who had her photographed in the chest. In due time she was sent on to Elmira, New York, where she married her lover, William Adams, and they lived happily together in that city.

E. M. Pettit, in his "Sketches of the Underground Railroad," mentions a number of interesting escapes, among the rest that of a mother and little daughter seven years of age, named respectively Statie and Lila, who escaped in a box from Washington, D. C., to Warsaw, New York. Statie was a very proficient house servant, belonging to a man by the name of Limes, living just opposite Washington on the Virginia side. Her master, owning more slaves than he could employ, hired out a number of them, their wages constituting his income. Statie was allowed to hire herself out on condition that she paid her master ten dollars a month, and furnished clothing for her little girl, who, like the mother, was nearly white, and quite attractive.

At first she hired herself to a farmer named Barbour, who was very kind to her and the child. Afterwards being offered much larger wages by a hotel keeper in Washington, she accepted the place, hoping to save enough money to buy her child's freedom. She would return to her master every three months, to see her child and pay him the wages. On one of these trips she learned of his intention to sell her little girl, and resolved at once to make her escape and take the child with her.

With the aid of her kind friend Mr. Barbour, a plan was soon arranged. It happened that Barbour had formerly lived in New York, and he now told his neighbors he was going to make a visit to his friends in that state. He had a splendid team, and a good strong spring-wagon. Procuring a box to fit his wagon, he put into it straw and quilts, plenty of provision and water.

According to previous appointment, he met the mother and daughter at night just outside of Washington, and Statie and Lila were soon comfortably stored away, en route towards the north star. Mr. Barbour passed himself off for a Yankee clock peddler, a veritable Sam Slick, and as he paid his hotel bills, drove a good wagon and team, no questions were asked. When out of sight of settlements, the fugitives would sometimes get out to pick berries, and when it was safe to do so, would walk about in the night for exercise. Thus they made the long journey through Pennsylvania to Warsaw, New York. Here he met Col. Charles O. Shepard of Attica, a popular member of the State Senate, who was there attending court. Col. Shepard was the very agent of the Underground Railroad he was in quest of; so Mr. Barbour gave his two passengers into his keeping, and he took them to Attica when he returned.

On account of its having been published in the papers, the master heard of them and employed slave-hunters to recapture and return them. But the men he sent were almost mobbed, so were glad to return without them. So mother and daughter lived happily together in Wyoming County, New York.

A gentleman took his little daughter with him to the Legislative Hall at Springfield to hear Owen Lovejoy make his great speech in favor of the bill to repeal the "black law" of Illinois.

Mr. Lovejoy showed that he had much of the same spirit of his martyred brother Elijah P., by denouncing the Fugitive Slave Law, as not only unjust and wicked, unnatural and dangerous to the stability of a free government, but also degrading and an outrage on every principle of humanity and religion. He endorsed the Underground Road in all its principles and results, and closed his speech with the following immortal words: "In so doing I accept the consequences of wicked legis-ration, and let it be known that Owen Lovejoy, of Princeton, Bureau County, Illinois, will hold himself ready at all times to give advice, food, shelter and aid in every possible way in the pursuit of freedom, to any poor, panting fugitive from the horrors of American slavery, so help me Almighty God."

On their way home the little girl asked, "Is that man an abolitionist?" "Yes," said he. "Well, papa, are you an abolitionist too?" "Yes," he replied, "but I was such a fool I did not know it!"

What Lovejoy thus expressed was the sentiment of thousands of people of the free states, who regarded the Fugitive Slave Bill as little short of an indirect attempt to abolish Christianity, and as absurd as the Pope's Bull against the comet.

Mr. Pettit related the following interesting story of Margaret, who, with her mother, was owned by a family who gave her religious instruction, and she became very pious. At the age of sixteen she went with her young mistress, who had married a planter living on the "Eastern Shore." Margaret married at the age of twenty; but in less than a year her husband was torn from her frantic embrace and sold South.

She incurred the displeasure of her master by grieving over her fondly cherished husband, and refusing to take another. In order to break her spirit, and bring her to terms, he put her into the tobacco field and instructed his brutal overseer to work her to the utmost of her ability, which command was enforced up to the day of the birth of her child. At the end of one week she was driven again to the field and compelled to perform a full task. It was customary at this time to have nur· series on the plantation, presided over by aged and decrepit slaves, where mothers could leave their infants during working hours. But this privilege was denied to Margaret; she was obliged to leave her child under the shade of a bush in the field, returning to it but twice during the long day.

On going to the child one evening, she found it apparently insensible, exhausted with crying, and a large serpent lying across it. Although she felt it would be better for both herself and child if it were dead, yet her mother's heart impelled her to make an effort to save it, so by caressing and careful handling she revived it. As soon as she heard its feeble wailing cry, she vowed to deliver her boy from the cruel power of slavery or die in the attempt. Falling on her knees like Hannah of old, she gave the child into God's keeping, and prayed for strength to enable her to perform her vow, for grace and patience to sustain her in suffering, toil, and hunger. Then pressing the child to her bosom, she fled with all speed, her course being northward. Having gone a mile or two, she was overtaken by Watch, the old house dog. Watch was a large mastiff, somewhat old, but he and Margaret had become great friends. She feared it would not be safe to let him go with her; still the dog had determined to go, and a mastiff has a will of his own, so she resumed her flight followed by her faithful escort.

At daybreak she hid herself in the border of a plantation, and was soon asleep. At dusk she was aroused by the noise of slaves returning to their quarters. Seeing a woman linger behind, she went up to her and telling her troubles, asked for food. About midnight the woman returned with a supply, which she divided with Watch, and immediately started on her journey.

The second day after she left, a slave-hunter, with his dogs, was employed to catch and return her. He started with a dog and three puppies, thinking, no doubt, that as the game was only a woman and baby it would be a good time to train the young dogs. He did not find her as easily as he expected, however, but about noon of the second day the old dog struck her trail where Margaret had made her little camp the day before; so she bounded off with renewed vigor, leaving the man and puppies far in the rear. The puppies soon lost the trail where Margaret forded the streams, and the old dog was miles away, leaving the hunter without a guide. Meantime Margaret had been lying in the woods on the banks of a river, intending to start again as soon as it was dark, when she was startled by the whining and nervous action of Watch, and listening, she heard the distant bay of a bloodhound. The peril of her situation now flashed upon her. She expected to witness the mangling of her babe by the savage brute, and then be torn to pieces herself. But she did not lose presence of mind, however, and determined to sell her life and that of her child as dearly as possible; she fastened him to her shoulder, and procuring a stout club waded out as far as she could into the river or inlet, which was too wide and deep to ford at this point.

Meantime the mastiff lay with his nose between his feet, watching the coming foe. The hound, ren-

dered more fierce by the fresh track, came bound-
ing on with her nose to the ground, scenting her
prey, and seemed not to see Watch, until, leaping
to pass over him, she found her throat seized by
the massive jaws of the mastiff. The struggle was
terrible but brief, for the mastiff did not loosen
his jaws until the hound was dead.

Margaret returned to the bank and would have
embraced her brave deliverer, but fearing this was
but the advance of a strong pack, she threw the
dead hound into the river and pushed on up the
stream.

A few hours after this she fell in with friends,
who hid her several days, then sent her to Philadelphia, from there to New York City over the
Underground Road.   Here she became a celebrated trained nurse, and was in great demand by
invalids.   She made a host of friends and earned
a competency.   Renting a comfortable house, she
kept the faithful old mastiff until he died of old
age some years afterwards.

Her boy, whom curiously enough, like Hannah
of old, she named Samuel, obtained the rudiments
of an education at a school in West Chester
County.   Afterwards, at the home of Gerrit Smith,
he enjoyed the advantages of a thorough education; became a devoted and eloquent minister
of the gospel in the Congregational church.   Like
his mother, he was so black it was said to grow
dark when he entered a room; but it grew light
when he began to speak.   Samuel afterwards
went to England, and was sent by the British
government on a mission of importance to Jamaica.

Samuel J. May, in his "Recollections of the

Anti-Slavery Conflict," mentions several interesting incidents of his personal experience as a station agent. "On one occasion," said he, "while
living at Syracuse, a squalid mortal came to my
back-door with a note stating that he was a passenger on the Underground Road. 'O massa,'
said he, 'I'm not fit to come into your house.'
'No,' I replied, 'you are not now, but soon shall
be.' So, stepping in, I got a tub of warm water,
with towels and soap. He helped me with them
into the barn. 'There,' said I, 'give yourself a
thorough washing and throw your clothing out
upon the dirt heap.' He set about his task with
a good will, and I returned to the house and brought
out to him a complete outfit of clean clothing,
from a deposit kept supplied by my parishioners.

"He received each article with unspeakable thank-
fulness, but the clean white shirt, with collar and
cravat, delighted him above measure. I found
him to be a man of much natural intelligence, but
ignorant of letters. He had had a very hard master and exulted on his new-found freedom. After
remaining with me two days, he went on to Canada."

Quite a contrast is shown by the following incident. One Saturday night Mr. May's eldest son
came to the parlor door and said, "Here, father,
is another living epistle to you from the South,"
and ushered in a fine looking, well dressed young
man. Mr. May took his hand in welcome and
said: "But this is not the hand of one who has
been doing hard work; it is softer than mine."
"No sir," he replied, "I have not been allowed to
do work that would harden my hands. I have
been the slave of a very wealthy planter in Ken-

tucky, who kept me only to drive the carriage for
mistress and her daughters, to wait upon them at
table and accompany them on their journeys. I
was not allowed even to groom the horses, and
was required to wear gloves when I drove."

Mr. May noticed he used good language, and
pronounced it correctly, and remarked, "You must
have received some instruction; I thought the laws
of the slave states sternly prohibited the teaching
of slaves." "They do, sir," he replied, "but my
master was an easy man in that respect. My
young mistresses taught me to read, and got me
books and papers from their father's library. I
have had much leisure time and have improved it."

By further conversation it was shown that he
was familiar with a considerable number of the
best American and English authors in poetry and
prose. Mr. May now asked, "If you had such an
easy time, and were so much favored, why did you
run away?" "O, sir," he answered, "slavery at
best is a bitter draught. Under the most favored
circumstances, it is bondage and degradation still.
I often writhed in my chains, though they sat on
me so lightly compared to others. I was often on
the point of taking wings for the North, but the
words of Hamlet would come to me, 'Better to
bear those ills we have, than fly to others we know
not of,' and I should have remained with my master had it not been that I learned a few weeks ago
he was about to sell me to a particular friend of
his, then visiting him from New Orleans. I suspected this evil was impending over me from the
notice the gentleman took of me and the kind of
questions he asked me.

"At length, one of my young mistresses, who knew my dread of being sold, came to me, and bursting into tears, said, 'Harry, father is going to sell you!' She put five dollars into my hand and went weeping away. With that, and with much more money I had received from time to time, and saved for this hour of need, I started that night and reached the Ohio River before morning. I immediately crossed to Cincinnati and hurried on board a steamer, the steward of which was a black man of my acquaintance. He concealed me until the boat had returned to Pittsburg. There he introduced me to a gentleman he knew to be friendly to us colored folks That gentleman sent me to a friend in Meadville, and he directed me to come to you."

Mr. May told him that since he was a coachman and waiter, he could get him an excellent situation in that city; which would enable him to live comfortably until he was acquainted with Northern manners and customs, and something better presented itself. But Harry hastily replied, "O, I thank you, sir, but I shall not dare to stop this side of Canada. My master, though kind to me, is a proud and passionate man. He will never forgive me for running away. He has already advertised me, offering a large reward for my arrest and return to him. I am not safe here and must go to Canada." So Monday afternoon he left with a letter of introduction to a gentleman in Kingston, where he arrived safely in a few days.

Mr. May also told of a beautiful octoroon who came to him from New Orleans. Her story was about as follows: "I was a slave in New Orleans;

my master was concerned in a line of packet steamers that ply between New Orleans and Galveston. For the past few years he had kept me on board one of his boats as the chambermaid. This was rather an easy and not a disagreeable position. I was very attentive to the lady passengers, especially when they were seasick, and made many friends. They often made me presents of clothes, trinkets and money, and what was better, they taught me to read. At each end of the route I had days of leisure, which I improved as best I could. I was often worried by the thought that I was a slave, but as I was comfortable in other respects, I might have remained in bondage, had I not learned that my master was about to sell me to a dissolute young man, and I knew it would be a life much more to be dreaded than the bondage I then endured; so at once I determined to escape.

"Being much of the time at the wharf in New Orleans, I could readily distinguish the vessels of the different nations. ·So I went to one I knew was an English ship, on board of which I saw a lady—the captain's wife. Asking and obtaining permission to come on board, and encouraged by her kind manner, I revealed to her my secret and my wish to escape. She could hardly be persuaded that I was a slave, being, as I supposed, the child of my master; but when all doubt was removed she readily consented to take me with her to New York.

"I succeeded in getting what money had saved and all my clothes on board, so we sailed next day. The captain was equally kind and I was

FERDINAND L. BARNETT,
Assistant State's Attorney of the State of Illinois.

able to pay as much as he would take for my passage. On arriving in New York the captain took pains to inquire for abolitionists, and being directed to Mr. Lewis Tappan, took me with him to the good gentleman. Mr. Tappan provided for my safety in that city, and the next day sent me to Mr. Myers at Albany, on my way to you."

Mr. May kindly offered to find her a place in some one of the best families in Syracuse; but she was afraid to remain there. She had seen in New York City her master's advertisement offering five hundred dollars for her restoration to him. She was positive there were slave-hunters on her track. Two men in the train between Albany and Syracuse had annoyed and alarmed her by their close observation. One had seated himself by her side and tried to engage her in conversation, and to look through her veil. At length he asked her to take off the glove of her left hand; by this she knew that he had seen the advertisement stating that one finger on the left hand was minus a joint. Instead of complying with this rude request she called the conductor, who gave her a seat by a lady, so reached Syracuse in safety.

After remaining with Mr. May several days, passing the time by reading French, he sent her to Kingston, Canada, where she was no longer a slave, but as God intended, enjoying her freedom.

CHAPTER XII.

HEROES AND MARTYRS.

On a marble monument at Canton Centre, New York, is to be seen this inscription: "In memory of Captain John Brown, who died in the Revolutionary War, at New York, September 3rd, 1776. He was the fourth generation from Peter Brown, who landed from the Mayflower at Plymouth, Massachusetts, December 22, 1620."

With such ancestors, the subject of this sketch could hardly fail to be a liberty-loving, slavery-hating patriot. John Brown, known in history as "Ossawatomie Brown," was born in Torrington, Connecticut, May 9th, 1800. He was nearly six feet tall, slender, wiry, and of dark complexion. His brow was prominent, with slightly Roman nose, which gave him quite a commanding appearance. He had great self-possession, conscientiousness and strong will-power. He was quick in his motions and elastic in his tread.

When Congress gave the Free State settlers of Kansas no protection, but was in reality trying to drag the territory into the Union with a slave constitution, many anti-slavery men rushed into Kansas, determined to maintain their rights and dispute every inch of ground, even if it led to a border war, as indeed was the inevitable result.

Among the champions of freedom who went to Kansas were John Brown and his sons. He was not in sympathy with either of the anti-slavery or political parties then in existence, but with his friends and followers formed a little party of his own which advocated carrying the war into the enemies' ranks, and aggressive measures for the freedom of slaves. In a speech at Ossawatomie about this time, he said: "Talk is a national institution, but it does no good to the slaves." He also said to a personal friend: "Young men must learn to wait. Patience is the hardest lesson to learn. I have waited twenty years to accomplish my purpose." These are the words of a practical, judicious leader, who had deep convictions of duty, a strong hold on truth, and "a conscience void of offense towards God and man." In short, he was a born ruler and leader of men, but had the misfortune to be a little in advance of public sentiment on the question of how to get rid of the hydra-headed monster, slavery.

One of Captain Brown's most successful expeditions was that in which he liberated eleven slaves in Missouri, conducted them through Iowa and Illinois to Canada, that haven of escaped slaves.

I think it was in 1847 that John Brown accepted an invitation to visit Boston from George L. Stearns, who proffered to pay his expenses. A full account of this visit was given by Mrs. Stearns in a letter. It was arranged for him to meet certain friends of freedom on Sunday, as this was the only time convenient to all parties. It was feared Brown would not approve of this, but he said in his characteristic way: "Mr. Stearns, I have a little ewe-lamb that I want to pull out of the ditch, and the Sabbath will be as good a day as any to do it." Mr. Stearns' oldest son, then a boy eleven years old, was greatly fascinated by this strange, kind-hearted man, and after obtaining his. father's permission, he brought out his spending money and gave it to Brown, saying: "Captain Brown, will you buy something with this money for those poor people in Kansas, and sometime will you write to me and tell me what sort of a little boy you were?" "Yes, my son, I will, and God bless you for your kind heart," he answered.

One of his sayings in Boston is quoted by Mrs. Stearns in the same letter, as follows: "Gentlemen, I consider the Golden Rule and the Declaration of Independence one and inseparable; and it is better that a whole generation of men, women and children should be swept away, than that this crime of slavery should exist one day longer." She also tells of her baby boy, little three year old Carl, coming into the room as Captain Brown was talking; and how he stood and looked at him intently with his beautiful, beaming eyes; but as the good man was simply irresistible to children, the little boy was soon on his knee playing with his beard or nestling his head in his bosom. We read, "A man may smile and smile and be a villain still;" but my observation teaches me that one who loves and is beloved by children is apt to be a candid and a noble man. Captain Brown had the same experience with the children of Frederick Douglass, when boarding in the family at Rochester, January, 1858. One of them still says: "The sun seemed to rise and set with me in John Brown." He even demonstrated his love for children by his request concerning the kind of mourners he wanted at his funeral, as mentioned in his last letter, which we will read farther on.

In the latter part of 1847 John Brown and Frederick Douglass spent the night together at Springfield, Massachusetts. The conversation which then took place between them is quoted from Frederick May Holland's work. In it Douglass tells his own story as follows: "He touched my vanity at the outset in this wise: 'I have,' he said, 'been looking over your people during the last twenty years, watching and waiting for heads to rise above the surface, to whom I could safely impart my views and plans. At times I have been almost discouraged, but lately I have seen a good many heads popping up, and whenever I see them, I try to put myself in communication with them.' John Brown's plan, as it was then formed in his mind, was very simple and had much to commend it. It did not, as some suppose, directly contemplate a general uprising among the slaves, and a general slaughter of the slave masters, but it did contemplate the creation of an armed force, which should constantly act against slavery in the heart of the South. He called my attention to a large map upon the wall, and pointed out to me the far-reaching Alleghanies, stretching away from New York into the Southern States. 'These mountains,' he said, 'are the basis of my plans. God has given the strength of these hills to freedom. They were placed here by the Almighty for the emancipation of your race. They are full of natural forts, where one man for defense will be equal to a hundred for attack. They are full of good hiding places, where a large number of brave men could be concealed and for a long time baffle and elude pursuit. I know these mountains well, and could take a body of men into them there, despite all the efforts Virginia could make to dislodge and drive me out of them. My plan, then, is this: to take about twenty-five brave men into those mountains, and begin my work on a small scale, supply them with arms and provisions, and post them in companies of five on a line of twenty-five miles. These shall for a time busy themselves in gathering recruits from the neighboring farms, seeking and selecting the most daring and restless spirits first.' In this part of the work, he said, the utmost care was to be taken to avoid treachery and discovery. Only the most conscientious and skillful of his men were to be detailed for this perilous duty. With care and enterprise, he thought, he could soon gather a force of one hundred hearty men, who would be content to lead the free and adventurous life to which he proposed to train them. When once properly drilled, and each man had found the place for which he was best suited, they would begin the work in earnest. They would run off the slaves in large numbers. They would retain the strong and brave and send the weak ones North by the Underground Railroad. His operations would be enlarged with the increasing number of his men, and they would not be confined to one locality. He would approach the slaveholders in some cases at midnight, and tell them they must give up their slaves, and also let them have their best horses upon which to ride away. Slavery, he said, was a state of war, in which the slaves were unwilling parties, and that they therefore had a right to anything necessary to their peace and freedom. He would shed no blood, and would avoid a fight, except when he could not escape from it and was compelled to do it in self-defense. He would then, of course, do his best. This movement, he said, would weaken slavery in two ways. First, by making slave property insecure, it would make such property undesirable. Secondly, it would keep the anti-slavery agitation alive, and public attention fixed upon the subject, and thus finally lead to the adoption of measures for the abolishing of the slave system altogether. He held that the anti-slavery agitation was in danger of dying out, and that it needed some such startling measures as he proposed, to keep it alive and effective. Slavery, he said, had nearly been abolished in Virginia by the Nat Turner insurrection; and he thought his plan of operation would speedily abolish it in both Maryland and Virginia. He said his trouble was to get the right kind of men with which to begin the work, and the means necessary to equip them. And here he explained the reason for his simple mode of living, his plain dress, his leather stock. He had adopted this economy in order to save money with which to arm and equip men to carry out his plan of liberation. This was said by him in no boastful terms. On the contrary, he said he had already delayed his work too long, and that he had no room to boast either his zeal or his self-denial.

From eight o'clock in the evening till three o'clock in the morning, Captain John Brown and I sat face to face, he arguing in favor of his plan, and I finding all the objections I could against it. Now mark! This conversation took place fully twelve years before the blow was struck at Harper's Ferry, and his plan was even then more than twenty years old. He had, therefore, been watching and waiting all these years for suitable heads to rise up, or 'pop up,' to use his expression, among the sable millions, to whom he could safely confide his plan, and thus nearly forty years had passed between this man's thoughts and his act."

The last interview between John Brown and Frederick Douglass took place in an old stone quarry near Chambersburg, Pennsylvania, August 20th, 1859. There were only four men present at this council of war, if it might be so termed; Douglass and a colored man named Shields Green, who had recently escaped from slavery in South Carolina, John Brown, and his secretary Mr. Kagai. Douglass now learned for the first time that Brown had changed his plan, and meditated an attack on Harper's Ferry at once and running the risk of getting to the mountains afterwards. With his usual far-seeing sagacity, Douglass told Brown he was running into a steel trap, and urged him to desist, as it could result only in ruin to himself, and injury to the cause they both loved. But it was unavailing; the man of iron will had made up his mind, and nothing could turn him from his purpose. When Douglass was about to separate from him, having declined to join him in his undertaking, Brown made one more pathetic appeal, and putting his arms around him in a manner more than friendly, he said: "Come with me, Douglass; I will defend you with my life. I want you for a special purpose. When I strike, the bees will begin to swarm and I shall want you to help me hive them."

Alas! how sadly mistaken he was in his theory remains to be seen.

John Brown purchased or leased a small farm about six miles from Harper's Ferry, on the Maryland side, July, 1859, and established here his headquarters and arsenal. He had one hundred and two Sharp's rifles, sixty-eight pistols, fifty-five bayonets, twelve artillery swords, four hundred and eighty-three pikes, one hundred and fifty broken handles of pikes, sixteen picks, forty shovels, besides quite a number of other appurtenances of war.

Captain Brown expected to make his attack on Harper's Ferry on the night of October 24th, 1859; but while in Baltimore in September, he was under the impression that there was a conspiracy in his camp. Fearing he would be betrayed and his plans frustrated, he determined, without informing his Northern friends, to strike the first blow on the night of October 17th.

The story is soon told. He was made a prisoner October 19th, and remained until November 7th without a change of clothing or medical aid. Forty-two days from the time of his imprisonment he was hanged, after a mock trial, by Governor Wise of Virginia. That this so-called raid was ill-timed and premature, all will agree; but the motive which inspired him to action was certainly a desire to imitate the example of Him who came "to bind up the broken hearted, to proclaim liberty to the captives, and the opening of the prison to them that are bound."

Whittier very pathetically describes the scene:

"John Brown of Ossawatomie, they led him out to die;
And lo! a poor slave mother with her little child pressed nigh;
Then the bold blue eye grew tender, and the old harsh- face grew mild,
As he stooped between the jeering ranks and kissed the negro's child."

He had gone into Virginia to save life, not to destroy it. This is proven by a statement made before the fight at Harper's Ferry: "And now, gentlemen, let me press this one thing on your minds. You all know how dear life is to you, and how dear your lives are to your friends, and in re-membering that, consider that the lives of others are as dear to them as yours are to you. Do not, therefore, take the life of any one if you can pos-sibly avoid it; but if it is necessary to take life in order to save your own, then make sure work of it." After the fight at Harper's Ferry he also said: "I never did intend murder, or treason, or the destruction of property, or to excite or incite slaves to rebellion, or to make insurrection. The design on my part was to free the slaves."

Congressman Vallandigham of Ohio, who ex-amined him in court, said afterwards in a speech: "It is in vain to underrate either the man or the conspiracy. Captain John Brown is as brave and resolute a man as ever headed an insurrection, and in a good cause, and with a sufficient force, would have been a consummate partisan commander.

He has coolness, daring, persistency, stoic faith and patience, and a firmness of will and purpose unconquerable! He is furtherest possible removed from the ordinary ruffian, fanatic or madman."

South Carolina, Missouri and Kentucky each sent a rope to hang him. But the one from Kentucky proving the strongest, was selected and used. It seems a little paradoxical that Kentucky, the home of Henry Clay the "Great Compromiser" of slavery, and the birthplace of Abraham Lincoln the great emancipator of slavery, should furnish the rope to hang John Brown, the forerunner of Lincoln, and one of the noblest and best men of any age or country.

His last letter was written to Mrs. George L. Stearns, his Boston friend at whose home he was entertained, and is as follows:

"Charlestown, Jefferson Co., Va., 29th Nov., 1859.

"Mrs. George L. Stearns,

Boston, Mass.

"My Dear Friend:—No letter I have received since my imprisonment here has given me more satisfaction or comfort than yours of 8th inst. I am quite cheerful, and never more happy. Have only time to write you a word. May God forever reward you and all yours. My love to all who love their neighbors. I have asked to be spared from having any mock or hypocritical prayers made over me when I am publicly murdered, and that my only religious attendants be poor little, dirty, ragged, bareheaded and barefooted slave boys and girls, led by some old gray-headed slave mother.

"Farewell, farewell. Your friend,
"JOHN BROWN."

Mr. Stearns helped to go through the formality of a defense, but it was in vain.

A well organized plan was made to rescue him, conducted by the brave Colonel James Montgomery of Kansas, but the prisoner sent word to them that his sense of honor to his jailer, Captain Acvis, prevented him from walking out should the door be left open.

A satchel belonging to Captain Brown was found when he was taken prisoner, containing letters which implicated Frederick Douglass. Warned by his friends, Douglass escaped first to Canada and from there to England. Buchanan's marshals were hot on his trail, coming to Rochester six hours after he left. Governor Wise made requisition on the executives of New York and Michigan, but the bird had flown. To show the temper of the Governor when he found his prey had escaped. I will quote from his speech made in Richmond, December 21, of the same year. He said, with tremendous applause: "Oh, if I had had one good, long, low, black, rakish, well-armed steamer in Hampton Roads, I would have placed her on the Newfoundland Banks, with orders, if she found a British packet with that Negro on board, to take him. And by the eternal gods, he should have been taken — taken with very particular instructions not to hang him before I had the privilege of seeing him well hung."

It seems that the death of John Brown and his followers had not mollified the rage of Governor and people. It might be said of Brown that, like Samson, he accomplished more in his death than during his life, for he lighted the torch of freedom, which was never extinguished. For though John Brown's body lay moulderng in the tomb, his soul went marching on, until freedom was proclaimed to four millions of slaves.

II. Calvin Fairbank:—The subject of this sketch is living at Angelica, New York, now upwards of eighty years of age. Although broken in health, he still takes great interest in passing events and keeps up an extensive correspondence with his friends. We have exchanged several letters with him and are glad to give him his true place in history by the side of Garrison, Brown and Lovejoy. Some years ago he wrote an interesting history of his life, and has recently published another book giving an exceedingly interesting account of "How the Way was Prepared" for the emancipation of slaves. He is a hero who has spent long years in jail in testimony of his devotion to the cause of human freedom. His career, one of daring and suffering, almost surpassing belief, has been unique and without parallel. The story of his life is best told in his own words and way:

"I was born in Pike, New York, eighty years ago. In my childhood my father was a farmer, but later he became a lumberman, engaged with an uncle of mine in clearing up a tract of timber land near Olean, the lumber from which they floated down the Alleghany and Ohio rivers and sold in the Cincinnati markets My father and mother were Methodists, and one of the most vivid recollections of my childhood is of going with them when I was about twelve years old to attend a quarterly meeting held in another town a dozen miles or so from Hume, N. Y., where we then lived. We remained over night, and as the large attendance at the meeting had filled every house in the town, I, being a boy, was sent to sleep at the home of an ex-slave family, the head of which had made his escape from Virginia some years before. Child though I was, the stories of the suffering and misery endured by slaves which the old Negro told me that night, as we sat together on the stone hearth in front of the open fireplace, settled the course of my after-life. I resolved, if I lived, to help right the great wrongs with which I had thus been made acquainted, and though it was not until many years later that I came to know of the existence of the Underground Railroad and the American Anti-Slavery Society, my resolution grew stronger as I grew older, and only needed fitting opportunity to bear fruit. The opportunity came in the spring of 1837, just before I was twenty-one years of age, when my father sent me down the river to Cincinnati in charge of a raft of lumber. It was a morning in April, sharp, crisp and clear, and we were rounding a bend in the Ohio River just below Wheeling when I caught sight of a strapping darky, an ax flung over his shoulder, jogging along on the Virginia bank of the river, singing as he went:

"De cold, frosty morning make a niggah feel good,
Wid de ax on de shoulder he go jogging to de wood."

"'Halloo, there! where are you going?' I called to him. 'Gwine choppin' in de woods!' 'Chopping for yourself?'

"'Han't got no self.' 'Slave, are you?' 'Dat's what I is.' 'Why don't you run away?' 'Case I don't know where to go.' 'I'll show you where to go.' 'White man mighty onsartin; niggah more so,' he said, shaking his head doubtfully.

"We talked for some time, I all the while urging him to make the break for the North, whither his wife had already escaped. Finally he asked where I was from, and when I told him from New York state my reply seemed to settle it, for he dropped his ax and jumped onto the raft. I pushed off and we swung over to the Ohio side. As we touched the shore the darky, whose name was Johnson, danced a jig for joy. I directed him to the house of a man named Snyder, who lived near by and who, I had been told, kept a station on the Underground Railroad, and continued on my way down the river. When I came back I learned that Johnson had remained in hiding for some time with the Snyders and had finally gone, no one knew where. I had now got my hand in as a slave stealer, and was anxious for more work to do. On the same trip down the river, near the mouth of the Little Miami, I helped across the Ohio a family of seven, Stewart by name, four men and three women, all of them over six feet tall.

"After I had marketed my lumber at Cincinnati I took passage on a steamer for Pittsburg. The steamer stopped at Maysville, Kentucky, to take on freight, and while it was loading I went for a walk about the town. On one of the back streets I met an extremely pretty girl of sixteen or seventeen who seemed in deep distress. I asked her what was the matter and she told me that she was a slave—you would not have known it from her color —and was trying to escape from her master, a man who lived a few miles out in the country from town, and who also was her father. I took the girl back to the steamer and introduced her to my sister, explaining to the clerk and captain that I had met her in Maysville by appointment. No questions were asked, and we made the trip to Pittsburg in safety. She was exceedingly bright and a skilled musician, and, I remember, made a deep impression on some of the male passengers, one of whom went so far as to ask the privilege of corresponding with her. She settled in New York, finally married well, and is now living in San Francisco in more than comfortable circumstances.

"In June, 1838, I was again in Cincinnati selling lumber, and while there heard of a slave family of fourteen, a few miles below the city, in Kentucky, who were anxious to escape. I engaged a scow and with a Negro named Casey paddled them across the river to the Ohio side. We were closely followed by their owner and a posse of officers, but succeeded in throwing them off the scent. Next day Henry Boyd, a wealthy Cincinnati colored man, guided the runaways in safety to Lawrenceburg, Indiana, whence they were sent further North. This made twenty-three slaves I helped to liberty before I was as many years old.

"I was anxious for a better education than the common schools I had thus far attended afforded me, and to secure it entered the seminary at Lima, N. Y., in 1839. Later I became a student at Oberlin College, Ohio, from which institution I graduated in 1844. While a student at Oberlin I made the acquaintance of Gerrit Smith, Joshua R. Giddings, Theodore Parker and other abolition leaders, and became thoroughly imbued with their ideas, coming to hold with Smith that the Federal constitution, instead of countenancing slavery, positively forbade it. During my college vacations, in order to obtain money with which to continue my studies, I taught school in Lexington, Kentucky. One of the first friends I made in Lexington was Cassius M. Clay. He was then, as now, a large-hearted, noble-minded man, and an attachment sprang up between us which to-day is as warm as ever. In those days he was editing the True American, the only anti-slavery paper published in the South. His boldness in attacking the lion in its very den, as it were, produced the most violent opposition, and upon a number of occasions I was among those who guarded his printing plant from destruction by mobs. Once, I remember, I manned for two days and nights a cannon loaded with grape and canister posted in front of his office door. There were one or two more cannons about the premises, and a mob, had it visited us, would have received a warm reception.

"One day in August, 1841, word came to me that an escaped slave, named Coleman, with his wife and three children, were in hiding in Lexington. The poor creatures had made their way from East Tennessee, but their owner was hot on their track, and they were afraid to go further

without a guide   I left my school in charge of
another, and started with them toward the Ohio
River at night and on foot.   We traveled for six
nights, lying in hiding during the day.   We finally
reached the Ohio, opposite Ripley, and crossed
the river in a skiff.   Just after we had crossed I
saw a Negro boy run along the Kentucky shore and
disappear.   I suspected he was trying to escape,
and went back to help him.   I found him behind
a log in the swamp, and got away with him,
though men with bloodhounds were hunting the
boy at the time.

"In April, 1842, I was in Covington, Kentucky,
and while there was told of the case of Emily
Ward, a handsome girl of eighteen, two-thirds
white, who had been sold and was about to be
taken South to become the mistress of her pur-
chaser.   She was kept in an attic facing the river.
I went at nightfall, and attracting her attention by
tossing pebbles against the windows, threw up to
her, tied to a stone, a note telling her I had come to
help her escape.   By the same means I got up to
her first a cord with a bundle of men's clothes
fastened to it, and finally a stout rope.   She put
on the clothes, and crawling through a rear window of the room in which she was locked, slid
down the rope to the ground.   When we were a
few feet away from the house we met her master,
who apologized for unintentionally brushing against
me in the darkness.   The girl's case was known to
every one in Covington, and I did not dare to hire a
boat to take us across to Cincinnati for fear of detection; so we got on board a raft, eight by twenty
rods, containing one million feet of boards and one

hundred thousand shingles, worked by twelve men besides myself, the pilot. Once in Cincinnati, we were safe. I took Emily to the house of Levi Coffin, Superintendent of the Underground Railroad in that department, and turned her over to him. He found her a comfortable home and she did well.

"Five days after helping Emily Ward to escape I again crossed the Ohio at night on a log. This time I had for a companion John Hamilton, a mulatto. He was a man of superior natural ability and made his mark. After the war he returned South and became a State Senator in South Carolina, only to be murdered by the Ku-Klux. This was my last log trip, but within a week I rescued the Stanton family, father, mother and six children. They had been sold and were about to be sent to a Louisiana sugar plantation. I packed them in the bottom of a load of straw bought just out of Covington ostensibly for livery use, and drove them in safety to Cincinnati, where Levi Coffin sent them North over the Underground Railroad.

"In August of the same year I spent several weeks in Montgomery County, Kentucky, as the guest of Richard McFarland. A girl of sixteen was anxious to escape and applied to me for help. Starting on a clear, moonlight night, we drove before noon next day to Lexington, a distance of ninety miles. On the way we were overhauled by a brother of McFarland, who was searching for a lost slave. When I heard the man's name my heart rose in my mouth, but by putting on a bold front I succeeded in getting off without disclosing the identity of myself and companion. My scruples against so gross a breach of hospitality as stealing the prop-

erty of my host were fully overcome by the fact
that both the girl and her mother were the children of their master. Kate was a pretty blonde,
with blue eyes and flaxen hair, showing not the
slightest trace of Negro blood. From Lexington I
took her to Cincinnati and gave her into the care
of Gamaliel Bailey, editor of the National Era, one
of the noblest and bravest soldiers in the abolition
army. Later, Kate's mother, brother and sister
escaped. The children were all educated by Mr.
Bailey and are still living in prosperous circumstances.

"The most remarkable incident of this period of
my life occurred in March, 1843. One day in the
latter part of that month, while looking through
the jail at Lexington, my attention was attracted
to one of the prisoners, a young woman of ex-
quisite figure and singular beauty. I asked the
jailer who she was, and to my surprise, for she
looked pure Caucasian, he told me that she was a
slave girl named Eliza and the daughter of her
master, who a few days later was to sell her upon
the block for the New Orleans market, impelled
by the jealousy of his wife because the slave girl
was superior to her own daughters. Then I talked
with the girl; I found that she was intelligent as
well as beautiful, and I resolved to exert every
effort to save so magnificent a creature from so
sad a fate. I told her I would go to Cincinnati
and do my best to raise the money with which to
purchase her freedom; if I obtained it I would be
back before the sale came off; if I did not return
she would at least have the sorry satisfaction of
knowing that I had done all I could. I hurried to

Cincinnati and sought out that old hero and apostle of freedom, Levi Coffin. He gave me prompt and generous assistance, and in a short time we raised seven hundred dollars. I then laid the case before Salmon P. Chase, afterwards Senator, Secretary of the Treasury, and Chief Justice, who gave me two hundred more and went with me to see Nicholas Longworth. The latter was worth millions, but we were afraid nothing would come of our appeal to him, but decided to make it, as it cost us nothing. 'Mr. Longworth,' said Chase, 'do you consider yourself a Christian?'

"'I am not a very good one,' was the reply.

"'Well, we have got a case here that appeals to both humanity and Christianity. Mr. Fairbank will tell you about it.' I told the story. Longworth listened in silence, and when I was through drew his check-book from a drawer and began filling out a check. A moment later Longworth wheeled around and handed me a check for one thousand dollars. A number of well-to-do Negroes raised and gave me several hundred dollars more, and when I went back to Lexington, the day before the time appointed for the sale, I carried two thousand two hundred and seventy-five dollars. Moreover, in my pocketbook was an agreement signed by Chase, Longworth and William Howard, another rich Cincinnatian, empowering me to draw upon them, if necessary, to the extent of twenty-five thousand. The sale took place and was attended by fully two thousand people, drawn there by descriptions of the girl's comeliness and rumors of the effort that was to be made to save her. The best people of the town were there, and a number of strangers from Boston, New York and Philadelphia were also present, curious and horror-stricken. But one man appeared to bid against me, a Frenchman from New Orleans, who I was told made it his business to attend sales of young girls and purchase them for a fate worse than death. Eliza, when placed upon the block, seemed ready to drop from fear and shame. The auctioneer began his work by pointing out her beauties, concluding with, 'What am I offered for her?' 'Five hundred,' I cried. The New Orleans man instantly raised my bid, until I raised his last bid to thirteen hundred, when he turned to me with an ugly look and said: 'How high are you going to bid?' 'Higher than you do, Monsieur,' I replied. He turned away and raised my bid, and we kept bidding until he turned to me and asked: 'How high are you going?' 'None of your business, sir, but you haven't enough money to buy this girl.' The auctioneer grew impatient and cried, 'Give, give.' Finally he dropped his hammer and tearing open Eliza's waist, exposed a bust as perfect as ever artist sculptured. 'Look, gentlemen,' he cried. 'Who is going to lose a chance like this. Here's a girl fit to be the mistress of a king.' 'Too bad!' 'What a shame!' ran through the crowd at sight of this indignity; but only to be followed by greater exposure of the poor girl's person. The hammer fell at fourteen hundred and eighty dollars, and the girl was mine. An instant later she tottered back into the arms of her aunt in a deep swoon. 'She is yours, young man,' said the auctioneer. 'What are you going to do with her?' 'Free her, sir,' and my answer awoke a cheer, which, rising to a Kentucky shout, rent the air. As soon as they could be made out, I handed Eliza the papers which formally set her free. Four days after the sale I took Eliza to Cincinnati, where she became a member of the family of Gamaliel Bailey. Under his care she received a finished education, married well, and to-day is a cheerful, charming matron. Only the members of her immediate family know the history of her early years; so you will understand why I do not give her full name.

"Lewis Hayden, who served as a member of the Massachusetts general court and in the Legislature of the same state, and who was long ago one of the honored citizens of Boston, was when a young man a slave, the property of Baxter and Grant, owners of the Brennan House, in Lexington. Hayden's wife, and his son, a lad of ten years, when I first knew them, were the slaves of Patrick Baine. On a September evening in 1844, accompanied by Miss D A. Webster, a young Vermont lady who was associated with me in teaching, I left Lexington with the Haydens in a hack, crossed the Ohio on a ferry the next morning, changed horses and drove to an Underground Railroad depot at Hopkins, Ohio, where we left Hayden and his family. When Miss Webster and I returned to Lexington, after two days' absence, we were both arrested, charged by their master with helping Hayden's wife and son to escape. We were jointly indicted, but Miss Webster was tried first and sentenced to two years' imprisonment in the penitentiary at Frankfort.

"My cell-mate in the jail in which I was con

fined before my trial was Richard Moore, a young mulatto, a slave under sentence of death for the murder of his mistress, a Mrs. Turner. The thing seemed impossible, but I determined to attempt his and my own escape. A week or so before the time set for his execution I suggested a plan for four or five slaves to break jail, and in this way secured two bars of iron, which I hid away. Early on the Tuesday night previous to the Friday upon which Moore was to hang, we attacked the wall of our cell. All night we worked without rest; the palms of my hands were worn to the tendons. We had reached the last bowlder on the outside of the four-foot wall when the city clock struck five. We were half an hour too late. 'I am a dead man,' said Moore, and fell almost to the floor. When what we had done was discovered we were hand-cuffed together, and remained so day and night until Moore was executed. Do you wonder that I have never forgotten this experience?

"While my case was still pending I learned that the Governor was inclined to pardon Miss Webster, but first insisted that I should be tried. When called up for trial, in February, 1845, I pleaded guilty and received a sentence of fifteen years. A little later Miss Webster received her pardon. I served four years and eleven months, was released August 23, 1849, by Governor John J. Crittenden, the able and patriotic man who afterwards saved Kentucky to the Union. His action was prompted by petitions in my behalf from all parts of the North. I returned to the North immediately after my release, and did what I could do to prevent the passage of the Fugitive

Slave ill. After it became a law by the signature of President Fillmore, I resisted its execution whenever and wherever possible.

"An incident which happened soon after I returned North showed me that my labors for the slaves had not been in vain. In the autumn of 1849 I was in Detroit, Michigan. In talking over my early experiences one day with General Lewis Cass I told him of Sam Johnson, the first Negro whom I had freed.

"'Why,' said the General, 'Johnson lives just out of this city. He has told me the same story a dozen times.' The General informed me that Johnson drove into the city almost daily, and next morning I waited at the place to which I had been directed for his appearance. He finally came, seated in a wagon loaded with grain and drawn by a six-horse team. 'Whose team is that?' I asked. 'Mine,' was the reply. 'Do you know that I am your master?' I continued. 'Hain't got no master,' said he gloomily. Then recognizing who I was, he leaped from his seat with a joyful, 'Blessed if you hain't de chap dat sot me free,' and caught me in his arms. He took me to his home, a few miles from Detroit, and I found him to be a well-to-do farmer, owning a well-stocked farm of one hundred and sixty acres, with his wife and children about him. Living near the Johnsons, and like them, contented and comfortable, I found the Stewart and Coleman families, for whom I had also lighted the path to freedom.

"My father had died of cholera at Lexington in 1849, while seeking to secure my release, and in October, 1851, I went South to get the body and bring it back to our old home here in New York. While waiting in Louisville for the cooler weather which would permit a fulfillment of my mission, I rescued a woman named Julia and her child. Crossing the Ohio in a skiff at night, I took them to an underground depot at Buckrams, Indiana I saw the mother afterward at Windsor, Canada, where she had married well. Two weeks later I carried off Tamor, a bright mulatto girl of twenty belonging to A. L. Shotwell of Louisville. I knew the undertaking was an extremely dangerous one and I laid my plans carefully. The girl met me one evening at a certain gate, dressed for the occasion. We walked through the busiest part of the city to the banks of the Ohio, which we crossed in a leaky skiff, which I propelled with a piece of board while Tamor kept the skiff from sinking by constant bailing with a large cup which we had brought along for the purpose. Resting as we might, during the night, chased from one retreat to another, I drove with her early next morning to a railroad station twenty-four miles from the river, and took her on the cars to Salem, Indiana, where I left her with a friend. This was the last slave whom I was ever able to help off. In fifteen years I had, unaided and alone, freed forty-seven slaves, besides lending assistance in many other cases.

"The freeing of Tamor again cost me my own liberty. One week afterwards I was kidnaped from Indiana soil, and without process of law taken to Louisville and lodged in jail. I was tried in February, 1852, the owner of Tamor appearing as my prosecutor, and though the evidence against me was of the flimsiest character, my reputation as slave-stealer secured my conviction. My sentence was fifteen years at hard labor in the state prison. My friends did little for me, and that was one reason why I fared so hard. They were afraid, so intense was the feeling against me in Louisville, that if they succeeded in securing my acquittal by a jury, a mob would take it up and lynch me. My own mind, however, was at rest on that point. I would have taken part in any lynching that might have been attempted and looked out for myself.

"I returned to the prison at Frankfort in March, 1852. Captain Newton Craig, the warden under whom I had served my first term, was still in charge. What was known as the lease system was then in vogue, the prison being leased to the warden for a certain sum a year, the warden looking to the labor of the prisoners for his profit. The prison during all the years that it was my home was in a horrible condition, unspeakably filthy and miserably ventilated. During my first imprisonment Craig had treated me kindly, but his bearing when I came before him for the second time plainly told me that my lot was to be a hard one. After being locked up for two days I was brought before the warden in the prison chapel, the Governor and other prominent citizens being present, and denounced for what I had done. 'Mr. Davis,' said the warden, 'take Fairbank to the hackling house and kill him.' To the hackling house I accordingly went. This was where the hemp, after being broken, was hackled. After a month's work in the hackling shop I was sent to the spinning shop, and finally to the weaving shop, where I remained for ten and a half years. While in the hackling shop I received my first flogging with the rawhide on the bare back, the blows cutting deep into the quivering flesh.

"Zeb Ward became warden of the prison in 1854. He leased it at six thousand a year and made one hundred thousand out of the lease in four years. To do this he literally killed two hundred and fifty out of three hundred and seventy-five prisoners. Ward was one of the strangest men I ever knew, physically handsome, socially magnetic, but utterly devoid of heart or conscience. He was a gambler, libertine and murderer under cover of the law. When he took the keys of the prison he said: "Men, I'm a man of few words and prompt action. I came here to make money, and I'll do it if I kill you all."

"He was as good as his promise. During his wardenship and that of J. W. South, who succeeded him in 1858, I received on my bared body thirty-five thousand stripes, laid on with a strap of half-tanned leather a foot and a half long, often dipped in water to increase the pain. All the floggings I received under Ward were for failure to perform the tasks set for me to do, generally weaving hemp—two hundred and eighty yards a day being what I was expected to perform, an utter impossibility. I was whipped, bowed over a chair or some other object, often seventy lashes four times a day, every ten blows inflicting pain worse than death. Once I received one hundred and seven blows at one time, particles of flesh being thrown upon the wall several feet away.

My weight, which was one hundred and eighty pounds when I entered the prison, was several times reduced to one hundred and eighteen pounds. I have seen new men in the hackling house fall at their work, weak from flogging, and when taken to the hospital die before morning from pneumonia and the strap. A remarkable constitution and great muscular strength were the only thing that saved my life. As it was, I was an old man at forty.

"But there was an occasional ray of sunshine in my prison life. Interest in my case constantly increased, and at last public opinion set in in my favor.

"In February, 1858, having been pressed for three years to do so, I stood in the prison chapel and addressed an audience of several thousand people, including the Governor and other state officials. In the course of my sermon—I had been ordained a minister just before my second arrest—I told them that war was inevitable, and that when it came slavery would be swept away like chaff. Lincoln was elected President, and in less than five years war followed.

"In September and October, 1862, General Bragg held Frankfort for six weeks, and during that period three times rebel soldiers came to kill me. Once with a rope in hand they came upon me in the prison yard and asked me where they 'could find that damned nigger-stealer, Fairbank.' I sent them another way, then hurried to Warden Whitesides, a kindly and humane man, who took charge of the prison in 1862, and he hide me. On their second visit we got word of their coming and

I was in hiding when they arrived. Their last visit was unexpected, and they found me in the prison kitchen. Brought to bay, I had to fight for my life. I caught up an ax and planting myself in the doorway, said: 'Come on, boys; you are not afraid of me!' None of them seemed inclined to attack me first, and finally the whole party, several hundred strong, marched out.

"The freedom for which I had waited so long came two years later. Among those whose friendship I gained during my confinement was Richard T. Jacobs, a wealthy planter of strong anti-slavery tendencies, who had married a daughter of Thomas H. Benton. Jacobs often talked about me with his brother-in-law, John C. Fremont, and the latter in turn told my story to President Lincoln, who, as after events showed, was deeply impressed by it. Early in 1864 General Speed S. Fry was sent from Washington to Kentucky with orders to enroll all Negroes whom he found fit for military service. Thomas E. Bramlette, then Governor of Kentucky, attempted to prevent General Fry from carrying out his orders, as President Lincoln had expected he would, and was ordered to Washington. Jacob s, who was Lieutenant Governor, became Acting Governor. On his first day in office General Fry said to him: 'Governor, the President thinks it would be well to make this Fairbank's day.'

"He called upon me that day and told me that he was going to turn me loose. Counting my previous imprisonment, I had spent seventeen years and four months of the best part of my life in prison. On the evening after my release I enjoyed at the Capital Hotel in Frankfort a cordial reception by the people of the city and distinguished persons from other parts of Kentucky, which I shall ever remember with pleasure as a reunion after victory. Twenty-four hours late I crossed the Ohio, and do not believe me sentimental when I tell you that when I found myself once more on the free soil of the Buckeye State I knelt down and kissed the ground.

"In the following June occurred the event anticipation of which had strengthened and encouraged me through all those dark and dreary years. Previous to my second imprisonment I had been betrothed to Mandana Tileston of Williamsburg, Massachusetts. True as the magnet to the poles, when misfortune again befell me she left her New England home, engaged as a teacher, first in Hamilton and then at Oxford, Ohio, waited and watched over the border, supplied me with every comfort within her power, worked and petitioned for my release without ceasing, and faithful to the last, refused honorable alliances to wait the uncertain fate of a prisoner. It was a happy day indeed when we were married."

III. WILLIAM LLOYD GARRISON.

"Seven Grecian cities fought for Homer dead,
  Through which the living Homer begged his bread."

If we estimate his life by labors performed, sufferings, amounting almost to martyrdom, endured; unswerving devotion to the principles of equal rights to all, William Lloyd Garrison was certainly the greatest of anti-slave leaders. He

JOHN B. FRENCH,
Of Chicago, represents energy and pluck. Is one of the
most successful Caterers in the country.

was born in Newburyport, Mass , December 10th, 1805.   His mother's maiden name was Fanny Lloyd; and his father, Abijah Garrison, though a sea captain, possessed some literary ability and ambition.

It is a little remarkable that the house in which our hero was born was overshadowed by the church under whose altar the remains of George Whitefield were buried.   Thus at the very spot where the life's work of this great advocate of slavery ended, God in his providence raised up a greater and more zealous advocate of anti-slavery, to rouse the people from the lethargy into which Whitefield and his disciples wooed them.

In 1808 Abijah deserted his wife and children, never returning, leaving them to struggle for exist-ence as best they could.   William Lloyd, or Lloyd as his mother called him, was apprenticed when quite young to learn the shoemaker's trade.   Not liking the work, he was next set to learn cabinet-making.   This proving uncongenial, his mother secured him a place in a printing office, where he mastered the business in happy contentment.

When but a youth, he wrote for the "Newbury-port Herald," and Boston papers; then at the end of his apprenticeship, became the editor of a new paper in Newburyport, called "The Free Press."

This paper was noted for its high moral tone, but like the most of such "felt wants," its exist-ence was brief.   We next find him in Boston, editor of "The National Philanthropist," said to be the first paper started to advocate the doctrine of total abstinence from intoxicating drinks.   The motto of the paper was this truism, "Moderate drinking is the down-hill road to drunkenness," which was at once expressive and original.

While editing this paper he became acquainted with Benjamin Lundy, and they felt mutual affinity of kindred spirits from the first.

In 1828 Mr. Garrison became editor of "The Journal of the Times," in Bennington, Vermont, a paper established to support John Quincy Adams for the Presidency. He earned his salary by ably supporting Mr. Adams, but he also earned adverse criticism by being the champion of temperance, peace and the emancipation of slaves.

Among his exchanges was Lundy's "Genius of Universal Emancipation." The reading of this little monthly paper intensified his hatred of slavery; so he wrote a petition to Congress for its abolition in the District of Columbia. Having obtained a large number of signatures by sending it to the different postmasters of Vermont, he sent it to Congress, where it caused no little commotion on being read. In the fall of 1829, Mr. Garrison went into partnership with his Quaker friend Lundy; so "The Genius of Universal Emancipation" was enlarged and issued weekly at Baltimore, Md. But a difficulty presented itself to the success of the paper under their joint management. Mr. Lundy favored a gradual emancipation, while Mr. Garrison advocated immediate emancipation. At last, at the suggestion of Lundy, each wrote from his own standpoint, signing his initials to the articles.

The rage of the slave-holders knew no bounds when Garrison demolished their sophistries and subterfuges, by which they eased conscience, with an invincible logic, and he insisted with voice of thunder that it was their duty to "break every yoke and let the oppressed go free."

About this time a vessel belonging to Francis Todd of Garrison's native town, Newburyport, took on a cargo of eighty slaves at Baltimore for New Orleans. He at once denounced it in his paper, saying it was not one whit better than if the slaves had been brought from Africa; and the law denounced foreign slave-trade as piracy. For this he was arrested and fined fifty dollars, in default of which he was sent to jail. To show that his brave spirit was neither crushed nor daunted by imprisonment, he spent his time in writing against slavery, and inscribing sonnets on the walls of his cell. One of them was as follows:

> "Prisoner! within these gloomy walls close pent,
>   Guiltless of horrid crime or venal wrong—
> Bear nobly up against the punishment,
>   And in thy innocence be great and strong!
> Perchance thy fault was love to all mankind;
>   Thou didst oppose some vile, oppressive law,
> Or strive all human fetters to unbind,
>   Or wouldst not bear the implements of war;—
> What then? Dost thou so soon repent the deed?
>   A martyr's crown is richer than a king's!
> Think it an honor with the Lord to bleed,
>   And glory midst in tensest sufferings!
> Though beat, imprisoned, put to open shame,
> Time shalt embalm and magnify thy name."

John G. Whittier, the rising young Quaker poet, had recently succeeded George D. Prentice as editor of "The New England Review," at Hartford, Connecticut, after Prentice had gone to Kentucky

to write the life of Henry Clay and edit "The
Louisville Daily Journal."

He was a friend to Mr. Garrison, who had published some of his maiden poems while editing
"The Free Press," and an admirer of Henry Clay.
Young Whittier knew that Mr. Clay was a slave-
holder, but he also believed him a true friend of
freedom, judging from his effort to check the spread
of slavery and to ultimately abolish it in Kentucky. So he wrote the great statesman on behalf
of the "guiltless prisoner," at Baltimore, begging
him to pay his fine and "let the captive go free."
Mr. Clay responded promptly, asking for partic-
ulars and indicating an intention of complying with
the request. While matters were thus pending,
Arthur Tappan, a wealthy merchant in New York,
paid the fine and costs; so the prisoner was
released.

The partnership between Mr. Garrison and Mr.
Lundy was now dissolved, with the most cordial
feeling of friendship, which existed ever afterwards.

Seeing the apathy in regard to slavery, even in
liberty-loving Massachusetts, Garrison resolved
to start a paper to be called "The Liberator,"
right under the shadow of Bunker Hill, and near
Faneuil Hall, the "Cradle of Liberty."

The first number of this paper appeared in January, 1831, containing this expressive motto, "Our
Country is the World, Our Countrymen are all
Mankind." At the expiration of four months "The
Liberator" appeared with an engraved head including a pictorial representation of an auction,
with a bill tacked up offering for sale "slaves,
horses and other cattle." Near by is a whipping-

post at which a Negro slave is receiving punishment. In the background is seen the capitol at
Richmond, with a flag floating over the dome inscribed with the word "Liberty." Even Garrison's friends trembled at his fearless denunciation
of slavery. One even suggested that he change
the name of his paper to "The Safety Lamp;" but
his only reply was, "I will be as harsh as truth,
and as uncompromising as justice; I am in earnest; I will not equivocate; I will not excuse, I
will not retreat a single inch; and I will be heard."

The following outrage on free speech is quoted
from the Columbia, S. C., "Telescope" of this period: "Let us declare, through the public journals of our country, that the question of slavery
is not and shall not be open to discussion—that
the very moment any private individual attempts
to lecture us upon its evils and immorality, in the
same moment his tongue shall be cut out and cast
upon the dunghill."

New Orleans offered twenty thousand dollars
to any man or set of men who would seize Arthur
Tappan of New York, Garrison's benefactor.
While in the year 1831, the Legislature of
Georgia, the governor, Wilson Lumpbin, concur-
ring, passed a resolution offering a reward of five
thousand dollars for the arrest, prosecution and
conviction under the laws of that state, of William
Lloyd Garrison, editor of "The Liberator."

The record of it is found in the laws of Georgia
for 1831, page 255. This of course was simply a
bribe to any ruffian to seize and kidnap these brave
defenders of Liberty.

On January sixth, 1832, in the midst of a tempest of wind and hail, "The New England Anti-Slavery Society" was organized, in the basement of the African Baptist church in Belknap Street, Boston. Of those present only twelve persons, all white, signed the constitution, as follows:

William Lloyd Garrison, Oliver Johnson, Robert B. Hall, Arnold Buffum, William J. Snelling, John E. Fuller, Moses Thacher, Joshua Coffin, Stillman B. Newcomb, Benjamin C. Bacon, Isaac Knapp, Henry K. Stockton. These might be called the "Twelve Apostles of Abolition;" but with this humble origin the society grew into a mighty influence against slavery. This was the first association organized on the principle of immediate emancipation. Arnold Buffum was chosen President, and William L. Garrison corresponding secretary.

The Quakers were in the main the friends of the oppressed, and opposers of slavery, but even this sect was by no means a unit in this particular, as the following colloquy shows: "Well, Perez, I hope thee's done running after the Abolitionists," said a leading Friend to one of his humbler brethren. "Verily I have," said Perez; "I've caught up with and gone just a little ahead of them."

Henry Clay, and many statesmen and divines of national reputation, favored the idea of colonizing the negroes in Africa, and a strong organization know as "The American Colonization Society" was formed. Mr. Garrison, having received protests against this society from a number of prominent colored men of many Northern cities, published their protest, together with his own views,

in a large pamphlet in the spring of 1832, called
"Thoughts on African Colonization." In it he
shows ten objections to the said society: "1. It
is pledged not to oppose the system of slavery.
2. It apologizes for slavery and slaveholders. 3.
It recognizes slaves as property. 4. It increases
the value of slaves. 5. It is the enemy of immediate abolition. 6. It is nourished by fear and sel-
fishness. 7. It aims at the utter expulsion of the
blacks. 8. It is the disparager of the free blacks.
9. It denies the possibility of elevating the blacks
in this country. 10. It deceives and misleads the
nation."

The society never fully recovered from this
pamphlet, which showed them up in their true
light. This colonization society, while claiming
to be in the interest of the Negro, never thought
of consulting a colored man, bond or free, any
more than a society for the prevention of cruelty
to animals would consult the animals they are
trying to protect. In sending the "niggers" from
a civilized to a barbarous land, it was—

> "Theirs not to reason why,
> Theirs not to make reply,
> Theirs but to 'go' and die."

Mr. Garrison crossed the ocean no less than
five times, his first trip occurring in the spring
of 1833. In London he was invited to an honor-
ary seat in conference on the slavery question,
where he mingled with such men as Wilberforce,
Brougham, Macaulay, O'Connell, Burton and
Clarkson. He put into their hands his "Thoughts
on African Colonization," and brought home a
"Protest" against this colonization scheme, signed

by four of the great names I have mentioned and others of equal weight.

He was sent as a delegate to. the Anti-Slavery Conference of London in 1840; but when he learned that the conference refused to receive the lady delegates on their credentials, he and those who came with him took seats in the gallery as spectators.

Mr. Garrison made his third voyage in 1846, this time by invitation of the Glasgow Emancipation Society, who desired him to lecture against the Free Church, for collecting money from the Southern slaveholders.

His fourth visit to Europe was made in May, 1867, two years after the close of the war of the rebellion. He joined his children in Paris, and after attending the Exposition, went to London, where a great public breakfast was held in his honor, at St. James' Hall. Among those present were Mr. F. H. Morse, the American consul in London, John Bright, John Stewart Mill, and other members of Parliament. John Bright presided, and made the first speech. He crossed the Atlantic for the fifth and last time in company with his son Frank in 1877.

The Boston Mob, of "gentlemen of property and standing," occurred October twenty-first, 1835. The occasion of it was an advertised meeting of the Boston Female Anti-Slavery society, to take place at Anti-Slavery Hall, 46 Washington Street.

The mayor of Boston took no steps to prevent or disperse the mob other than by being present and commanding the ladies to retire. Seeing they could hope for no protection, they adjourned to meet again at the home of one of their number. The mayor now advised Garrison to escape by a window at the rear of the building. This he attempted to do, but was seized by the mob and dragged through some of the prominent streets of Boston with a rope about his body, amid the jeering and curses of men thirsting for his blood. At last the two strong men who supported him on either side, and a few friends and policemen with superhuman effort forced their way with him into the city hall. From here he was committed to jail ostensibly as a disturber of the peace. After being hustled into a carriage in waiting at the door, which the mob tried in vain to upset or capture, he was driven by a circuitous route to the jail and locked behind the prison bars. Was he crushed and discouraged? No, a thousand times no! It is true a new suit of clothes was torn to shreds; it is true he was buffeted and bruised; it is true he barely escaped with his life; but he slept as sweetly that night as if he had been in the bosom of his family. The next morning he wrote on the walls of his cell the following lines:—

"William Lloyd Garrison was put into this cell on Wednesday afternoon, Oct: 12th, 1835, to save him from the violence of a 'respectable' and influential mob who sought to destroy him for preaching the abominable and dangerous doctrine that, 'all men are created equal,' and that all oppression is odious in the sight of God.

"Reader, let this inscription remain till the last slave in this despotic land be loosed from his fetters."

"When peace within the bosom reigns,
 And conscience gives the approving voice,
Though bound, the human form in chains,
 Yet can the soul aloud rejoice.

'"Tis true my footsteps are confined,
 I cannot roam beyond this cell,
But what can circumscribe the mind?
 To chain the winds attempt as well!"

"'Confine me as a prisoner—but bind me not as a slave.
 Punish me as a prisoner—but hold me not as a chattel.
 Torture me as a man—but drive me not as a beast.
 Doubt my sanity—but acknowledge my immortality."

Mr. Garrison, like the immortal Bunyan, seemed to have his loftiest inspiration when behind the prison bars. Like flowers which exude their fragrance only when crushed or bruised, persecution drove him to poetry. Garrison was released from prison in the afternoon of the next day, and at the request of the city authorities, took his wife, who was in critical health, and left the city for a few days, until the excitement abated. But he lived to edit "The Liberator," until his demands were granted, and four million slaves were made free. This having been accomplished, in part through the influence of his paper, he deemed it unwise "to run the mill after the grist was out," and the last issue was published the last week in December, 1865, making the paper cover the full period of thirty-five years. But he continued the same kind friend to the freedmen he had been to the slave, until his labor ended with his life in New York City, Saturday night about eleven o'clock of May 24th, 1879, in the seventy-fourth year of his age.

IV. ELIJAH PARISH LOVEJOY.

Perhaps with the exception of John Brown's attack at Harper's Ferry, or the bombardment of Fort Sumter, no event in connection with slavery produced more widespread excitement north and south than the murder of Lovejoy at Alton, Illinois, Nov , 1837.

Before describing this startling event, it is well to consider something of the man, and the circumstances which led up to his untimely and cruel murder.

He was born in Albion, Maine, November, 1802, and was thirty-five years of age when killed by the mob. His father, Daniel Lovejoy, was a Congregational minister and a graduate of the well known college at Waterville, Maine.

When Elijah was a young man there was a great tide of emigration from New England to the mighty West; drifting with this tide, he came to St. Louis, where after teaching school for a time, he became editor of a Whig paper called the St. Louis Times. The ready pen and stirring style of the young editor soon brought the paper into prominence, and made it a great expose of Whig sentiment in Missouri and Illinois, and he bid fair to make his mark as a politician and moulder of public sentiment.

In 1832 he experienced a remarkable conversion to the Christian faith, and became deeply impressed with the duty of preaching the gospel. Yielding to this conviction, he at once went east and entered the Princeton Theological Seminary, and the next year, 1833, was licensed to preach. A few months after this he returned to St. Louis, where he was known as a ready writer, and soon secured a position as editor of the "St. Louis Observer," the leading organ of the Presbyterians of Missouri and Illinois. His was a remarkable career at this time, when we consider that he was not converted until 1832, when he was thirty years of age, and became a minister, and an influential religious editor the next year; thus obtaining at a single bound, among the cultured and conservative Presbyterians, that which with them was often the work of a lifetime.

His biographer, Henry Tanner, who was with him at the time of his death, describes Mr. Lovejoy as being "of medium height, broadly built, muscular, of dark complexion, black eyes, with a certain twinkle betraying his sense of the humorous, and with a countenance expressing great kindness and sympathy." He said further, "There probably had not lived in this century a man of greater singleness of purpose in bearing witness to the truth, more courageous in maintaining principle in the face of passionate opposition."

When we read quotations from the "St. Louis Observer" of this period we are astonished that such mild editorials should so provoke the wrath of the pro-slavery people. But they were evidently determined to nip in the bud and crush out in its incipiency, any agitation of the slavery question, knowing their position was untenable, and could not stand the light of investigation.

As a summary of his views at this time, I would say he favored the idea of gradual emancipation of slaves, to be followed up by colonization. Surely this was a very mild view of the situation, when

we consider that many of the Southern slave-holders themselves advocated the same measure.   But
his heart was grieved at the brutal treatment many
slaves of this period received at the hands of masters and overseers.   Here he thought the reform
should be thorough and immediate.   "For," said
he, "it is fearfully true that many professed Chris-
tians habitually treat their slaves as though they
had no immortal souls, and it is high time such a
practice as this were abolished."   But   Garrison
and his associates were throwing red-hot shot into
the pro-slavery ranks.   "The Liberator" and
"Emancipator" were read in St. Louis and enraged the advocates of slavery.   In their excitement they regarded all Abolitionists as one and the
same in their views, and persistently ignored Mr.
Lovejoy's plea for "cool and temperate argument,
supported by facts," and the following editorial
from his pen: "It has been with pain that we
have seen, recently, the heated and angry meetings and discussions which have taken place
amongst our eastern brethren of the abolition
and colonization parties."

The excitement increased during the summer of
1845, until the slaveholders of St. Louis were
not willing to have the subject discussed, however
mildly.   The articles of Mr. Lovejoy, although
written in a kind, Christian spirit, became very
offensive to them.   The slaveholders were ready
to tar and feather him, as an Abolitionist, while
the rabble termed him an amalgamationist.   Yet
nothing was farther from his views.

It soon became evident that the main issue between Lovejoy and his enemies was freedom of

speech and the freedom of the press. He resolved to defend this at all hazards, and they were equally determined to suppress it.

Seeing he could have no protection in St. Louis, from insult and threatened mob violence, Mr. Lovejoy now determined to move his paper to the then thriving city of Alton, Illinois, just above St. Louis on the river. Alas! as is so often the case, he escaped Scylla only to wreck on Charybdis, as we shall see.

The "St. Louis Observer" of June 21, 1836, announced the editor's intention, but before the move could be made, some ruffians forced an entrance into his office and destroyed much of the property, including some of the editor's furniture, which was broken up and thrown into the river. The remnant, including the press, was shipped to Alton, where it remained on the landing during Sunday, and was broken to pieces and thrown into the river before Monday morning. But a public meeting was promptly held, in which the citizens denounced those who destroyed the press and raised money to buy a new one. The new press was soon received and the first number of the "Alton Observer" was issued September 8th, 1836.

For nearly a year Lovejoy enjoyed a period of comparative tranquility, but it was only the calm before the storm. Many Southerners and pro-slavery men came to the thriving young city These could not tolerate even the mild anti-slavery tone of the "Observer," and used their influence with the "lewd fellows of the baser sort," who were to be found in every western city, especially

river towns. Then, too, the great dailies of St.
Louis continued to harass him, and insist that
"something must be done" to rid the country of
this pestilential fellow, who actually taught that
all men were created equal. This actually caused
a mob at Alton on Aug. 21st, 1836.

The mob first attempted to assault Mr. Lovejoy on the street about nine o'clock at night, while
returning home from the drug-store with some
medicine for his sick wife. Having surrounded
him, the cry was, "Rail him, rail him," "Tar and
feather him!" Turning to the leaders, he said in
calm tone, "I have one request to make of you,
and then you can do with me what you please.
My wife is at home sick in bed; send one of your
number to take this medicine to her, and let it be
done without alarming her." This they promised
to do, and one of the men started with the medicine at once. But the calm demeanor of Lovejoy,
together with the self-sacrificing spirit in reference to his sick wife, touched the hearts of some
of them and he was permitted to go home undis-
turbed. But the same night they destroyed his
second press, type and other material; yet money
was quickly raised, partly from different states,
and partly from friends of free speech at Alton;
and a third press was on hand September 21st,
1837. It was taken to a warehouse and stored.

The mayor, John M. Krum, offered to guard it,
and did so by placing one constable at the door
of the warehouse until about midnight. But, as
might have been expected, the officer had hardly
gone, when about a dozen ruffians broke in the
warehouse door, dragged the press to the river and

after demolishing it, threw the fragments into that common receptacle of Lovejoy's property, the river. About ten days after this event, Mr. Lovejoy, with his wife and babe, were spending some time with his wife's mother at St. Charles, Missouri. He had preached morning and evening on that peaceful Sabbath, and about nine o'clock was enjoying a conversation with his friend Rev. Mr. Campbell, when a knock was heard at the docr. On opening it, he saw a number of men on the portico and in the yard. The two leaders, formerly from Virginia and Missouri, rushed into the house and attempted to pull him out. But with the help of his heroic wife, her mother and sister, the two men were driven from the room. The drunken mob again returned to the charge, and rushing into the room, they attempted to drag him out, and might have succeeded, had it not been for his friend Campbell. It required the utmost exertion of their united efforts to force the mob from the room and clear the house. The fiends even made a third attempt to force an entrance, after which it was thought best for Lovejoy to leave the house that night. Groping through the darkness to a house of a friend, he procured a horse and arrived at Alton the next day.

Money for a fourth press was raised, it is thought by friends of free speech in Ohio, and was shipped from Cincinnati to Alton. It was received by the friends of Mr. Lovejoy, about midnight of November 6, 1837, and stored in the warehouse of Godfrey and Gilman, the leading firm in the city. Mr. Gilman, one of the owners of the warehouse, called for volunteers to guard it during the night;

nineteen responded, among them Mr. Lovejoy.
The mob soon began to gather, when two of their
number, Keating and West, were unwisely admitted inside the building to confer with Mr. Gilman.
Of course they saw how few were on guard and
immediately demanded the surrender of the press,
threatening to blow or burn up the building in
case of refusal. Most of those in the warehouse
were anxious to fire on the mob from the window
as soon as they got in range, hoping to repulse
them at once. But Captain Long would not let
them fire until the mob was close up to the building and had fired into the door. He then ordered
one of his men to return the fire; he did so and
killed one of the mob, a man named Bishop. This
caused a cessation of hostilities for a moment, but
the mob was soon reinforced by a lot of ruffians
who had been drinking to stimulate their courage.
They now made a desperate charge, shouting "Fire
the building, and shoot every Abolitionist as he
tries to escape!" An effort was now made to fire
the building. For this purpose a long ladder was
placed on the side where there were no windows.
Soon a man mounted the ladder with a lighted
torch and attempted to set fire to the shingles,
which fortunately were damp with a heavy dew,
and slow to kindle into a flame. Captain Long
now called for volunteers to fight their way to the
ladder and throw it down. Amos B. Roff, Royal
Weller and Elijah P. Lovejoy, against the protest
of his friends, promptly attempted this fatal mission. As they stepped from the door into the
bright moonlight a perfect fusillade was fired at
them from a pile of lumber near by. Roff and

DR. I. B. SCOTT,
Editor of the Southwestern Christian Advocate, New Orleans, La.

Weller were both wounded, but the fire seemed to be concentrated upon Mr. Lovejoy, who must have been recognized in the bright moonlight. He received five balls in his body, but had strength enough to run back into the house and up the stairs, crying as he went, "I am shot! I am shot! I am dead!"

These were his last words; his friends laid him on the floor, where he instantly expired.

The mob then seized the fourth press and destroyed it. The citizens of Alton generally, appeared to sympathize with the mob; for when Mrs. Graves, the wife of the Presbyterian pastor, in his absence, rang the bell of her church, not far off, until she exhausted herself, not one of the citizens appeared to defend a minister who was about to be murdered. It seems, too, that Mr. Lovejoy rather expected to be murdered, as was seen by perhaps, the last public speech he made after being mobbed at St. Charles. At his own request he was buried at Alton. Thus lived and died one of the noblest and bravest defenders of free speech and civil liberty the century has produced. Mob law was thus triumphant, but it was a dear-bought victory for Alton. She could destroy four presses for Mr. Lovejoy, but she could not destroy that mighty palladium of liberty throughout the Union. All the invective of contemporary journalism was hurled at Alton. Commerce shunned it as a plague-spot, and emigrants avoided it as a valley of death A store built by Mr. Tanner at a cost of twenty-five thousand was sold by him for less than half that amount, and offered back to him for two thousand.

Many of her best and wealthiest citizens moved away. Her empty warehouses crumbled into the river, or became the haunts for bat and owl.

As a city, it seemed to be under the bane of Him who came "to proclaim liberty to the captives," saying also, "Touch not mine anointed and do my prophets no harm."

CHAPTER XIII.

BLACK PHALANX IN THE REBELLION.

From the time the first mutterings of Rebellion were heard, and the war cloud no larger than a man's hand appeared on our country's horizon, the Negro believed, with an unswerving faith, that slavery was the one cause of war; that God was now ready to punish the despoiler, and let the oppressed go free. The chorus of his favorite song of this period was, "It must be now that the kingdom am coming, and the year of jubilee."

Naturally he was anxious to do all in his power to help save the country by putting down the Rebellion, and thereby proving himself worthy of the coveted boon of freedom.

But alas for the suicidal policy of the Government, he was forced to conquer race prejudice, and the most determined opposition, before he was permitted to face the enemy on the field of battle. In short, they did not believe that the Negro would fight, and seemingly demanded that he should prove himself a soldier before facing the enemy; reminding one of the father who told his boys never to go near the water until they had learned to swim; or the Irishman who could not get on his boots until he had worn them awhile.

The New York "Times" of February 16, 1863, in an editorial summed up the objections to enlisting Negroes as follows: "First—That the Negroes will not fight. Second—It is said that the whites will not fight with them, that the prejudice against them is so strong that our citizens will not enlist or will quit the service if compelled to fight by their side, and thus we shall lose two white soldiers for one black one that we gain. Third—It is said we shall get no Negroes—or not enough to prove of any service. In the free states very few will volunteer, and in the slave states we can get but few, because the rebels will push them southward as fast as we advance upon them. Fourth— The use of Negroes will *exasperate* the South. We presume it will; but so will any other scheme we may adopt which is warlike and effective in its character and results. We are not ready with Mr. Vallandigham, to advocate 'immediate and unconditional peace.' The best thing we can do is to possess ourselves in patience while *the experiment* is being *tried*."

The President and Secretary of War and a large majority of the generals in the army acted on the theory, "This is a white man's war, and the Negro has no lot or part in it." They seemed to be blind to the fact that Negro slavery had been the disturbing element in the nation for about a century and was the real casus belli, the election of Lincoln being only the immediate occasion. Moreover, the Union army was turned into a gigantic slave-catching institution.

Even General McClellan, "whose pen was mightier than his sword," when commander-in chief, paused long enough in his demands on the war department for more men (to drill and send home on furloughs), to issue a proclamation from "Headquarters, Army of the Potomac, July 7, 1862," in which among other things he announced that "neither confiscation of property, political execution of persons, territorial organization of states, nor forcible abolition of slavery, should be contemplated for a moment."

In a speech made in the early days of the war at Worcester, Massachusetts, Charles Sumner said, "I do not say carry the war into Africa, but carry Africa into the war."

The honor of organizing the first regiment of colored soldiers during the civil war belongs to General David Hunter, who, while commanding the Department of the South, gave the necessary orders from Port Royal, South Carolina, in May of 1862.   General Hunter was in advance of public opinion, however, and Hon. Edwin M. Stanton, Secretary of War, wrote for full information concerning the matter.   The reply of General Hunter tended to bring public opinion up to his standard; especially where he informed the Secretary of War that no regiment of "fugitive slaves" had been organized in his department.   He stated that there was, "however, a fine regiment of persons whose late masters are 'fugitive rebels'—men who everywhere fly before the appearance of the national flag, leaving their servants behind them to shift as best they can for themselves.   So far, indeed, are the loyal persons composing this regi-

BISHOP DANIEL A. PAYNE.

ment from seeking to avoid the presence of their late owners, that they are now, one and all, working with remarkable industry to place themselves in a position to go in full and effective pursuit of their fugacious and traitorous proprietors." General Hunter explained to Mr. Stanton, that he was acting under instructions issued by Hon. Simon Cameron, late Secretary of War, to his predecessor General Thomas W. Sherman, who turned them over to him for his instruction and guidance. Said instruction authorized him "to employ all loyal persons offering their services in defense of the Union, and the suppression of this Rebellion."

He continues: "The loyal slaves everywhere remaining on their plantations to welcome us, aid us, and supply us with food, labor and information," filled this requirement exactly, and as they were the only men who were loyal, he had organized them into a regiment and detailed officers to drill them. He closed his letter by stating, "The experiment of arming the blacks, so far as I have made it, has been a complete and even marvelous success. They are sober, docile, attentive and enthusiastic; displaying great natural capacities for acquiring the duties of the soldier. They are eager, beyond all things, to take the field and be led into action; and it is the unanimous opinion of the officers who have had charge of them that in the peculiarities of this climate and country they will prove invaluable auxiliaries."

With General B. F. Butler, the idea of using Negroes as soldiers seems to have been a gradual growth in grace, but he was at last soundly converted. While in Maryland he offered to co-operate with Governor Hicks in suppressing any insurrection of the slaves against the laws of the state. In New Orleans he permitted a rebel slaveholder to enter his camp, and seize a mulatto, who was nearly white, after he had enlisted and donned the Federal uniform. Before this, General Butler had called the slaves who came into his lines, "contraband of war" and set them to work, thus recognizing property in man, and rating Negroes with mules, muskets or other munitions of war. But he seemed to think more favorably of free Negroes, and finding the idea growing popular at the North, he on the twenty-second of August, 1862, issued an appeal to the free men of color in New Orleans, to volunteer their services as soldiers in defense of the Union, which met with a hearty response. From this time on he was a strong advocate of employing Negro soldiers, and afterwards ably championed their cause on the floor of Congress.

General John Charles Fremont, having been appointed to the command of the Western Department with his headquarters at St. Louis, gave a new claim to his title of "pathfinder" by finding at once a way of success for the Union army, and freedom for the slave, by the aggressive action of an emancipation proclamation. This was issued August thirty-first, 1861. It proclaimed that "the property, real and personal, of all persons in the State of Missouri who shall take up arms against the United States, or shall be directly proven to have taken active part with their enemies in the field, is declared to be confiscated to the public use, and slaves, if any they have, are hereby declared free men." You will observe that he did not refer to Negroes as personal property or "contraband of war," but free men.

President Lincoln regarded this proclamation as premature, and annulled it; still it tended to pave the way for his great Emancipation Proclamation.

After the fall of Fort Donelson, February sixteenth, 1862, General Grant had backbone enough to send out the following order, which was the first of the kind issued during the war, and was not only in accord with the highest military wisdom, but consonant with the dictates of humanity and common sense.

"Headquarters, District of West Tenn.
Fort Donelson, Feby. 26, 1862.

"I. General Order No. 3, series 1861, from Headquarters Department of Missouri, is still in force and must be observed. The necessity of its strict enforcement is made apparent by the numerous applications from citizens for permission to pass through the camps to look for fugitive slaves. In no case whatever will permission be granted to citizens for this purpose.

"II. All slaves at Fort Donelson at the time of its capture and all slaves within the line of military occupation that have been used by the enemy in building fortifications, or in any manner hostile to the Government, will be employed by the quartermaster's department for the benefit of the Government, and will under no circumstances be permitted to return to their master.

"III. It is made the duty of all officers of this

command to see that all slaves above indicated are promptly delivered to the chief quartermaster of the district."

"By order of Brigadier General U. S. Grant.
"John A. Rawlins, A. A. G."

The "silent-man-on-horseback" did not often speak, but when he did, it was to the point and purpose.

The honor belongs to Governor Sprague of Rhode Island for making the first official call for Negro troops at the North. This appeal to the colored citizens of that state was issued August fourth, 1862. But the palm for actually raising the first colored regiment was won by one of the youngest of the sisterhood of states, even bleeding Kansas. This regiment was recruited in the summer and fall of 1862. Was organized at Fort Scott by Colonel James M. Williams January fourth, 1863, and was ready to take the field the following May. It is thought the reason Kansas led the Northern States in raising colored troops, was the fact that she had not yet accomplished the days of her mourning for the martyrdom of John Brown.

Governor Andrew of Massachusetts, having obtained authority from Secretary Stanton to raise a number of colored regiments, hurried home from Washington and sent out his first order February ninth, 1863. But owing to past disappointment, having been spurned and insulted when they were eager to preserve their country, the response of the "persons of African descent" was not hearty. Moreover, Massachusetts had but a small colored population. In this emergency the Governor sought help from the adjoining state. He dispatched Mayor G. L. Stearns to lay the case before the great leader and champion of his race, Frederick Douglass, then living and publishing his monthly at Rochester, New York.

As a result of the visit Mr. Douglass published a stirring appeal in the March number of his monthly of that year. This appeal had the desired effect; large numbers (including two of Douglass' sons) went over into Massachusetts and helped them fill up the ranks. When ready to take the field they intended marching through New York City, but the chief of police notified Governor Andrew that he would be unable to protect the colored troops from being mobbed by the foreign ruffians, and rebel sympathizers who had already tasted blood by mobbing inoffensive Negroes, looting and burning a colored orphan's home.

Tammany is usually represented by a tiger, but this time a dog in the manger would have been more appropriate. Not wishing to complicate matters, or spill unnecessary blood, they sailed around New York to meet the other rebels in the South.

But a change of sentiment rapidly took place and the colored troops scored a victory, even against the mobocracy of the metropolis. When the Twentieth Regiment Colored U. S. Troops was ready to leave its rendezvous on Ricker's Island for service, the members of the Union League Club and other friends proposed to give it a reception in New York City, but some of the committee

did not wish to expose the soldiers to mob violence and were timid, to say the least. It was decided to inform the commander of the regiment,
Colonel Bartram, of their apprehensions, and ask
him if he thought he could get through the city.
To which the brave commander replied: "Give
me room to land my regiment, and if it cannot
march through New York, it is not fit to go into
the field." This settled the matter. The police
cleared a space for it to land at Thirty-sixth
Street; and with fixed bayonets, loaded muskets,
martial music and company front, they marched
through the most aristocratic streets of the city.
Their manly appearance and military bearing produced the wildest enthusiasm and cheering among
the very cowardly ruffians who had wreaked their
vengeance on an orphan's home, a short time since.
The march became a triumphal procession, a perfect ovation, as a hundred thousand loyal citizens,
including some of the most wealthy and refined
ladies and gentlemen, showed their approval by
encouraging plaudits, enthusiastic cheering, waving handkerchiefs and showering them with bou-
quets.

But if Frederick Douglass could by his matchless eloquence inspire his people to go to war, a
worthy contemporary, Aunty Sojourner Truth,
could by means of a song which she composed
keep up the inspiration after they reached the front.
She composed this song for "her boys," the colored
regiment from Battle Creek, Michigan, but it soon
became a favorite with all the colored soldiers.
An old veteran told the writer he once heard a black
regiment sing it just before a battle and they made

the welkin ring, and inspired all who heard it.
Imagine a thousand Negro soldiers singing the
following lines to the tune of "John Brown's
Body."

THE VALIANT SOLDIERS.

We are the valiant soldiers who've 'listed for the war;
We are fighting for the Union, we are fighting for the law,
We can shoot a rebel farther than a white man ever saw,
   As we go marching on.

 CHORUS.—

  Glory, glory, hallelujah! Glory, glory, hallelujah!
  Glory, glory, hallelujah, as we go marching on.

Look there above the center, where the flag is waving bright;
We are going out of slavery, we are bound for freedom's light,
We mean to show Jeff Davis how the Africans can fight,
   As we go marching on.—CHO.

We are done with hoeing cotton, we are done with hoeing corn;
We are colored Yankee soldiers, as sure as you are born;
When Massa hears us shouting, he will think 'tis Gabriel's horn,
   As we go marching on.—CHO.

They will have to pay us wages, the wages of their sin;
They will have to bow their foreheads to their colored kith and
  kin;
They will have to give us houseroom, or the roof will tumble in,
   As we go marching on.—CHO.

We hear the proclamation, massa, hush it as you will;
The birds will sing it to us, hopping on the cotton hill;
The possum up the gum tree couldn't keep it still,
   As he went climbing on.—CHO.

Father Abraham has spoken, and the message has been sent;
The prison doors have opened and out the prisoners went
To join the sable army of African descent,
   As we go marching on.—CHO.

But how did they behave themselves under fire, what did they do in battle? They did what would be naturally expected, when it is remembered that behind them were chains and slavery; in their immediate presence the rebel proclamation of "no quarter for Negroes," while before them was the bright star of freedom beckoning them on to a happier and independent life.

> "They fought like brave men" nobly well;
> "They piled the ground with" rebels slain;
> "They conquered, but" a thousand fell,
> "Bleeding in every vein."

Truly does George W. Williams, himself a colored veteran, say in his "History of the Negro Troops in the Rebellion," "The part enacted by the Negro troops in the war of the Rebellion is the romance of North American History." But it may be objected that *he* is a partial witness. True, but he was *there*, and a man who was present certainly knows more about it than another who was afraid to go. We will presently introduce witnesses who were opposed to the use of the Negro as a soldier.

Even President Lincoln remarked to Dr. Patten of Chicago, when urged to press the Negro into service, "If we were to arm them I fear that in a few weeks the arms would be in the hands of the rebels." So it was with many misgivings they were at last permitted to face the enemy. Early in their military career they were given an opportunity to prove their valor by a desperate encounter at Fort Wagner, Port Hudson, and the mine explosion at Petersburg; still each time they met the enemy like heroes and veterans, and by their indomitable courage and enthusiasm conquered the prejudice of the Union men who at first opposed their enlistment.

At Fort Wagner near Charleston the wealthy and cultured young Colonel R. G. Shaw commanded the Fifty-fourth Massachusetts colored regiment. To get to this battle they had made a forced march of a day and night without food or rest; over shifting sands and under a broiling sun, during the day, and through darkness and a drenching rain at night. They reached General Strong's headquarters at six o'clock on the memorable morning just as they were forming the line of battle, and without stopping for rest or food, they proudly took their place at the head of the assaulting column.

General Strong and Colonel Shaw each made burning patriotic speeches inspiring their men to be eager for deeds of valor or a glorious death. After about half an hour General Strong gave the order to charge, and onward swept the troops led by the gallant Negro regiment, nor were they checked by the galling fire from the ramparts of Fort Wagner, or the destructive cross-fire which raked them from Cummings Point and Sumter. Rushing across the ditch with irresistible force, the regiment reached the parapet and there planted their flag. But at this critical moment the gallant General Strong was mortally wounded, "and here," in the language of Williams, "the brave, beautiful and heroic Colonel Shaw was saluted by death and kissed by immortality." But his regiment in this charge through the very jaws of death had actually gained the *inside* of the fort, and had

they been strongly supported Wagner would undoubtedly have been taken.

Colonel Shaw's regiment numbered about six
hundred enlisted men and twenty officers which
helped in this battle.   Of the privates, thirty-one
were killed, one hundred and thirty-five wounded,
and ninety-two missing.   Of the twenty-two
officers three were killed and eleven wounded.
Thus we find that more than half the officers were
killed or wounded, and nearly half of the privates
were either killed, wounded or missing.   Although
the assault on Wagner was a military failure, for
in war nothing succeeds but success, still it effec-
tually demonstrated that the Negro troops were
among the bravest of the brave, and it tended to
silence the scoffing contempt and ridicule of the
stay-at-home Negro-doubters.

Delighted with their gallant conduct, General
Gillmore presented medals to the following soldiers
of the glorious Fifty-fourth colored regiment: Sergeants Robert J. Simmons and William H. Carney;
Corporal Henry F. Peal and Private George Wilson.   In this charge John Wall, the Negro color
bearer, was killed, but William H. Carney seized
the standard and bore it to the parapet, but after
receiving several severe wounds, one of which
mangled his arm, he brought the tattered banner
to the rear in his clenched teeth, stained with his
own blood, and shouted to his comrades, "Boys,
it never teched the ground!"

When a flag of truce was sent to the enemy to
claim Colonel Shaw's body, a rebel officer replied,
"We buried him with his niggers " They thought
thus to heap odium on this dead hero, but the

effort was a failure. At the request of his parents, the body was not disturbed, but the gallant young officer and his black comrades were permitted to sleep on in a common grave. Thus united in life, in death they were not separated.

> "'They buried him with his niggers!'
>   Together they fought and died;
> There was room for them all where they laid him,
>   (The grave was deep and wide)
> For his beauty and youth and valor,
>   Their patience and love and pain;
> And at the last day together
>   They shall all be found again.
>
> 'They buried him with his niggers!'
>   Earth holds no prouder grave;
> There is not a mausoleum
>   In the world beyond the wave
> That a nobler tale has hallowed
>   Or a purer glory crowned,
> Than the nameless trench where they buried
>   The brave so faithful found.
>
> 'They buried him with his niggers!"
>   A wide grave should it be;
> They buried more in that shallow trench
>   Than human eye could see.
> Ay, all the shams and sorrows
>   Of more than a hundred years
> Lie under the weight of that Southern soil,
>   Despite those cruel sneers.
>
> 'They buried him with his niggers!'
>   But the glorious souls set free
> Are leading the van of the army
>   That fights for liberty,
> Brothers in death, in glory
>   The same palm branches bear,
> And the crown is as bright over the sable brows
>   As over the golden hair.'"

The Union army was anxious to capture Port Hudson, that the "Mississippi might go unvexed to the sea."

Two of the colored companies or "Corps d' Afrique," which had been organized by invitation of General Butler at New Orleans, the First and Third, took part in this their first engagement. They numbered one thousand and eighty men, and were commanded respectively by Colonel C. J. Bassett, and Colonel Henry Finnegas. Though comparatively raw recruits, they appeared eager for the command to charge for the enemy's guns on the bluff. At the word they moved off in quick time, which was soon changed into double quick. The rebels in the fort reserved their fire until the charging column was within four hundred yards, then instantly evey gun discharged a fusillade of death-dealing missiles. In the midst of fearful slaughter the shattered columns wheeled to the rear in good order, reformed and again charged the enemy, but the unceasing fire of grape, canister, minie-b⋅ll and sixty-two pound shot, were to much for infantry in the open field with no chance to return the fire. Moreover, there was a deep bayou to cross and an almost perpendicular bluff to scale before the guns of the fort could be reached.

Seeing it was impossible to take the fort from these natural obstructions, Colonel Nelson dispatched an aide to General William Dwight, then in command, explaining the difficulty. To which the General sternly replied, "Tell Colonel Nelson I shall consider that he has accomplished nothing unless he takes those guns." So they were again sent into the jaws of death. Six times did these colored troops charge desperately into this veritable slaughter pen, before the inexorable General saw it was a useless waste of the lives of his brave men, so ordered them back.

One of the most gallant men killed that day was Captain André Cailloux of Company E, First Regiment Native Guards. Though phenomenally black, he was a gentleman of broad culture, commanding presence, considerable wealth, and a born leader of men. While urging his soldiers on, first in English, then in French, his left arm was mangled, but he faltered not. Leading his company to the edge of that fatal bayou, a shell struck him, and he fell dead with his face to the enemy, like the hero that he was.

When the first regiment was ready to leave New Orleans, the colonel, who for some cause was not going, deliverd its colors with these words: "Color guard, protect, defend, die for, but do not surrender these flags." To which Anselmas Planciancois, the color sergeant, on receiving them nobly replied, "Colonel, I will bring back these colors in honor, or report to God the reason why." Poor Anselmas was gallantly bearing his colors in front of the regiment, near the enemy's works, when a shell cut away part of the beautiful banner, together with part of the sergeant's head, and as he embraced it in death it became baptized in his blood and brains. Doubtless he reported to the Great Commander-in-chief of us all, "the reason why."

The following is an extract from a letter written by a sable warrior, to a friend in Chicago, describing the deeds of heroism performed by his company, in the tragedy of the crater at Petersburg:

"The rebels poured a deadly fire upon us, wounding Corporal Maxwell severely, and he was compelled to let the colors fall. Corporal Stevens then seized the colors and bore them up to the top of the works. He was quickly cut down. Corporal Bailey seized the flag and was killed instantly. Thomas Barrett, a colored private, seized the colors and bore them up to the top of the fort again. He quickly fell dead. Captain Brockay then seized the flag and was mortally wounded and obliged to let the colors fall. Col. John A. Bross of Chicago, attired in his full uniform, with the evident intention of inspiring his men, then seized the flag, rushed upon the top of the fort, planted it upon the parapet, drew his sword, took his hat in his hand, and cried: 'Rally, my brave boys, rally!' The boys did instantly rally up to him; but he quickly fell in death."

We will not harrow the feelings of the reader by portraying all the details of the heart-rending Fort Pillow massacre. Suffice it to say that the garrison included two hundred and ninety-five men of the 13th Tennessee Union Cavalry, commanded by Major W. F. Bradford, and two hundred and sixty-two colored troops of the 6th U. S. Heavy Artillery, making five hundred and fifty-seven all under the command of Major L. F. Booth, of the artillery. On April twelfth, 1864, a strong rebel force, under the command of Major-General N. B. Forest and General Chalmers, appeared before the fort and demanded its surrender, which being refused, they uttered the rebel yell of "No quarter!" and charged on the fort. After a desperate resistance in which Major Booth, the commanding officer, was killed, the weak garrison overpowered and the fort taken by assault; then began an indiscriminate massacre of men, women and children, white and black, which has no equal in civilized warfare. As fast as the Negroes surrendered they were shot down. The wounded were dragged into houses, and after the doors had been barricaded the torch was applied* and the houses and contents burned; others were nailed to the doors of burning houses, while a number were burned alive. At least three fourths of the entire force were annihilated, most of them after the fort was taken. But never was a braver defense made. What Thermopylæ was to the Greco-Persian war; what the Alamo was to the Mexican war, that Fort Pillow was to the Rebellion. Right nobly did the black troops avenge this massacre of their comrades, on many hard-fought battle fields after this, when the cruel rebel yell of "No quarter!" was answered by their battle cry, "Remember Fort Pillow!"

Volumes would be required to chronicle the daring deeds of valor and patriotism performed by these black heroes in the *four hundred and forty-nine* battles in which they participated. We can only sketch a few more instances of their bravery. At Bermunda Hundred, they captured seven pieces of artillery and six redoubts with their connecting rifle pits. At Ship Island, they successfully repulsed rebel veterans twice their number. At Millikin's Bend, the rebels came on like madmen, shouting, "No quarter!" only to be soundly whipped and driven back by the Negro troops, many of whom were raw recruits in their first action. The rebels were glad to get for themselves what they denied the Negro.

At Fort Powhatan, the ex-slaves repulsed the very flower of Virginia chivalry, led on by the valorous Fitz Hugh Lee. The fight lasted five hours, during which the Virginia masters made three desperate charges, only to be mowed down like grass by the enemy from behind their fortifications. Chivalry at last retired disgusted, his ranks fearfully depleted, and the chattel having gained the day.

Fort Harrison, five miles from Richmond, was the key to the rebel position on the north of the James. General Butler sent his Negro troops under the invincible Birney to take this fort at point of bayonet. The Confederate garrison cried out tauntingly, "Come on, darkies, we want your muskets " The darkies did come on in the face of a galling fire, shouting, "Remember Fort Pillow!" The cavaliers did not get the guns, but received their contents, which checked the flight of many, but the others ran for four miles, and the fort was taken by the Negroes.

Of this exploit General Butler said on the floor of Congress: "It became my painful duty, sir, to follow in the track charging column, and there, in a space not wider than the clerk's desk, and three hundred yards long, lay the dead bodies of five hundred and fifty-three of my colored comrades, slain in the defense of their country, who laid down their lives to uphold its flag and its honor as a willing sacrifice; and as I rode along among them, guiding my horse this way and that way, lest he should profane with his hoofs what seemed t › me the sacred dead, and as I looked on their bronzed faces upturned in the shining sun as if in mute appeal against the wrongs of the country for which they had given their lives, and whose flag had only been to them a flag of stripes on which no star of glory had ever shone for them— feeling I had wronged them in the past, and believing what was the future of my country to them—among my dead comrades there I swore to myself a solemn oath: 'May my right hand forget its cunning, and my tongue cleave to the roof of my mouth if I ever fail to defend the rights of those men who have given their blood for me and my country this day, and for their race forever;' and God helping me, I will keep that oath."

A Negro soldier having been clad in rags all his life, the very Federal garb he wore tended to inspire him with self-respect and patriotism. He was on picket duty in a Virginia town, when a Southern sympathizer came along and shoved him off the sidewalk. At this the soldier cried out, "White man, halt," but no attention was paid to him. Whereupon he brought his musket to a *ready*, with an ominous click of the trigger, and loudly shouted: "White man, halt!" Hearing *shoot* in his tone, the man stopped, and turning around found himself looking down a gun barrel. His next order was, "White man, come here;" this was obeyed, when the soldier remarked, "Dis nigger is of no particular account, but you must 'spect dis uniform; white man go on."

They fully comprehended the issues, as when

a former slave, standing guard and seeing his late master brought in as a prisoner, thus greeted him: "Ah, master, bottom rail on the top this time."

There were 178,975 colored volunteers, of whom 141,252 were from the slave states and 37,723 from the free states. Of this large number 36,847 were killed, wounded or missing. As we have stated, they participated in 449 battles, and filled with distinction almost every military department of the Federal army. This was the largest army of civilized Negroes of any war in the world's history, ancient or modern, Christian or pagan.

Massachusetts was the first state to commission Negro officers; she had ten; Kansas three; and the two regiments of Corps d' Afrique from New Orleans had black officers.

It is believed there were at least seventy-five colored men who bore commissions for a short time in the Department of the Gulf. There were also quite a number of colored surgeons and chaplains who were given commissions.

The Negro historian, Williams, in his "Honor Roll," gives a list of ten colored regiments which were commanded by General Butler, and presented with banners inscribed with the names of the places where they won their laurels. He also has on his "Roll" the names of sixty-seven heroes. Of this number ten were publicly commended by the General, twenty-four received medals for gallantry, thirty were promoted for their deeds of valor, while three others were doubly honored with medals and promotion.

Secretary of War Stanton says of colored

troops at Petersburg: "The hardest fighting was done by the black troops. The forts they stormed were the worst of all.   General Smith said they cannot be excelled as soldiers."

Adjutant-General Lorenzo Thomas wrote Senator Henry Wilson concerning Negro troops, "Experience proves that they manage heavy guns very well.   Their fighting qualities have been fully tested a number of times, and I am yet to hear of the first case where they did not fully stand up to their work. At Millikin's Bend, where I had three incomplete regiments, one without arms until the day previous to the attack, greatly superior numbers of the rebels charged furiously up to the very breastworks.   The Negroes met the enemy on the ramparts, where both sides freely used the bayonet, and the rebels were defeated with heavy loss."

General Thomas Morgan, speaking of the courage of the Negro troops in the battle of Nashville, said: "Those who fell nearest the enemy's works were colored."   Gen. James Blount says of the First Colored Regiment at Henry Springs, Arkansas: "The Negroes were too much for the enemy, and let me here say that I never saw such fighting as was done by that Negro regiment.   Too much praise cannot be awarded them for their gallantry. The question that the Negroes will fight is settled; besides, they make better soldiers in every respect than any troops I have ever had under my command."

General Butler, in an address to the army of the James before Richmond, October, 1864, made the following statement concerning the campaign just ended: "In the charge of the enemy's works by the colored division of the Eighteenth Corps at Spring Hill New Market, *better men were never better led, better officers never led better men.* This war is ended when a musket is in the hands of every able-bodied Negro who wishes to use one."

Thus it is not an exaggeration to say that colored troops turned the tide of war against slavery and the Rebellion, in favor of freedom and the Union.

In proportion to numbers, they were equally gallant and useful on the high seas, and in the navy. During the month of June, 1861, the schooner "S. J. Waring," bound from New York to South America, was captured by the privateer "Jeff Davis." A prize crew consisting of a captain, mate and four seamen were put on board and the vessel headed for Charleston. Three of the original crew were retained on board; a Yankee, who was put in chains, a German as steersman and a black man named Wm. Tillman, the steward and cook of the schooner, who was put to work at his business, and informed that he now belonged to the Confederacy and would be sold on arriving at Charleston. But the Negro was as brave as a lion, and resolved that the ship should never reach Charleston. With him to resolve was to act. After putting the captain out of the way, he was master of the cabin. Ascending the deck, he made way with the mate. Seizing the mate's revolver, he drove the crew below deck, and proclaimed himself master of the ship. He then ordered the release of the Yankee, whom he armed, and put the enemy in irons.

With the stars and stripes flying, they turned "The Waring" towards New York. A storm arose, more men were needed to work the ship. Tillman ordered the rebels to be released and brought on deck. They were put to work, but informed that the least disobedience meant death. Five days after this "The Waring" arrived in the port of New York under the command of William Tillman, the Negro patriot.

The New York "Tribune" said of this event:— "To this colored man was the nation indebted for the first vindication of its honor on the sea."

The Federal government awarded Tillman six thousand dollars prize money for the capture of the brig.

On the morning of May 13, 1862, the rebel gunboat "Planter" was captured by her colored crew, while lying in the port of Charleston, and delivered to the Federal squadron then blockading that port. Following is the dispatch from Commodore Dupont to the Secretary of War, announcing the fact:

"U. S. Steamship, Augusta, off Charleston, May 13, 1862.

"Sir:—I have the honor to inform you that the rebel armed gunboat 'Planter' was brought out to us this morning from Charleston by eight 'contrabands,' and delivered up to the squadron. Five colored women and three children are also on board. She was the armed dispatch and transportation steamer attached to the engineer department at Charleston, under General Ripley. At four in the morning, in the absence of the captain, who was on shore, she left her wharf close to the government office and headquarters, with the

Palmetto and Confederate flags flying, and passed the successive forts, saluting as usual, by blowing the steam whistle. After getting beyond the range of the last gun, they hauled down the rebel flags and hoisted a white one. 'The Onward,' the inside ship of the blockading squadron, was about to fire, when her commander discovered the white flag. The armament of the steamer is a thirty-two pounder on a pivot, and a fine twenty-four pound howitzer. She has, besides, on her deck, four other guns, one a seven inch rifle, which were to be taken on the following morning to a new fort. One of the four guns belonged to Fort Sumter and had been struck in the rebel attack on the muzzle.

"Robert Small, the intelligent slave, and pilot of the boat, who performed this bold feat so skillfully, is a superior man to any who have come into our lines, intelligent as many of them have been. His information has been interesting, and portions of it of the utmost importance. The steamer is quite a valuable acquisition to the squadron, by her good machinery and light draught. The bringing out of this steamer would have done credit to any one. If in view of the Government, the vessel will be considered a prize, I respectfully submit to the Department the claims of the man Small, and his associates.

"Very Respectfully, S. F. Dupont, Flag Officer Commanding."

It is gratifying to be able to state that the "Planter" was received as a prize and Robert Small appointed captain. In this position he showed great courage and ability.   The "Planter" was ordered to Charleston just after that city was taken and there Captain Small received a perfect ovation.

We cannot shut our eyes to the verdict of history, nor to the glamour of romance that surrounds many of our colored brethren, and are compelled to admit that whether on land or sea, 'n army or navy, there is but one verdict, "The Colored Troops Fought Nobly "

HON. R. L. SMITH,
Member of Texas Legislature and Founder of the Farmer's
Improvement Society, an organization doing great
good among the farmers of Texas.

CHAPTER XIV.

EXODUS, AND SETTLEMENT IN THE NORTH AND WEST.

The great hegira of the blacks from the South, or "the Negro Exodus," as it was called, began about February 1st, 1879. The Negroes had all heard of Kansas, made memorable by the struggles, on their behalf, of Jim Lane and John Brown, and naturally when they decided to leave the South they turned their eyes toward that "Promised Land."

But what caused them to leave the South in such large numbers? There were two answers to this question, but both of them could not be true. Said a Southern Democrat to a correspondent of the "Atlantic Monthly" of that period: "I tell you, it's all owing to the radical politicians at the North; they've had their emissaries down here, and deluded the niggers into a very fever of emigration with the purpose of reducing our basis of representation in Congress and increasing that of the Northern states."

It has been shown repeatedly that nothing could have been more foreign to the truth than the statement just uttered; the movement had no political significance except in the fact that the Negro was denied a free ballot and fair count in the South, and sought a country where he could have both, with "none to molest or make him afraid."

Not one of the states in which they settled, through the officials, invited them; but to their credit be it said, they received them kindly when they arrived. This was especially true of the Prohibition Governor of Kansas, John P. St. John.

Not one dollar of public funds soever, national, state or municipal, was used in buying land or furnishing supplies for these poverty-stricken black imigrants, and the only known contribution from any man engaged in politics, was one hundred dollars from Vice-President Wheeler. Congress could, without the slightest qualms of conscience, vote away millions of acres of the richest lands to railroad monopolies. The government could appropriate millions of acres of land and millions of dollars in money to support the wild Indians, many of them drinking, gambling, and living a life of idleness, vagrancy, and crime. It could wring from the people millions for the benefit of railroad magnates, factory kings, the coffee and the sugar trust, when every pound of Southern sugar was made by the brawn and sweat of the poor negro, but it could not give one dollar for the benefit of the colored man, who had spent two and one-half centuries in unpaid toil to enrich the South, from which he is now forced to flee empty-handed and almost naked. Verily consistency is a jewel.

All the action taken by Congress was the adoption of a resolution offered by U. S. Senator D. W. Voorhees of Indiana, providing for an investigation of the causes of the migration of the colored people from the Southern to the Northern states. Thus, with its usual recklessness, congress appropriated thousands of dollars to find out what was already known to every intelligent person, and almost every schoolboy in the country, that the Negroes were leaving the South because of systematic robbery, and political cruelties. Thousands of dollars to ascertain the cause of the poor Negroes' distress, but not one cent to relieve it.

An intelligent Negro told the same correspondent for the "Atlantic Monthly," who interviewed the Bourbon democrat: "We've been working hard for fourteen long, dreary years, and we ain't any better off than when we commenced." The same statement was substantially made by many of the dusky emigrants. "Now, Uncle Joe, what did you come for?" "Oh law! Missus, I follers my two boys an' the ole woman, an' then 'pears like I wants a taste of votin' afore I dies, an' de ole man doan' want no swamps to wade in afore he votes, kase he must be Republican, ye see."

"Well, old Aunty, tell us what you think of leaving your old home." "I doan' have no home nohow, if they shoots my ole man an' the boys an' give me no money for de washin'."

A sprightly woman of twenty-five frankly stated: "I hadn't much real trouble yet, like some of my neighbors, who lost everything. We had a lot an' a little house, an' some stock on the place. We sold all out kase we didn't dare stay when votin' time came again. Some neighbors bet-

ter off than we, had been all broken up by a
pack of 'night-riders'—all in white, who scared
everybody to death, run the men to the swamps
before elections, run the stock off, an' set fire to
their places. A poor woman might as well be killed
and done with it." Though not voters, and consequently free from personal assaults, the women
suffered as much from the general terrorism that
prevailed in certain districts, especially in Mississippi and Louisiana, as the men. "We might as
well starve or freeze to death in Kansas," they say,
"as to be shot-gunned here."

There is certainly just cause for complaint of
systematic extortion and robbery, through the in-
iquitous "Plantation Credit System." The Negroes'
necessities have developed at the cross-roads or
steam-boat landings an offensive class called merchants by courtesy, who are frequently Jews and
live by extortion. In any Northern or Western
community they would be called sharks, harpies,
or vampires, and would not be tolerated more
than one season. But many stores claiming to
do a legitimate credit business, are owned in whole
or in part by the planters, and were almost as
exorbitant. Every store-keeper has a cash and
credit price, and the latter was usually double
the former.

Besides, it is claimed on good authority, that
in Mississippi five years prior to the Exodus, not
one white man was convicted and punished for an
offense against a colored man, or made to pay a
debt due a colored man; while in Texas, Alabama and Georgia, laws were passed under which
freedmen were arrested for debts, and their labor,

(which is virtually themselves) sold at auction. The usual bid was twenty-five cents per day, with rainy days and Sundays deducted and board exacted for them. The following items were taken from a planter's contract, and store-keeper's receipted bill, brought with them to Kansas: "Rent of land for one season, five and ten dollars per acre" (more than its assessed valuation, and more than it would bring at public sale). "Hire of mule to cultivate crops, thirty dollars" (the mule was sold at the end of the season for twenty-five dollars). "Mess pork thirty-five dollars per barrel. Corn-meal, nine dollars per barrel. Bacon sides and shoulders, twenty cents per pound. Common brown sugar, twelve and one-half cents per pound. Rice, twelve and one-half cents per pound. Molasses, common black strap, one dollar and twenty-five cents per gallon. Tobacco (ordinary "dogleg"), one dollar and fifty cents per pound. Cotton drilling, forty cents per yard. Domestic prints, fifteen and sixteen cents per yard."

By a strange coincidence, the man who sold these particular goods was one of a delegation of planters who came from the South to Kansas to persuade some of the best of the Negroes to return. When confronted with this bill, he acknowledged that it was genuine, and in his own hand-writing. It is unnecessary to state that he got no Negroes to return with him.

The poor unsuspecting Negro, unable to read or calculate, and paying such prices as we have quoted, generally found himself from twenty-five to two hundred dollars in debt at the end of each year. This, of course, necessitated another engagement for the next year, in order to pay that debt, then another engagement, until the poor Negro was a veritable slave, for it was impossible to get out of debt. But political persecution was as patent a factor in causing the Exodus, as systematic robbery.

When a prominent pastor of St. Louis said a few years ago at a National Baptist Anniversary: "In the South the whites are going to rule, by fair means if they can, but they are going to rule," he expressed the sentiment of the Solid South, and they were absolutely unscrupulous in their methods, especially after they became thoroughly exasperated with the carpet-baggers, and Negro rule in the South, during the period of reconstruction.

Many of the Negroes were terrorized by "night-riders," "Kuklux," or "bull-dozers," as they were variously called, and driven to the swamps just before elections. Numbers were murdered outright, as the following letter from General. P. H. Sheridan, written from New Orleans, January 10th, 1875, shows:

"Since the year 1866, nearly thirty-five hundred persons, a great majority of which were colored men, have been killed and wounded in this state. In 1868 the official record shows that eighteen hundred and eighty-four were killed and wounded. From 1868 to the present time no official investigation had been made and the civic authorities, in all but a few cases, have been unable to arrest, convict or punish the perpetrators; consequently there are no correct records to be consulted for information. There is ample evidence, however,

to show that more than twelve hundred persons
have been killed and wounded during this time,
on account of their political sentiments.   Frightful massacres have occurred in the parishes of Bas-
sier, Caddo, Catahoula, Saint Bernard, Grant, and
Orleans.   .   .   .   Human life in this state is
held so cheaply that when men are killed on account of political opinions the murderers are
regarded rather as heroes than as criminals in the
localities where they reside."

   In the year 1867-8, a reign of terror prevailed
in Louisiana. A massacre of Negroes began in St.
Landry parish Sept. 28, 1868, lasting from three
to six days, and resulting in the killing of from
three to four hundred men.   "Thirteen captives
were taken from the jail and shot, and a pile of
twenty-five dead bodies were found burned in the
woods." As a result of this campaign, not one
Republican vote was cast in the election which
followed a few days later, though prior to this
they had a registered majority of one thousand
and seventy-one.

   A similar massacre occurred between the 20th
and 30th of Sep., 1867, lasting three or four days.
In this there were two hundred Negroes killed.
There were one thousand nine hundred and thirty-
eight Republican votes in the parish by official
registry, but at the ensuing election only one
Republican vote was cast.

   About forty Negroes were killed in Caddo parish
during the month of October, 1868. The result
of this massacre was, that General Grant only
received one vote out of a Republican registered
vote of 2,894.

It is shown from official sources that over one thousand Negroes were whipped, maimed, or murdered for political reasons in the months of Sept., Oct , and Nov., 1867, with the result that out of 47,923 registered Republican votes, only 5,360 were cast for General Grant. The same policy was pursued in the Presidential campaign of 1876 and with a like result.

When it became as much as a poor Negro's life was worth to persist in voting the Republican ticket, he did what might have been expected under the circumstances, stopped voting. Now, among business men of our Northern cities voting is considered a disagreeable duty, because it takes them away from the pursuit of wealth for a few hours. It never seems to occur to them that it would be money in their pockets, to attend the nominating conventions and ward meetings, to nominate and elect men who would be a help and honor to their country. The result is, the saloon keepers, gamblers, and hoodlums run the politics of our Northern cities. But the Negro of the South (especially Louisiana and Mississippi) regarded the ballot as forbidden fruit, and desired it with as much eagerness "as the hart panteth after the water brooks."

Governor St. John had in his office over three thousand letters on file, from the Negroes of the South, and the burden of their inquiry was: "Can we be free, can we have work, and can we have our political rights?" Surely they made a very modest request.

There were two charitable organizations designed to aid these colored emigrants until they could obtain homes or employment. The first was organized at St. Louis in 1878. This was known as "The Refugee Relief Board." Its President was the famous colored minister and friend of his race, Rev. Moses Dickson, the founder of the International Order of "Twelve Knights and Daughters of Tabor."

The Exodus proper had not commenced or was just in its infancy, but this sagacious colored leader seemed to expect his people en route for the mighty West, so made ready to receive them at St. Louis, and help them on to their destination. This society received and cared for about sixteen thousand men, women and children, fleeing from Southern oppression. It was the medium for collecting and distributing to those needy ones thousands of dollars in money; also hundreds of boxes containing clothing and provisions.

The other society was organized in May, 1879, as, "The Kansas Freedmen's Relief Association," with headquarters at Topeka. This was composed of the state officers, with a few other leading citizens, and was designed to provide for the destitute emigrants who had come among them, rather than to encourage others in coming.

Mrs. Comstock, a kind, motherly old Quaker lady, came forward and offered her services free of charge. She was then in her sixty-fourth year, having spent twenty-five years of her life in relieving suffering humanity.

John M. Brown was appointed general superintendent of the Freedmen's Relief Association; he proved to be the right man for the place, and as great a benefactor to the negro as "Old John Brown." When the facts of their destitution were known, together with its true cause, the hearts of a great people were touched. Money, food and clothing poured into the Association, and during the year about forty thousand dollars in money and five hundred thousand pounds of clothing and bedding were distributed.

Mrs. Comstcok was well known, even in England, for her noble deeds of philanthropy; her friends there sent her eight thousand dollars in money, and fifty thousand pounds of goods. One third of the remainder was furnished by the society of Friends, and the Christian women of America contributed a large amount in small sums, through their mite societies and sewing-circles. Ohio led the states in the amount of their contribution; followed by New York, Pennsylvania, Massachusetts, Michigan, Illinois and Iowa in the order named; but nearly every state sent something. The largest individual gift was one thousand dollars from John Hall, a Quaker of West Chester, Pennsylvania.

During their first year the freedmen got possession of twenty thousand acres of land, and cultivated three thousand of it. They also accumulated thirty thousand dollars, and built three hundred cabins and dug-outs. But this was not accomplished without prodigious labor, and overcoming difficulties apparently insuperable.

Henry Carter, a refugee, who in 1879 had come to Kansas from Tennessee, started on foot from Topeka to Dunlap, a distance of sixty-five miles. He was accompanied by his wife, who carried their bed-clothes, while he carried his tools. By 1880 he had forty acres of land cleared, and had made the first payment. He had built a good stone cottage, sixteen by ten feet, owned a good horse, two cows, etc., having earned his money by daily labor on sheep ranches and elsewhere in the neighborhood. In one instance a black man in Graham County "broke" five acres of raw prairie with a common spade.

According to the report of John M. Brown, Superintendent of the Relief Association, about sixty thousand refugees had come to the state of Kansas to live, up to February of 1880. Nearly forty thousand of them were in a destitute condition when they arrived, and had been helped by the Association. They had received sixty-eight thousand dollars, which had been used to the best advantage possible under all circumstances. Of the number reported, five thousand had gone to other states, thirty thousand had settled in the country on their own or rented lands, or hired out to the farmers, leaving about twenty-five thousand in or around the different towns or cities of Kansas.

Referring to the fact that the refugees managed, by the help of this Association, to get through the winter in tolerable comfort, a correspondent for Scribner's Monthly of that period remarks: "Fortunately, they long ago learned to be content with a very meager diet, and seem able to make a feast on what would haunt white persons with visions of starvation. 'Gimme a sack o' meal an' a side o' meat,' said one of them, 'an' my folks kin git along han'som', and many of them did get along throughout the winter with little more than corn-bread and bacon—and there were chickens roosting in the neighborhood too. All things considered, they

have given convincing evidence of their disposition
to work, and to be honest, and sober, and frugal. . .
Such as got work at any price, did not ask assistance; those who were compelled to apply for aid
did it slowly, as a rule, and rarely came a second
time.   Not a single colored tramp was in Kansas
all winter; and only one colored person was convicted of any crime."

Stearns has beautifully said, "God tempers the
wind to the shorn lamb." This certainly was true
in the case of these poor, half-clad colored refugees from man's oppressions, who blindly yet
beautifully trusted "de good Lord," with a faith
that was seldom equaled, for the first winter of
their stay in Kansas was the mildest in the history
of that state. As one of their preachers expressed
it, "God seed dat de darkies had thin clo's, an'
he done kep' de cole off."

The state officers in time withdrew from the
Relief Association, and left its work in the hands
of representatives of the different denominations,
with immediate executive control vested in the
Society of Friends.   The Negro found, as in the
anti-slavery struggle, that a Friend in need was a
Friend indeed.   Too much praise cannot be given
to this band of philanthropists, whose hearts were
ever touched by the cry of distress. But the effort
of the Friends was promptly and ably seconded by
the other denominations, and right nobly was the
arduous task performed.

The Southern people were greatly agitated over
this wholesale emigration of their laboring class.
For in their moments of calm reflection they
knew full well that three things were indispensable

to the South, the Negro, the mule, and cotton;
and as their white men would not work, the Negro
and mule were necessary adjuncts to a cotton crop.
The exodus wrung from a number of independent
Southern Journals a confession of the fiendish
practice of bulldozing and kukluxing, by their demands that such practice should be abandoned before it drove all the better class of Negroes from the
South. In short, the Southern leaders began to
realize that they must treat the Negro justly, and
give him his political rights, or lose his labor; and
the only way to stop the exodus was fair treatment
to those who remained The subject was also discussed from the pulpit and rostrum of the South.

C K Marshall, D.D.,of Vicksburg, Mississippi,
in an address on the exodus delivered January 21,
1880, seems to favor the idea, but urges the Negroes to go to Africa, "the land of their fathers,"
instead of remaining in this country. If the gentleman had noticed the large number of mulattoes all
over the South, and especially in Vicksburg, he
would have decided with us, that the negro was
already in the land of his fathers.

As might have been expected, this Southern
white man is blinded by prejudice, and cannot do
the Negro justice. Hear him: "Trades they cannot
learn. Ask the 'Trades Unions' of Boston, New
York, Philadelphia, or Baltimore how many Negroes belong to them? And the answer would be,
nearly none, practically none." But he does not tell
us *why* the Negro does not learn trades—Simply
because he is debarred from them, on account of
his black skin and because of his "previous condition of servitude." But if the Negroes of the

South do not learn trades (because they are not permitted), no more, as a rule, do the Southern white men, with nothing on earth to prevent them but their own indolence and foolish pride, a legacy of their "peculiar institution." Our best mechanics are still the Yankee and the foreigner.

Nevertheless the good Doctor continues, unmindful of the fact that his whole argument is a straddle, and series of contradictions. The parentheses, of course, are ours: "Briefly view the situation from what point of the political, social, and industrial compass you may, the Negro must forever remain a dwarf on American soil." Near the close of his address he says, "They will return (to Africa) with stalwart physical, manly vigor," (he has just said 'he must forever remain a dwarf') womanly culture, refinement, and piety. They will carry a higher type of intelligence, and a wider range of powers than was dreamed of by their most enlightened ancestral seers; a knowledge of science, agriculture, mechanism, law, medicine, and divinity." (How can they learn all this except among other people?) "They will go back with the Bible, the hymn-book, and the knowledge of the one true God, and Jesus Christ the adorable Savior. They will build the school-house, the college, the university," (if in Africa, why not here?) "they will issue periodicals from their own presses, cloth from their own looms, shoes from their own shops, coin from their own mints, cargoes of merchandise from their own wharves, justice from their own courts, and laws from their own congress." If the Negro must "forever remain a dwarf," and "trades they cannot learn,"as Mr. Marshall has informed us, how

can the colored man accomplish all these mighty
deeds he predicts, in Africa? And if he can do
all this in Africa, and we do not question it, why
can he not do it, and more, in happy, free America, 'the land of his fathers?' We believe he can
and will. The Negro certainly has greater facul-
ties for acquiring knowledge, and picking up trades,
in spite of the Trades Union, in this great free
country, than he could hope to enjoy among the
uncivilized Negroes of the Guinea Coast.

Here is the black man's home and here he will
remain. He is over nine millions strong, and a
peace-loving, native-born American citizen. And
if the Trades Union continue to debar him, he will
simply have a Trades Union of his own, where the
young colored men can learn trades.

The worthy Doctor's statements are not only
contradictory, but he is plainly trying to resurrect
that old dead and buried African Colonization Society, which Wm. Lloyd Garrison rendered an
object of ridicule, by showing that in the zenith
of its glory, a great many more slaves were brought
from Africa each year than the Society had ever
sent there during all the years of its existence.

Contrast, if you please, this strange address,
which was clearly made for buncombe, with the
following manly and eloquent review of the exodus by a colored statesman and orator, Hon.
John M. Langston, ex-minister to Hayti. This
address was delivered by invitation, before the
Emigrant Aid Society, at Lincoln Hill, Washington,
D. C., October 7, 1879.

"Herodotus tells of a Scythian general who, returning with his army after a protracted expe-

dition, found their slaves had taken possession of their households, their wives and the management of public affairs. He counseled his comrades to throw away their weapons, their arrows and their darts, and meet their opponents without any means of defense save the whip which they used upon their horses Said he: 'Whilst they see us with arms, they think themselves our equals in birth and importance, but as soon as they shall see us with whips in our hands, they will be impressed with a sense of their servile condition and resist no longer.' The plan was adopted and proved a success. This illustrates the feeling generally entertained between the old master and his former slaves.

"How shall the American ex-slave, who has served for two hundred and forty-five years in slavery, be released from the control of a class heretofore his masters? The history of the world offers but one solution to this question, and that solution is found in his exodus. Let him go forth, where sympathy and the recognition of liberty and usual rights are accorded him; where labor is to be performed; where struggle is to be made, where the stern realities of life are to be met; there let him demonstrate his courage, his self-reliance, his manly independence. Under such new conditions, his capacities, his power, and his efforts will win the crown which befits the brow of noble manhood. . . The South has not changed a great deal for the better. Nor has the feeling of the non-slave-holding class of the South undergone any material change with respect to the freedmen. Indeed, it seems to be true that this class hates the colored man more now than when he was a slave, and stands ready at the command of the aristocratic class to do its bidding even to the shedding of his blood. As showing that this condition of affairs is true, and that little advancement has been made, one has only to pronounce in your hearing certain terrible words coined in connection with the barbarous, cruel treatment that has been meted out to the emancipated class of Mississippi, Louisiana, and other states formerly slave-holding. What is the meaning of the frightful words 'Kuklux,' 'Bulldozers,' and the terrible expressions, 'the shot-gun or Mississippi policy?' The meaning is clear. It is that neither the old slave-holding spirit, or the old slave-holding purpose or control is dead in the South; that plantocracy, with its fearful power and influence, has not passed away; that the colored American under it, is in a condition of practical enslavement, trodden down and outraged by those who exercise control over him. Such things will continue so long as the spirit of slavery exists in the South; so long as the freedman consents to remain in a condition more terrible than any serfage of which history gives account. How can this condition of things be broken up? How can the master class be made to realize that it is no longer slave-holding, and the slave has been set free? And how can the freedman be made to feel and realize that having been emancipated, practical liberty is within his reach, and that it is his duty to accept and enjoy it, with its richest fruits?

"To the intelligent and sagacious inquirer, there can be, as it seems to me, but a single answer. It is this. Let the freedman of the South, as far as practicable, take from the old plantocracy, by his exodus, the strong arms, broad shoulders, stalwart bodies, which, by compulsion, have been made to prop and sustain such system too long already in this day of freedom. Let him stand from beneath, and the fabric will fall, and a new and necessary reconstruction will follow.

"But is it possible to transfer all the freedmen from the Southern part of the country? Perhaps not. It is, however, possible and practicable to so reduce the colored laborers of the South by emigration to the various states of the North and West, as to compel the land-holders—the planters—to make and to observe reasonable contracts with those who remain, to compel all white classes there to act in good faith, and address themselves to necessary labor upon the plantation, as well as elsewhere obeying the law and respecting the rights of their neighbors.

"Even the exodus movement just commenced, small as it is, insignificant as it appears to be, has produced in this regard a state of feeling in the South which justifies entirely the opinion here expressed. Where shall he go? It has already been indicated that the North and West furnish the localities open to the freedman and to which he should go. It certainly would not be wise for him in large numbers to settle in any one state of the union; but even in thousands, he would be received, welcomed to kind, hospitable homes in the various states of the sections named, where labor, educational advantages, and the opportunity to rise as a man, a citizen and a voter would be furnished him.

Objections—" But it is claimed that the Negro should remain in the South and demand of the Government protection from the wrongs which are perpetrated against him. Here it must be remembered that in emigrating from the South to the North or West, the freedman is simply moving from one section of our common country to another, simply exercising his individual right to go, when and where it suits his convenience and advantage. In the next place, it is in exercising such constitutional rights that he leaves a section of the country where slavery has created a barbarous and oppressive public sentiment, the source of all the abuses which he suffers.

"But it is claimed that the freedman cannot endure a Northern and Western climate, that the winters are too severe for him.

"Never was a greater mistake. While it is true the colored man, as he goes North into colder regions, adapts himself with ease to the climate. In no part of our country does he show more robust health, finer physical development and endurance, and consequent longevity, than in the Western and Northern portion of our country. It is where the zymotic and malarial disorders prevail, that the Negro sickens and dies, and this is abundantly shown in the fearful death rate that is given by sanitarians, as connected with the warm and tropical regions of our own and other countries.

"Again it is urged that the freedman is too poor to emigrate. Those who urge this objection ought to remember, that it is the poor and oppressed in all ages and in all countries who have emigrated. One never emigrates only as he seeks to improve his condition, to relieve himself and family of want, to escape oppression and abuse. It is wise for the poor, starving, oppressed Irishman to quit the country of his nativity to seek a new home in our goodly land, where opportunity of culture, the accumulation of wealth, advancement and success await his endeavors. Then let no man either despise or oppose the exodus of the freedman, who now, realizing his real condition, emigrates from the old plantation and Negro quarter, from the scene of his former enslavement, from the hateful and oppressive control of a stupid and tyrannical landed aristocracy, from poverty, from ignorance, from degradation, to a home among those who value freedom, free institutions, educational and material, moral and Christian worth, individual efforts and achievement—to a home among those who, loyal to God and man, never fail to give sympathy, success and hospitable welcome to the needy son of Ireland, or the yet more needy son of Mississippi, who comes seeking, not only liberty, but the opportunity to labor, to live and achieve in their midst. I do most reverently and heartily accept the lesson contained in the words: 'I have surely seen the affliction of my people which are in Egypt, and have heard their cry by reason of their taskmasters, for I know their sorrows and I am come down to deliver them out of the hand of the Egyptians, and to bring them up out of that land unto a good land, and large, unto a land flowing with milk and honey.'"

One of the best plantation songs we have heard, was written by Thomas P. Westendorf, commemorative of this event, entitled:

GOING FROM DE COTTON FIELDS.

"I's going from de cotton fields, I's going from de cane,
I's going from de ole log hut dat stands down in de lane;
De boat am in de ribber dat hab come to take me off,
's gone and jined de 'Exodus' dat's making for de Norf.
Dey tell me out in Kansas, dat's so many miles away,
De colored folks am flocking, 'cause dey're getting better pay;
I don't know how I'll find it dar, but I is bound to try,
So when de sun goes down to-night I's going to say good-bye.

> CHORUS.—I's going from de cotton fields,
> And ah! it makes me sigh;
> For when de sun goes down to-night,
> I's going to say good-bye

"But Dinah she don't want to go, she says we're getting old,
She's 'fraid dat she will freeze to death, the country am so cold;
De story 'bout de work and pay she don't believe am true,
She's begged me not to do the thing dat I am bound to do.
And so I's sold de cabin and de little patch of groun',
Dat good ole master gave us, when de Yankee troops came down;
My heart am awful heavy, and de tears am in my eye,
For when de sun goes down to-night I's going to say good-bye.

> CHORUS.—

"It grieves me now to leave the place where I was born and bred,
To leave de friends dat's living, and de graves of dem dat's dead;
De flow'rs dat grow where master sleeps will miss my tender care,
No hand like mine will ever go to keep dem blooming there.
But den de times hab got so hard, and I is ole and poor,
De hungry wolf am looking in and snarling at my door;
I's got to help de chil'ren some before I comes to die,
So when de sun goes down to-night I's going to say good-bye."

> CHORUS.—

CHAPTER XV.

KENTUCKY'S HOSPITALITY.

Some of the pioneer settlers of Kentucky, contemporary with Boone and Kenton, brought their negro servants with them. Naturally these shared with their masters the hair-breadth escapes and perilous adventures of that period, and often displayed bravery unsurpassed.

In Collin's history of Kentucky, the following incident is recorded: "In the year 1781 or 2, near Crab Orchard, in Lincoln County, a very singular adventure occurred at the house of a Mr. Woods. One morning he left his family, consisting of a wife, and daughter not yet grown, and a lame Negro man, and rode off to the station near by, not expecting to return until night. Mrs. Woods, being a short distance from her cabin, was alarmed by discovering several Indians advancing towards it. She instantly screamed loudly in order to give the alarm, and ran with her utmost speed, in the hope of reaching the house before them. In this she succeeded, but before she could close the door the foremost Indian had forced his way into the house. He was instantly seized by the lame Negro, and after a short scuffle, they both fell with violence, the Negro underneath.

"Mrs. Woods was too busily engaged in keeping the door closed against the party without to attend to the combatants, but the Negro, holding the Indian tightly in his arms, called to the young girl to take the ax from under the bed and dispatch him by a blow on the head. She immediately attempted it, but the first attempt was a failure. She repeated the blow and killed him. The other Indians were at the door endeavoring to force it open with their tomahawks. The heroic Negro now rose and proposed to Mrs. Woods to let in another, and they would soon dispose of the whole of them in the same way. The cabin was only a short distance from the station, the occupants of which, having discovered the perilous situation of the family, fired on the Indians and killed another, when the remainder made their escape."

Not even the name of this black hero is given, when he justly merited his freedom for this brave deed.

Mrs. Connelly's "Story of Kentucky" gives the following incident:

"When Kentucky was first settled, a night attack was made by a band of Indians upon the home of Edmund Cabell, during his absence in Virginia. The family were left in the care of an uncle to Mrs. Cabell, and black Sam, a brave, able-bodied slave.

"The day preceding the massacre had been very

HON. H. A. RUCKER,
Collector Internal Revenue, State of Georgia.

hot and sultry, so Sam was sleeping on a bunch of hay in the edge of the woods. About midnight he was awakened by a blaze of light at the cabin, which he now discovered to be in flames. At the same instant he saw that the house was surrounded by Indians, who now began a general massacre of the family, all of whom, with one exception, were killed by the light of their burning home. The exception was a little girl, who was carried out of the building by one of the Indians and laid down about halfway between the house and where our colored hero was crouching behind the hay. The Indians now returned to the house to get more plunder; this was Sam's opportunity; creeping cautiously through the grass and weeds at imminent danger of being seen by the light of the burning house, or attracting the attention of the Indians by any disturbance he might make among the bushes.

"Providence favored him, and he reached the child in safety, clasped her in one strong arm, and retraced his steps in the same cautious manner. He was well acquainted with the child, and managed to keep her quiet, until there was quite a distance between him and the Indians. He aimed for the nearest Fort and traveled all night. About noon next day, having lost his direction, he was weak from hunger and exhaustion. He found a spring of water, and ripe berries which kept him and the child from starving. Traveling for the most part at night, and hiding at every sound for fear of Indians, he reached the Fort with the little girl, both of them more dead than alive, for they had spent three nights and a portion of the intervening days in the woods.

"Sam now returned to his master's farm to look after whatever live stock was left. And when the master returned from Virginia and was viewing the blackened ruins of his once happy home, faithful Sam appeared before him, and kept him from utter despair, by giving him the first intelligence that little Augusta, the darling of his heart, was alive and safe at the Fort.

"Mr. Cabell now gladdened Sam's heart by telling him that he had brought his family with him from Virginia, in consideration of his faithfulness and lonely condition in the wilderness. So Sam was in some measure rewarded for his heroism and fidelity.

"Augusta Cabell became in time one of the most beautiful young ladies in Kentucky, and was very grateful to her dusky defender."

On March 22, 1794, William Bryant, of Lincoln County, advertised for his negro man, Sam, and offered ten dollars reward for securing him, so that the owner could get him again. This was the first slave advertised in Kentucky. Such advertisements became quite common, not only in this state but throughout the South, sometimes offering rewards for runaway slaves, alive or dead. There were, perhaps, fewer such advertisements in Kentucky papers than any Southern state.

The truth is, in the words of N. S. Shaler, "the Negroes of Kentucky were not generally suffering from any bonds that weighed heavily upon them. Slavery in Kentucky was of the domestic sort; that is, it was, to most of their race, not a grievous burden to bear. This is well shown by the fact that thousands of them quietly remained with their masters in the counties along the Ohio River, when in any night they might have escaped across the border.

"Still the Underground Railroad System, although it did not free many slaves in Kentucky, greatly irritated the minds of their owners, and even of the class that did not own slaves."

"Perhaps," wrote Mrs. Stowe, "the mildest form of the system of slavery is to be seen in the state of Kentucky. The general prevalence of agricultural pursuits of a quiet and gradual nature, not requiring those periodic seasons of hurry and pressure that are called for in the business of more Southern districts, makes the task of the Negro a more healthful and reasonable one, while the master, content with a more gradual style of acquisition, had not those temptations to hard-heartedness which always overcome frail human nature, when the prospect of sudden and rapid gain is weighed in the balance with no heavier counterpoise than the interests of the helpless and unprotected."

There is much truth in this statement, but it occurs to me as a Kentuckian, and the son of a slave-holder, that a number of circumstances contributed to make the lot of the Kentucky slave much easier than those in the cotton or sugar belt.

In the first place, the nature of the country is better adapted to labor, being for the most part elevated and rolling. As there are no swamps to produce chills and fever, it is a remarkably healthy country, with a delightful and invigorating climate. Then too, in the agricultural portions of the state, instead of vast plantations of thousands of acres, and a small army of slaves, driven from morning until night by a brutal overseer, or still more brutal negro driver, small farms and few slaves were the rule. As a general rule the Kentucky farmer, or one of his sons, managed the farm without the aid of a regular hired overseer, although he would often put one of the slaves in for foreman. This foreman was generally the best worker and most trustworthy hand on the farm, and was expected to lead, not drive the work.

It must not be forgotten that the Kentucky staples, such as live stock, the cereals, tobacco and hemp (she leads the world in the two last), did not yield such immense profits as to tempt the cupidity of the farmers, or require such forced and exhausting labor. We are also inclined to the opinion that this mild form of servitude was largely due to the fact that the average Kentucky farmer was and is a whole-souled, big hearted man. Happy, prosperous, and well-fed himself, he liked to have even his slaves share in his good cheer.

Patty B. Semple, a correspondent for the Atlantic Monthly, writing of an old Kenutcky home in the ante-bellum days, says: "After breakfast, there was always a group of Negroes about the porch, each one armed with a tin cup or plate, and waiting for the daily allowance of molasses, sugar, and coffee to be given out from the store-room, hoping also for some special tidbit from the family table." We do not recall having read any account like that about any other state.

In describing the Blue Grass farmer, she does it so perfectly that we know she must have been there. "He was not a hard master, although perhaps not a particularly indulgent one. A practical

farmer, he insisted that the work should be properly done, and to keep the indolent, careless Negroes
up to the mark required an immense amount of
oversight. His horse was saddled before breakfast, and he was mounted, and about the farm
early and late, knowing the old maxim that the
eye of the master will do more work than both
his hands. He went to bed early, usually rose
between three and four o'clock in the morning,
and smoked a meditation pipe on the back porch
before any one else was about, and then at 'sun-
up' his stentorian voice would be heard starting
the hands. His constant companion was a corn-
cob pipe filled with Kentucky tobacco, which was
always lighted by a live coal, and one of the most
common sounds about the place was his call to
one of the little darkies, 'Bring me a coal of fire,
Polly,' or Lizzie, or Tom, as the case might be.
The piece of glowing wood was carried in a pair
of short tongs from the kitchen fire, and as he blew
away the ashes and applied it to his pipe, he put
good-natured, teasing questions to the little Negro
who had brought it. These colloquies were the
source of infinite enjoyment to him and embarrassment to his victim, who stood uneasily on
one foot, twisting the other about and boring into
the ground with one great toe, until the tongs
were handed back with some extravagant compli-
ment, and the interview ended."

We are inclined to believe what contributed
most to alleviate the condition of the Kentucky
slave was the constant lashing of conscience. A
large number, perhaps a majority of the people
of the state did not believe slavery was right. Now,

we know this bare statement, unbacked by strong evidence, would not pass unchallenged; but the evidence, is at hand. There is abundant proof that the conscience of the great body of the people was ever sensitive concerning the right of one man to own another.

The institution was recognized at first, simply because most of the early settlers were from the slave-holding states and brought their slaves with them. From an early period they began to emancipate them, and to place statute restriction on their importation.

When the new constitution was to be adopted, thirty thousand votes, representing the wealthiest and most intelligent slave-holders, were cast in favor of an open clause, by which gradual emancipation should become a law, as soon as practical. One religious denomination after another denounced slavery as a moral evil. Additional proof that there was a growing sentiment against this institution and in favor of a gradual emancipation, is found in Dr. J. Freeman Clark's "Anti-Slavery Days." He was a citizen of Kentucky from 1833 to 1840; and states that slavery existed there in a comparatively mild form, and the sentiment of the better class of people was decidedly against it, for the reason that they considered it a wrong and an evil, that should be abolished.

A young man from Boston called upon Dr. Clark in Louisville, and was invited to take a drive with him into the country to visit some of the plantations. The Boston youth was a member of one of the very conservative New England families who opposed abolition as a fanatical movement, and thought the abolitionists endangered the safety of the union.

The first place they came to was the home of Judge Jno. J. Marshall, who belonged to one of the old families of Virginia and Kentucky, Mrs. Marshall being the sister of Jno G. Birney, afterwards a candidate for the Presidency on the Free Soil ticket.

As the Marshalls owned slaves, and there were a large number of Negro children about the yard, the young man thought it opportune to speak favorably of the institution. "Mrs. Marshall," said he, "I think our people at the North are very much mistaken in attacking slavery as they do. It seems to me there is nothing so very bad about it." Mrs. Marshall replied: "It will not do, sir, to defend slavery in this family. The Marshalls and the Birneys have always been abolitionists." Of course the young man was surprised at that statement coming from the wife of a slave-holder, but a still greater surprise awaited him at the next house at which they called, the home of Judge John Speed, who had a large plantation and about sixty slaves.

The Boston youth, thinking no doubt that Mrs. Marshall was an exceptional person, and it would be safe this time to advocate slavery, said: "Judge, I do not see but the slaves are as happy as our laboring classes at the North." "Well" answered the Judge, "I do the best I can to make my slaves comfortable; but I tell you what it is, you cannot make a slave happy, do what you will. God Almighty never meant a man to be a slave, and he cannot be happy while he is a slave." The young man continued in amazement, "But what can be done about it, sir? They are not able to take care of themselves, if they were free. How could they manage if slavery were abolished?"

"I think I could show you three men on my plantation," replied Judge Speed, "who might go to the Kentucky legislature; I am inclined to believe they would make just as good legislators as the average men that you find there now." This statement, coming from such a source, astonished the young man still more; but it was a plain statement of the exact truth.

With the Kentuckian's characteristic fondness for fair play, the question in all its bearings was freely discussed. "The Louisville Journal," then edited by Geo. D. Prentice, was ever ready to welcome and print articles showing the evils of slavery.

Dr. Clark recalls a discussion in Louisville which lasted three nights; in that time the whole question of slavery was covered; one side assuming that it was right, and a good thing, and ought to be maintained; and the other that it was an evil, morally, socially, and politically, and as such should be abolished. This was not an ordinary debate, some of the most cultured and intelligent gentlemen in the city, including Dr. Clark, participating on either side, and, strange as it may seem, a majority were on the side of those who contended that it was an evil and a wrong.

The best article on slavery in Kentucky we have seen was written by James Lane Allen. In his "Uncle Tom at Home in Kentucky," he quotes the following extract from a letter to him from Mrs. Stowe, dated Apr. 30, 1886: "In relation to your letter, I would say that I never lived in Kentucky, but spent many years in Cincinnati, which is separated from Kentucky only by the Ohio River, which, as a shrewd politician remarked, was nearly dry one half of the year and frozen the other. My father was president of Lane Theological Seminary at Walnut Hills, near Cincinnati, and with him I traveled and visited somewhat extensively in Kentucky, and there became acquainted with those excellent slave-holders delineated in Uncle Tom's Cabin. I saw many counterparts of the Shelbys— people humane, conscientious, just and generous, who regarded slavery as an evil and were anxiously considering their duties to the slave. But it was not till I had finally left the West, and my husband was settled as professor in Bowdoin College, Brunswick, Maine, that the passage of the fugitive slave law and the distress that followed it drew this from me."

Thus we find that Mrs. Stowe testifies to the fact that there was a strong undercurrent of intense opposition to slavery in Kentucky at that time, and that the slaves she saw there were well treated.

A close analysis of "Uncle Tom's Cabin" will impress one with the thought that she first introduced the reader to slavery in Kentucky, because it was of the mildest form; that she might cap the climax by an introduction to Legree's Red River cotton plantation, where it was seen in its most hideous and brutalizing aspect.

Another proof that the slaves in this state fared better than elsewhere, is seen in the code of laws framed to regulate slavery. According to this, "if slaves were inhumanly treated by their owner, or not supplied with proper food and clothing, they could be taken from them and sold to a better master."

A few cases are recorded, of slaves who had been liberated and sent to Canada, voluntarily returning into service under their former masters.

Even in Kentucky there were slave-holders, and slave holders, some good, some bad, and some very bad. Those who were kindest to their slaves were ready to put down an abolitionist, whom they regarded as interfering with their affairs, and bitterly hated.

The saddest feature of slavery in this state was the internal slave trade. That negroes were regularly raised for the Southern market cannot be denied. That in some cases brutalized white men sold their own sons and daughters, knowing them to be such, goes unchallenged; but these were the exceptions rather than the rule.

The sentiment of a majority of their people being against it, the slave trade was not as large as is generally believed. Sometimes a farmer would have among his slaves one that was unruly and even vicious; such a one was invariably sold South. But the chief reason for which slaves were sold was embarrassment by debt on the part of their master. In this case it often happened that the most valuable slaves on the farm were sold, as in the case of Uncle Tom, for the rascally slave buyers, knowing the master's condition, would have none but the best.

There is a hint of the cause of such sales, in the pathetic strain, seldom appreciated:

"By'n by *hard times* comes a-knocking at the door;
Then my Old Kentucky Home, good-night."

On one occasion, all the slaves in a tobacco field

dropped their hoes and chased a rabbit the dogs had started. A meddlesome neighbor reported the fact to their master. But he received the indignant answer from the old gentleman, "Sir, I'd have whipped the last black rascal of 'em if they hadn't run 'im!"

A sketch of slavery in Kentucky would be incomplete without some mention of Cassius Marcellus Clay, "the noblest Roman of them all;" certainly the greatest of Southern Abolitionists, and perhaps the equal of any in the nation. This remarkable man is the son of General Green Clay, and was born in Madison County, Oct. 19, 1810. After taking a course of study at Transylvania University, Lexington, the same school Jefferson Davis attended, he graduated at Yale College in 1832.

He took a great interest in politics when a young man, and represented Madison and Fayette Counties each in the Legislature, where he made a brilliant record.

He issued the first copy of the "True American," from Lexington, June 3, 1845. This paper was devoted to the overthrow of slavery in Kentucky. It required great courage in those turbulent times to edit an anti-slavery paper in the South. It seemed like bearding the lion in his den. But Cassius M. Clay was the "boldest of all the enemies of slavery." His soul was aflame with hatred and disgust for human servitude. Naturally a paper edited by such a man would be a powerful philippic hurled against the detested institution; and while it made many friends for the cause he espoused, it heated its enemies seven times more than they were wont to be heated.

Accordingly on Aug. 18, 1845, there was a great mass meeting held in Lexington, of citizens from all over central Kentucky, irrespective of party. At this meeting it was resolved that the press and materials of the "True American" should be sent beyond the confines of the state. A committee carefully boxed up all his outfit and shipped it, expenses prepaid, to Cincinnati; after which they sent Mr. Clay the address of the house to which they consigned it, subject to his order.

The Kentuckian's love of fair play is again reflected in this incident, when it is remembered that in the case of Lovejoy the pro-slavery ruffians from Missouri and Illinois murdered him outright, after destroying four presses.

Mr. Clay afterwards obtained judgment against two of the committee for twenty-five hundred dollars, which was paid by citizens of Fayette and adjcining counties.

Mr. Clay commanded the Old Infantry in the Mexican War. Returning home, he was presented with a sword for gallant conduct. He was also minister to Russia in 1861, Major General of Volunteers in 1862, and again minister to Russia from 1863 to '69.

He was once nominated for governor of Kentucky, with George P. Blakey of Logan County on the ticket for lieutenant-governor.

He now resides at his beautiful home, White Hall, Kentucky. The sunset of his long life is as peaceful and quiet as his earlier years were turbulent.

His nephew and namesake, Cassius M. Clay, Jr., of Bourbon County, is now a strong candidate for governor. This Mr. Clay has been a member of the Kentucky Legislature, and was President of the late constitutional convention of that state. As he is from the county where the author spent his "boyhood's happy hours," and where his people still live, most of whom are Clay men, and as he is thoroughly competent to fill the high place to which he aspires, it is to be hoped he will be elected.

The two greatest sons of Kentucky were Henry Clay and Abraham Lincoln, for she claims them both, the one by adoption, the other by birth. Each was strangely identified with the question of slavery; each was a pure patriot who loved his country; each was strictly conscientious in the belief that his own view was the true solution to the vexatious problem, and for the best interests of the nation. Kentuckians always believed in Henry Clay; her cardinal points of political faith might be summed up in the dictum, "There is a just God who presides over the destiny of nations, and Henry Clay is his prophet." But this hero-worship was not confined to Kentucky. I remember when a boy hearing Theodore Tilton deliver a lecture at Paris. In speaking of his visit to Henry Clay's grave and monument, while at Lexington the day before, he said: "As I neared that sacred spot I imagined I heard a voice saying unto me, 'Put off thy shoes from off thy feet, for the place whereon thou standest is holy ground.'" It is an imposing, awe-inspiring monument Kentucky has erected over his remains, and can be seen several miles from Lexington, in almost any direction.

Illinois has built a still more imposing monument in honor of her greatest adopted son, at Springfield. The author stood once and viewed first the monument, and then a group of dusky freedmen, as, with heads reverently uncovered and tears in their eyes, they were gazing at Lincoln's statue, that the image might be photographed on their minds and hearts.

It would not have taken them long to decide that Lincoln was not only a greater man than Clay, but in some respects the greatest man America ever produced.

The contrast between the great compromiser and the great emancipator might be stated in this way.

Henry Clay said, "I would rather be right than to be President," but he was neither right nor President. Lincoln made no such boast, but he was *both right* and *President.* Clay no doubt did the best he could for his day and generation, under all circumstances. He was frequently misunderstood and misquoted, because his enemies would persistently put the words of Cassius M. Clay, the abolitionist, into the mouth of Henry Clay, the compromiser; the opposite party could not, or would not, understand that there were two Clays from Lexington, Kentucky, each of whom was a prominent politician and statesman, and the leader of his party in that state, but their views on the slavery question were as wide apart as the two poles.

An amusing incident is told by Mrs. Pickard. It seems that Mr. Clay had a favorite servant named Aaron, who was his carriage driver. He was very competent, but would take a drink of whisky every opportunity, and sometimes become intoxicated. "On one occasion he drove Mrs. Clay into Lexington, and while she was shopping, he was drinking. By the time she was ready to go home Aaron was incapable of driving.

"Much to her mortification, she was compelled to hire a driver in order to get home. Justly indignant, she resolved that Aaron should be punished; so she told her husband all about it. Calling the overseer to the house the next morning, Mr. Clay repeated the circumstance and instructed him to take the offender to the carriage house and give him a light whipping. "Now, do it quietly, said he, and be sure not to cut his skin. I don't want to hear any disturbance. Do it as gently as possible."

The overseer assented and went out. One of the maids happened to overhear the conversation, and slipping out of the house, she told Aaron all about it.

"Forewarned is forearmed, and fortifying himself with a drink of whisky, he meekly responded to the overseer's call and went with him into the carriage house, and the door was fastened on the inside. 'I am sorry to have to whip you,' said the overseer, 'but it is Mr. Clay's orders; he said your drinking habits had annoyed your mistress and you must be punished.' 'Well, if Massa say so, then it must be so, but you needn't tie me—I won't be tied!' 'Very well,' replied the overseer, throwing down the rope, 'you need not be tied if you will stand still; but you must take off your coat.' 'Yes, sir, but if I takes off my coat to be whipped, you ought to take yourn off first, to whip me!'

"The overseer saw that he had been drinking and knew he must indulge his whims if he would obey Mr. Clay's orders and keep quiet; so he pulled off his coat, and the slave laid his beside it. Next followed the two vests. 'Now your shirt, Aaron,' said he. 'Yes, sir, but you must take off yourn first.' This was going farther for quiet's sake than the overseer had intended, but he thought it would be best to humor him. He had long wished for a chance to humble Aaron, and the time had come. But behold! no sooner had he lifted his arms to pull his shirt over his head, than Aaron seized the garment, a strong new one, and twisting it around his neck, held him fast. Then catching the whip, he applied it vigorously to the overseer's naked back, raising the skin at every stroke. His victim screamed and threatened him with vengeance, but all in vain; the blows fell hard and fast.

"Mr. Clay heard the outcry and grew angry. 'I told him,' said he, 'to make no noise, and to be sure not to whip the poor fellow severely. He must be cutting him to pieces.'

"He hastened to the carriage house and heard the whizzing of the whip as it descended on the sufferer's back. 'Open the door,' he cried! 'Didn't I tell you not to whip him hard? Open the door, I say.'

"'O, Mr. Clay! it's Aaron whipping me! I haven't given him a blow.'

"'Aaron,' cried the master, 'open the door!' Instantly the slave obeyed. With his right hand, in which he still held the whip that he had used to such good purpose, he opened the door, while with his left he retained his vice-like grasp of the twisted shirt. His face was all complacency, yet his eyes twinkled with mirth, and a roguish smile lurked at the corner of his mouth.

"Mr. Clay stood for a moment mute with astonishment. But when he fully comprehended the strange scene, he burst into a hearty laugh, and although the overseer, as soon as he was released, proceeded to explain to him the manner in which he had been caught, and insisted that he should now be allowed to whip Aaron, his arguments were lost. The master quietly expressed his opinion that there had been whipping enough—it was not necessary to go any farther."

Almost my earliest recollection was the sale which followed my father's death, at the old homestead in Fayette County. I remember after the miscellaneous assortment of farming implements, stock, grain, etc., was disposed of, the negroes were put up on the block and knocked off to the highest bidder. And when Uncle Lewis, the foreman, who had made me whistles and toys, and let me ride with him to the field and back, was put up, and his age was inquired, and his teeth and muscles examined much as they did the horses at the barn, it cut me to the heart. But when I afterwards saw Aunt Ann, my black "mammy," who had carried me in her arms and nursed me on her bosom, and my little black playmates, who were as dear to me as any I ever had, put up and disposed of, the iron entered my soul. Child as I was, I knew that what I that day witnessed was wrong; and as first impressions are the most lasting, I have never for a moment thought differently. My opposition to slavery, thus aroused, has grown with my growth and strengthened with my strength, until now "I loathe, abhor, my very soul with strong disgust is stirred, whenever I hear or write or tell of this dark institution of hell."

My oldest sister married a well-to-do farmer, stock-dealer, and slave-holder in southern Kentucky. After my mother's family moved to Paris, this sister, with her husband, baby girl and nurse, came on a few weeks' visit. My mother's cook, Aunt Dinah, was very industrious, but a genuine Guinea negro and a veritable virago. She ruled over the nurse and house girl with a rod of iron, for she frequently brandished the poker, as she scolded and berated them for some misdemeanor. Every one on the place except the mistress, stood in awe of her.

Now, my little niece was devoted to her nurse Ellen; and though little more than a baby, was a precocious child; she seldom spoke, but when she did it was plain and pointed.

Of course this little tot stood in awe of Aunt Dinah and seldom played around the kitchen. But one day when the cook was administering her usual tongue lashing to the nurse, the baby girl plucked her apron to attract attention, and said, her eyes flashing, "I thinks you treats my Ellen mighty mean!" At this the cook jumped back and threw up both hands in amazement, and said, "Fo de Lord, whar dat chile come from? never know'd she could talk!" She never abused Ellen after this.

On one occasion while visiting relatives in the country I went fishing in company with my cousin, a boy older and larger than myself. We had good luck and caught a nice string of small fish.

Late in the afternoon, a black girl, nearly grown, named Seeley, rode out into the pasture on horseback where we were, to drive up the cows. Like every other town boy, I was eager for a ride, and as my cousin was willing to carry the poles and fish, I was soon on the horse behind the girl, and we were galloping to the back part of the pasture.

Just as she was whipping the horse into still greater speed, the girth broke, and the saddle turning, threw us both to the ground with violence. She landed on her feet and was not hurt, but I broke a leg by the fall. My cousin, who saw the accident, turned back; between them they caught the horse, and having re-saddled it, put me on its back, and while one of them led the horse, the other walked by my side and supported the broken leg.

The girl was in great distress, and said "she knew the white folks would kill her for that." My cousin thought so too, and to prevent her being severely punished, who was not in any way to blame, except that she rode too fast thinking to please me, we contrived a very plausible explanation of the accident. "Let us tell them," said the girl, "that you raised up a rock to get a fishing worm, and accidentally let it fall back against your leg and broke it." This we agreed to do, and even decided which rock it was, namely, the one nearest the stump at the end of the dam. Well, it was a deliberate falsehood, but I believe the recording angel blotted it out under the circumstances. For years afterwards the identical rock that fell against the boy's leg and broke it, was pointed out to passers-by.

Every one has read of "Jimmie Butler and the owl," but I propose to tell you about Tom Butler and the mule. The circumstance happened on my Uncle's farm, about seven miles from Paris, where I spent several vacations when a boy. There were seven hundred acres in the farm, and of course he employed a good many hands, mostly Negroes. Among them was this Tom Butler, a young man about twenty years of age; and with the work stock, was a big one-eyed sorrel mule named Jack, who could jump a fence even if it was mule high, and throw his rider without any apparent effort. One day I was riding him out to work, when Tom Butler rattled his shoes, while sitting on the fence on the blind side of the mule; immediately he arched his back and shot skyward; I found myself on the ground, but not hurt. My cousin, who was manager, happened to see it, and made the Negro get on the mule, and took me up behind him on his horse. We rode on ahead and left the other hands to follow. Now we had occasion to go up on one side of a "branch" through the corn-field to get to our work. Here there were some tall horse weeds beside the path. At the suggestion of my cousin, I concealed myself in those weeds, armed with a long, sharp stick. When the mule and his rider came along I punched him in the ribs on the blind side with my stick; you can readily imagine what happened. My cousin was looking backward at the time, and he declared that the mule's feet actually got up higher than the corn tassels. The first jump was not sufficient to throw him, for though the Negro was elevated some distance in the air, he fell back straddle of the mule.

Jack now saw that he had more than an ordinary rider, and as he had never failed before, and had his reputation at stake, he arched his back and shot up

ward like a rocket; and the Negro, well, he fell flat
on his back in the mud and water of this little creek.
I fully expected a fight or a foot race, but no, the
good-natured fellow was not hurt; he arose, pulled
himself out of the mire, and with a grin on his face
said, "We is eben now; less quit."

After my sister was left a widow, I made my home
with her for five years, and managed her farm and
other business. Tobacco was the great staple, and
in its culture we sometimes had poor whites from
Tennessee, and colored people, as tenants or hired
hands. But the blacks were infinitely more satisfactory. They had been taught to work in a cruel and
exacting school, and the lesson was well learned.

Among the black people on the place was an intelligent mulatto named Griffin Taylor, and his family.
He had belonged to a wealthy but hard master; had
also been a soldier during the war. He was now getting old, and being afflicted with rheumatism, so that
he worked under great pain and disadvantage, and
having a large family, he was always hard pressed
to make a living. I remarked to him one day,
"Griffin, did you not fare better when a slave than you
do now?"

"Boss," was the reply, "have you read the fable of
the fat cur dog and the lean wolf? Well, in those
days I was a fat cur dog; I was fed, passably clothed,
and well worked, and if I ventured off the farm at
night without a pass I was liable to be well whipped.
I was simply chained to the place, a mere machine
or animal. Now I am like that lean wolf; I have a
hard scuffle to get enough to eat, but I am free to go
where I please and no man can stop me. Better a
thousand fold liberty with poverty, than plenty with
slavery." And this sentiment is practically endorsed
by all with whom I have ever talked on the subject.

It was at this time I made a study of the Negro race. I found much in their dispositions and characters that was admirable. In the first place, they were ambitious to excel in their work. This ambition could be aroused by just and honest settlements, by discreet and honest commendation, not flattery, and by getting up a friendly rivalry between two champions, or set of hands. Put them on their honor and show that you have confidence in them, and you will seldom find your confidence misplaced.

For instance, my sister had for a cook a colored auntie, Aunt Mandy, or "Black Mammy" as we sometimes called her. She was brought up and trained under the old régime, and the very soul of honor. My sister and her family could go and leave her any length of time, knowing that when they returned, everything would be in as good condition as when they left.

In the Blue Grass Region, most of the Negroes have settled in little villages of their own, around the large towns. Here the more thrifty of them own their homes, and others can rent on reasonable terms. The men go in numbers and work for the farmers from Monday morning until Saturday night. There are no better farm laborers in America than those Kentucky black men. The women, however, are not inclined to be as industrious. Often during harvest or thrashing, a farmer can get more help than he wants of the very best quality, but his wife can hardly get help in the kitchen for love or money, when at the nearest colored town there are scores of strong young women absolutely idle; they will not go into the country to work. Still a few of the women are as industrious as the men.

The colored farm hands have monopolized the work in hemp, especially cutting and breaking; this is due to the fact that such work is very heavy, and unpleasant owing to the dust which is constantly flying. White men cannot endure the dust and refuse to work at it.

The work they seem to take the most pride in is around the stable where the trotting or race horses are trained.   Here the negro is in his glory as a rubber, rider, driver, or even trainer; for some of the most successful premium and race winners in Kentucky have no other trainers but colored men. They take as much pride in a horse they train or drive in a race, as the owner, and of course could not be bribed to "throw off" a race.

However, a colored man could not fail to take interest in horses if he lived in that favored state; it is simply contagious, especially around Lexington, the fast horse center of the universe.   Office and parlor of the leading hotels are filled with paintings of horses in the very poetry of motion.   If two men are engaged in an earnest conversation, nine times out of ten they are talking "horse."   I was in the Phœnix Hotel office one day, when a gentleman introduced two others as follows: "Allow me to present my friend Colonel Blank, better known as the owner of Membrino." Indeed "horseology," to coin a word, is considered one of the essential accomplishments of a Blue Grass belle; while the young men imagine the "halo around the moon to be a glorious celestial race track."

Another characteristic of the Negro I have often noticed.   They are never willing to acknowledge that they are perfectly well; you can often hear a conversation about like this: "How you do dis mo'nin'?" "I'm tol'able."

"How you, Unc' Dick?" "I'm tol'able, bless God!" "How Rachel?" "She's tol'able."   "How Unc'

Billy?" "He's tol'able." "The chil'un all well?" "Yes'um, dey all tol'able." When probably every individual inquired about was in almost perfect health.

However, we think with Judge W. M. Beckner of the Winchester Democrat, that "the Negro population of Kentucky is of a better class than that of the cotton states."

The circle of those who recognize the "Brother in Black" as a useful element in the social forces of the South, is widening from year to year.

He has a record of moral and intellectual inprovement without a parallel in the history of the world."

FREDERICK DOUGLASS.

335

CHAPTER XVI.

FATHERS TO THE RACE.

I. FREDERICK DOUGLASS:—It is not known just when this remarkable man was born; but he supposes it was in February, 1817, in the village of Tuckahoe, Maryland.

His mother's name was Harriet Bailey, and he remembers that she was the only black person in the village who could read; he also recollects that she was quite black and glossy; and as he is many shades lighter, his father must have been a white man. Frederick had an older brother named Perry, and four sisters. His mother, as if anticipating his future career of greatness, gave him a name in keeping with it; she called him Frederick Augustus Washington Bailey; but after his escape, wishing to conceal his identity, he took the name he has since borne.

The Negroes on his master's plantation received the usual cruelty accorded slaves in Maryland at this time. Many were the floggings the boy witnessed, which brought blood from the backs of the victim of an overseer's lash.

However, there were a few bright spots in his plantation life to which he could look back with pleasure.

His master's daughter, Mrs. Thomas Auld, called by the slaves "Miss Lucretia," treated him with great kindness; indeed he became quite a pet with her, and often when hungry, his usual condition, would sing under her window, receiving for his pay a slice of bread and butter. When struck on the forehead by another slave boy, she it was who dressed his bleeding wound.

After this, he was sent by his master to Baltimore, where his new mistress, the wife of Hugh Auld, was very kind to him, and began teaching him to read; but was prevented by her husband, who said in the presence of the boy, that "learning would ruin any nigger" and if Fred was taught to read the Bible it would be impossible to keep him a slave. The words of his master were treasured up by our young hero, who resolved at all hazards to get learning, and with all his getting to "get understanding."

He always carried a Webster's spelling book in his pocket, and induced his little white playmates to give him instructions. He turned bootblack, and earned fifty cents with which he bought a "Columbian Orator," and read with such avidity he might be said to have devoured it.

In 1834 Frederick's master hired him to one Covey, a prominent Methodist in the same county, who talked religion on Sunday to his slaves, and prayed before them morning and evening; but his treatment of them was not in keeping with his profession. When he had been there but a few days, Covey sent him with a yoke of unruly oxen to draw in wood from the forest. This would have been a difficult task for an experienced ox driver; but our hero had never driven oxen before, and as might have been expected, they became unmanageable, tangling themselves and the cart, until it was hard work releasing them; however, this was finally accomplished, and with his load on he started to the house; but the oxen ran away even with the load on the cart; breaking the gate to pieces, they almost crushed the driver between the wheel and the gate-post. He did not reach the house until late noon, but Covey at once ordered him back for a second load; and following after saw what had been done.   He now cut three black gum sprouts, noted for their toughness, from four to six feet long; tearing off Frederick's clothes, he wore them out on his bare back, one at a time, and his coarse shirt kept the sores rubbed and open for weeks.   On another occasion during a hot afternoon in August, Frederick was taken deathly sick while carrying wheat to a fan. Covey saw him lying on the ground, and with a brutal kick in the side, ordered him to rise; he made an effort and fell back, but a second heavy kick brought him to his feet, only to fall helpless on attempting to pick up the tub of wheat and chaff.   Upon which Covey struck him over the head with a stick, causing the blood to gush out, saying, "I will cure your headache." His victim was still too weak to rise, and was left bleeding in a fence corner.   The flow of blood relieved his dizziness, and he determined to go and complain to his master; seeking a moment when Covey's back was turned, he crept into the woods, where, after resting a while, he made his way almost exhausted to St. Michaels, and reported to Captain Auld, only to be sent back the next day. He did not present himself before Covey until Sunday morning, having spent Saturday night with a slave named Sanday and his wife, who gave him food and ministered to his wants.   Brother Covey received him kindly, for it was the Sabbath, and the good man (?) was just starting to church.

He attempted to whip Fred once more after this, but the worm turned on him. The slave had noticed, "men are whipped oftenest who are whipped easiest." He determined to resist, and did so with such success that he drew blood from Covey without losing a drop himself.

LOUIS B. ANDERSON,
Assistant County Attorney Cook County, Illinois.

He never attempted to whip him afterwards. He was a slave four years longer, but was never again whipped, for whenever it was attempted he always gave as good as he received, sometimes better.

In 1835-6 he was hired from his master by one Mr. Freeland; here he received kind treatment, and found a way to open a Sunday-school. He also determined to preach the gospel, and after all had retired to bed would go out and address the pigs as "Dear Brethren."

After this, he was sent to Baltimore and apprenticed to a ship-builder. From here he escaped, disguised as a sailor, and fled to New York. Here he was joined by his sweetheart, Anna Murray of Baltimore, a free woman of color, and they were married. The bride and groom pushed on to New Bedford, where he hoped to get work at his trade, that of calking ships.

He worked in New Bedford at shoveling coal, sawing wood, digging cellars, or any other odd job that came to hand, until he finally secured work at calking whalers in the ship yard.

On August 11th, 1841, he was invited for the first time to address an audience of white people in a convention at Nantucket. He arose with fear and trembling, being much embarrassed, but managed to stammer through a short speech, wherein he thanked the champions of liberty for what they had done and were doing for his enslaved race. He made a good impression, however, and after urgent solicitation opened the convention next morning.

Douglass on this occasion and afterwards, amused the people and proved that he had been a slave, by giving the following extract from a slave-holding minister's sermon to an audience of slaves on the text, "Servants, obey in all things your masters."—

"The Lord in His Providence sent pious souls over to Africa—dark, heathen, benighted Africa, to bring you into this Christian land, where you can sit beneath the droppings of the sanctuary and hear about Jesus. The Lord has so established things that only through the channel of obedience can happiness flow. For instance—Sam, the other day, was sent out by his master to do a piece of work that would occupy about two hours and a half. At the expiration of that time, Sam's master went out; and, lo and behold! there lay Sam's hoe in one place, and Sam in another, fast asleep. The master remembered the words of scripture: 'He that knoweth his master's will and doeth it not shall be beaten with many stripes!' So Sam was taken up and whipped, so that he was disabled from doing any work for the space of three weeks and a half. For only through the channel of obedience can happiness flow."

It was after he had spoken at Oakland, Ohio, that one Irishman remarked to another: "And what do you think of that for a Naygur?"

"Be aisy," was the answer, "he's only half a Naygur."

"And if half a Naygur can speak like that, what could a whole one do?"

His companions soon learned it was wise to have Douglass the last speaker on the program, if they wanted to hold their audience to the end.

At Grafton, Massachusetts, he advertised his own meeting by ringing a bell through the streets and crying, "Notice! Frederick Douglass, recently a slave, will lecture on American slavery, on Grafton Common, this evening at seven o'clock." He was greeted by a great audience, and offered the largest church in town for his other meetings.

His matchless eloquence was the "Open Sesame" which secured this favor.

Having written the true "Narrative of the Life of Frederick Douglass," he thought it discreet to put the ocean between him and his enraged master for a season.   Accordingly he embarked for Liverpool Aug. 16, 1845.

His book was eagerly read on board, and an invitation extended to its author to deliver an address upon the saloon-deck.   This he attempted to do; but a number of Southern slave-holders on board interrupted him by giving the lie to everything he said and shaking their fists under his nose.   The captain was at last forced to clear the deck, and even threatened to put the leader of the mob in irons.   An account of this suppression of free speech on the high sea was published in the English papers and gave the black orator an immense amount of free advertising; so that his lecturing tour through Ireland, Scotland and England was almost an ovation.   While in Ireland, Father Mathew gave him a soiree, and administered to him the *temperance* pledge.   In making a speech in St. Patrick's Temperance Hall,   Douglass said of those who spoke of the Irish as slaves, that "they do not sufficiently distinguish between certain forms of oppression, and slavery.   Slavery is not what takes away any one right or property in man; it takes away man himself, and makes him the property of his fellow.   It is what unmans man, takes him from himself, dooms him as a degraded thing, ranks him with the bridled horse and muzzled ox, makes him a chattel, a marketable commodity, to be swayed by the caprice, and sold at the will of his master."

At Belfast, Jan. 6, 1846, the local branch of the British and Foreign Anti-Slavery Society presented him with a Bible splendidly bound in gold.   He remarked on receiving it, "I accept thankfully this Bible; and while it shall have the best place in my house, I trust also to give its precepts a place in my heart."

While in London he was lionized because of his oratorical gifts.

He took breakfast with Sir John Bowring, and met Lord Brougham and Douglas Jerrold.

A young man from one of our Southern states was being entertained by an English gentleman, who said, "I want particularly to have you look at my bust of your countryman, Mr. Douglass." "With the utmost pleasure," he answered. "Senator Douglass is one of our most distinguished men." What was his amazement when he discovered that the bust was of our hero and in *black* marble!

While he was in England Mrs. Ellen Richardson collected money and bought Douglass' freedom from Hugh Auld, and his papers were presented to him on his return to America; but he told his English friends in his parting address, that he had just as much right to sell Hugh Auld as Auld had to sell him; and said he, "If any of you are disposed to make a purchase to-night just say the word."

Mr. Douglass began to publish the "North Star," at Rochester, New York, Dec. 3, 1847. It was aggressive and ably edited from the first. But in order to avoid confusion, he changed its name with the fourth volume to "Frederick Douglass' Paper." "For," said he, "there were I know not how many stars in the newspaper firmament." He furnished each member of Congress a copy of his paper, with good results. In 1858 he started a magazine called "Douglass' Monthly," mainly for circulating in England. The weekly paper was merged in the "Monthly" in August, 1860.

On one occasion, Mr. Douglass received the following letter: "I have been informed that you had

an only daughter, and that you desire her to marry a
whight man; whereupon you give $15,000 or $20,000
dollars to any respectable whight man that would
marry her and cherish her through life. If there is
any truth in this report, P. S. let me know and
I will marry your daughter on these conditions, and
will endeavor to make myself agreeable."

To which Douglass in replying remarked, that as
a total stranger his correspondent should have given
at least one reference, and then continued: "You
date from Auburn, and tell me to direct to Auburn,
but do not name the street. Pardon me for regarding this as a suspicious circumstance. You may be an
inmate of the State Prison, or on your way there; a
fact which you see would interfere with the fulfillment of your part of the proposed bargain, even if I
could fulfill the part you assign to me. You want
$15,000 or $20,000; this is a common want, and you
are not to blame for using all honorable means to
obtain it. But candor requires me to state, that if
you were in every respect a suitable person to be
bought for the purpose you name, I have not the
money to buy you. I have no objection to your complexion; but there are certain little faults of grammar and spelling, as well as other little points in your
letter, which compel me to regard you as a person
by education, manners, and morals, wholly unfit to
associate with my daughter in any capacity whatever.
You evidently think your white skin of great value;
I don't dispute it; it is probably the best thing about
you; yet not even that valuable quality can commend
you sufficiently to induce even so black a Negro as
myself to accept you as his son-in-law."

Can any fair-minded man read the foregoing letter
and still insist that the Negro is an inferior race?

When the war came on, Douglass did all he could

with tongue and pen, to have the Negroes enlisted to help fight for their own freedom; two of his sons, Charles, and Lewis H., afterwards Sergeant-Major, enlisted. Mr. Douglass afterward called on President Lincoln, in the interest of fair treatment to Negro soldiers. The following extract is from a speech delivered in Philadelphia, Dec. 4, 1863: "When I went in, the President was sitting in his usual position, I was told, with his feet in different parts of the room, taking it easy. As I came in and approached him the President began to rise, and he continued rising, until he stood over me; and reaching out his hand, he said, 'Mr. Douglass, I know you; I have read about you and Mr. Seward has told me about you;' putting me quite at ease at once. He told me that I had made a speech somewhere in New York and it had got into the papers, and among other things I had said that if I were called upon to state what I regarded as the most disheartening feature of our present military situation, it would not be the various disasters experienced by our armies and navies, on flood and field, but it would be the tardy, hesitating, vacillating policy of the President of the United States. And the President said to me, 'Mr. Douglass, I have been charged with being tardy, and vacillating, but I do not think that charge can be sustained; I think it cannot be shown that when I have once taken a position I have ever retreated from it.'

"I told him that he had been somewhat slow in proclaiming equal protection to our colored soldiers and prisoners; and he said the country needed talking up to that point. He hesitated in regard to it, when he felt the country was not ready for it. He knew that the colored man was a despised man, and that if he at first came out with such a proclamation, all the hatred which is poured on the head of the Negro race would be visited on his administration. He said that there was preparatory work needed, and that this work had now been done. And continued, 'Remember this, Mr. Douglass: Milliken's Bend, Port Hudson, and Fort Wagner are recent events; and these were necessary to prepare the way for this very proclamation of mine.' I thought it was reasonable, but came to the conclusion that while Abraham Lincoln will not go down to posterity as Abraham the Great, or as Abraham the Wise, or as Abraham the Eloquent, although he is all three—wise, great, and eloquent, he will go down to posterity, if the country is saved, as Honest Abraham; and going down thus, his name may be written anywhere in this wide world of ours side by side with that of Washington without disparaging the latter."

I think one of the best things Douglass ever said was in a jubilee meeting held in Faneuil Hall, Boston, just after Richmond was taken. Said he: "I tell you the Negro is coming up. He is rising. Why, only a little while ago, we were the Lazarus of the South; the Dives of the South was the slave-holder. But now a change has taken place. That rich man is lifting up his eyes in torments down there, and seeing Lazarus in Abraham's bosom; and he is all the time calling on Father Abraham to send Lazarus back. But Father Abraham says, 'If they hear not Grant and Sherman, neither will they be persuaded though I send Lazarus unto them.' I say, we are way up yonder now, no mistake."

The war over, Mr. Douglass continued to support the Republican party, and was appointed by President Hayes Marshal of the District of Columbia. He presided over the colored people's convention at Louisville, July, 1880. In May, 1881, he was appointed Recorder of Deeds for the District of Columbia.

HON. W. L. MARTIN,
Graduate of Oberlin College, a Member of the Chicago Bar,
and Member of the Illinois State Legislature.

When Harrison was elected President he appointed him Minister to Hayti. And at the World s Fair Mr. Douglass had general charge of the exhibit from that Republic.

Fred Douglass is unquestionably America's greatest colored man, and will go down in history as one of her greatest orators. A gentleman who heard his great oration on Lincoln at the Rochester Courthouse, said: "I have heard Webster and Clay in their best moments, Channing and Beecher in their highest inspirations; I never heard truer eloquence. I never saw profounder impression."

Colonel F. W. Higginson said of Douglass: "I have hardly heard his equal in grasp upon an audience, in dramatic presentation, in striking at the pith of an ethical question and in single illustrations and images."

Most of Frederick Douglass' public life was spent at a period which tried men's souls and tended to produce great orators; but he showed that he was more than an orator; he was a statesman of sound judgment, and was almost invariably right. Garrison claimed that the constitution was pro-slavery, and even favored secession and disunion as a means of putting down slavery. But Douglass maintained that the constitution, if rightly interpreted, was emphatically anti-slavery. And he rightly favored fighting for emancipation under the constitution and the stars and stripes. He also favored arming the strong black hand as well as the white, and this was the very policy which proved a success.

II. TOUSSAINT L'OUVERTURE:—The subject of this sketch was born about the year 1745, on what was called the Breda estate, near the town of Cape Haytien, Hayti. His full name was Francois Dominique Toussaint. He earned the surname L'Ouverture because of his great prowess in battle. An admiring Frenchman said of him, "Cet homme fait l'ouverture"-- "This man makes an opening everywere." After this his soldiers called him L'Ouverture, "the opening."

Toussaint showed such marked intelligence, and purity of conduct, as to give him great influence over his fellow slaves, and attracted the attention of the manager of the plantation, M. Bayou de Libertas, who taught him reading, writing and arithmetic. This was a great accomplishment, when we consider that only one slave in ten thousand possessed these elements of knowledge. His master also made him postilion, a position which gave him advantage over the plantation hands.

When the insurrection took place in 1791 Toussaint was urged to join them, but he declined until he had aided his benefactor M. Bayou, and his family on board a ship to escape to Baltimore.

St. Domingo was a bone of contention between the Spanish and French. Finding the latter weakened by being divided into opposing factions of Republicans and Bourbon Loyalists, the Spanish determined to seize the whole island. In their extremity the French invited the English of Jamaica to come to their relief. At first the Governor of Jamaica sent them a few hundred soldiers; afterwards, the English government sent General Maitland, who landed with four thousand troops and gained great success.

The French Governor now saw he had as much to fear from his English allies as his Spanish foes, for England had determined to seize the island for her own.

In his extremity, the Governor thought of the mulattoes who had assisted him in putting down an insurrection of the whites five years before. But he had forfeited his solemn oath to grant them civil privileges, and they would not be deceived a second time.

He now thought of the enslaved blacks, and sent a deputation to Toussaint, who even then had great influence with his people. But he was a diplomatist, and asked the envoys, "Where are your credentials?"

"We have none," was the answer. "Then," said he, "I will have nothing to do with you." The envoys next went to Francois and Biassou, two other slave leaders of considerable influence, and said, "Arm, assist the government to put down the Spanish on one side, the English on the other."

Having been previously advised by Toussaint, who, like Cromwell, preferred not to be in the lead at first, they placed themselves at the head of fifteen thousand blacks, who had been supplied with arms from the government arsenal. This was in August, 1791.

With the help of this army of blacks, Blanchelande gained the ascendency over the combined Spanish and English, and was reinstated as Governor. Having accomplished this, the black leaders, speaking for their people, said to the Governor they had created, "Now grant us gradual emancipation, give us one day in seven; give us one day's labor; we will buy another and with the two buy a third, and so eventually be free." Surely this was a very mild request, coming from men who had saved his government from overthrow. But the same Blanchelande, who was false to his mulatto benefactors, proved doubly false to his black allies. He sneeringly replied, "Disarm! Disperse!" But they stood their ground, and replied, "The right hand that has saved you, the right hand that has saved the island for the Bourbons, may perchance clutch some of our own rights." Thus began the insurrection. The Blacks refused to disband or lay down their arms, as they had been mortified by two insults. First, their commissioners sent to meet

the French Committee were ignominiously dismissed;
after this Francois, their general, being summoned to
a second conference, went to it on horseback, attended by two officers. Here he met a young French
lieutenant, who had known him as a slave, who seeing him in the uniform of an officer, became enraged
and struck him a heavy blow with his riding-whip
across the shoulders. The Negro troops did not hear
of the insult to their commander for twenty-four
hours. When they did, the cry was heard, "Death
to every white man!" They soon had fifteen hundred
white prisoners ranged in front of the camp, intending to shoot them. Just at this critical time, Toussaint reached the camp, having been offered the
position as second in command. Mounting a hill in
front of the army, he gained their attention and said
in a loud voice heard by all: "Brothers, this blood
will not wipe out the insult to our chief; only the
blood in yonder French camp can wipe it out. To
shed that is courage; to shed this is cowardice, and
cruelty besides." They heard his words and the lives
of fifteen hundred men were saved. Shortly afterwards he became the commander-in-chief of the
black army, and in seven years' time accomplished
the following results:

He conquered the Spanish, even in their own cities,
over which he caused the French banner to wave; he
fought pitched battles with the English general, Maitland, whom he defeated, with great slaughter, but
afterwards he permitted him to retreat with the remnant of his army to Jamaica; he subdued the mulattoes to his sway, and when the French army turned
on their general, Loveaux, and put him in chains,
Toussaint defeated them, rescued Loveaux from
prison and placed him at the head of his army. The
French, in their gratitude, now named him General-in-

Chief of the armies of St. Domingo. From this to the position of governor of the island was for Toussaint but a short step.

Under his government the island continued happy and prosperous.

In the year 1800 he appointed a committee of nine to draft a constitution for him.   Out of this number there were eight white proprietors, and one mulatto, not a single Negro or soldier in the number.   With the instinct of a true statesman he said to this committee: "Put at the head of the chapter of commerce that the ports of St. Domingo are open to the trade of the world."   Catholic as he was, he took his place beside Roger Williams in securing to all, religious liberty, for he said to the committee: "Make it the first line of my constitution that I know no difference between religious beliefs."

This constitution worked admirably during the time it was tried, even if it did make Toussaint President for life with the power to choose his successor.   The commerce of the world visited St. Domingo, her coffers were filled, and her plantations, worked by free labor, blossomed like the rose.

The same year in which the constitution was drafted, Toussaint made the following proclamation: "Sons of St. Domingo, come home; we never meant to take your houses and your lands The Negro only asked that liberty which God gave him.   Your houses wait for you, your lands are ready."   And the exiled planters returned from Baltimore and New Orleans, from Madrid and Paris, and lived contentedly on their estates, protected by the pledged word of this black ruler, which was never broken.   Then turning to his armies—in their rags and poverty, he said: "Go back and work on these estates you have conquered; for an empire can be founded only on order and industry, and you can learn these virtues only there."

Within a week his army was transformed into laborers.

Thus did Toussaint establish what bid fair to be the best governed republic on earth. But this very fact was an eyesore to Napoleon Bonaparte, who was about to seize the crown of France. Moreover, Toussaint had written Napoleon a letter in which occured this language, "The first of the blacks, to the first of the whites." And when the satirists of Paris spoke of Toussaint as the "Black Napoleon," it enraged Bonaparte more than the defeat of his army by this Negro chieftain.

So Napoleon called a council and asked, "What shall I do with St. Domingo?" The slave-holders present said, "Give it to us." But a letter was read from Colonel Vincent, formerly private secretary to Toussaint, and his answer was: "Sire, leave it alone; it is the happiest spot in your dominions; God raised this man to govern, races melt under his hand. He has saved you this island; for I know of my own knowledge that, when the Republic could not have lifted a finger to prevent it, George III. offered him any title and any revenue if he would hold the island under the British crown. He refused and saved it for France." But Napoleon had already decided what to do before calling the council. He had sixty thousand idle republican soldiers, and he dare not seize the crown until they were sent to a distant realm, or the ocean rolled between him and them. Accordingly in an evil hour he put thirty thousand of them under the command of his brother-in-law, Leclerc, and sent them to Hayti, with instructions to overthrow the Republic, bring Toussaint a prisoner to France, and re-establish slavery on the island.

Toussaint, in company with his friend Christopher, rode on horseback to the eastern extremity of the island, where from a high promontory he saw the approaching fleet.

Counting the ships, he found they numbered sixty, each crowded with the best drilled, best armed soldiers in all Europe. He then exclaimed to Christopher: "All France has come to Hayti; they can only come to make us slaves; and we are lost!" He now deplored his misplaced confidence in Napoleon which caused him to disband his army. But he resolved to give the invaders a warm reception and sell his liberty and that of his people as dearly as possible. Accordingly he issued the following proclamation:

"My children, France comes to make us slaves; God gave us liberty; France has no right to take it away. Burn the cities, destroy the harvests, poison the wells, show the white man the hell he comes to make;" and they obeyed him.

Marching into battle singing the Marseillaise Hymn, the Negro soldiers under such a leader were invincible, and at first routed the invading army in every encounter.

Defeated in battle, Leclerc resorted to lying, and issued this proclamation:

"We do not come to make you slaves; this man Toussaint tells you lies; join us and you shall have the rights you claim." Deceived by these lying promises, all the officers laid down their arms except Pierre, Toussaint's brother, Christopher and Dessalines; finally these, too, went over to the enemy, and the great leader was left alone, with a remnant of his army. He now sent the following message to Leclerc. "I will submit. I could continue the struggle for years,—could prevent a single Frenchman from safely quitting your camp. But I hate blood. I have fought only for the liberty of my race. Guarantee that, I will submit and come in." He took the oath to be a true citizen, and the French general swore on the same crucifix, that the island should be free, and that Toussaint should be faithfully protected. But the white man never intended to keep that sacred oath, as all the circumstances show. Leclerc was struck by the contrast between his own splendidly equipped soldiers and the ragged followers of the black commander, whose arms were in keeping with their clothes, and he said to him, "L'Ouverture, had you continued the war, where could you have got arms?" "I would have taken yours," was the Spartan-like answer.

The story is soon told. Relying upon the pledges of Leclerc, Toussaint, who never broke his word to friend or foe, retired to his plantation, only to be treacherously seized in the night, and conveyed on board a man of war, bound for France. As he caught the last glimpse of his beloved Hayti, he remarked to the captain, "You think you have rooted up the tree of liberty, but I am only a branch; I have planted the tree so deep that all France can never root it up."

He was taken to Paris, and incarcerated in prison. Here the great (?) Napoleon sent Caffarelli, one of his secretaries, to interrogate him concerning supposed buried treasures. After listening a few minutes he answers, "Young man, it is true I have lost treasures, but they are not such as you come to seek."

Toussaint was now sent as a prisoner to the Chateaux de Joux and confined in a stone dungeon twelve by twelve feet, with a single narrow window, looking out on Switzerland's mountains of snow. It is said that ice covered the floor in winter, and dampness in summer. From this dungeon tomb he wrote the following letter to Napoleon:—"Sire, I am a French citizen. I never broke a law. By the grace of God,

I have saved for you the best island of your realm. Sire, of your mercy grant me justice."

This letter was never answered. And when Napoleon learned that five francs a day were allowed him for food and fuel, he cut it down to three. Still the iron constitution did not yield to slow assassination fast enough, and the jailer was ordered to go into Switzerland with the keys of the dungeon, and remained four days. When he returned the Black Prince was dead.

This sad event was in April of 1803, and when it became known raised a cry of horror, and indignation against Napoleon, who would thus destroy in this barbarous manner one of the noblest and bravest of the African race. But God is just, and twelve years afterward the imperial assassin was a closely guarded prisoner on the rocky island of St. Helena, whining his life away, saying "he did not live, he simply existed."

In a few years he died of disappointment and a broken heart; and nothing he accomplished while living exists. Even the monarchy for which he fought so many battles, has been superseded by a republic.

Contrast this with the fact, that while no monument marks the resting place of Toussaint, thus cruelly murdered, still the republic he founded exists to day as a memorial of his valor and statesmanship.

It is significant, too, that the last claimant of the Bonaparte dynasty, Prince Napoleon, was killed by the Zulus in Africa, the very people from which Toussaint sprang, the blood of whose kings flowed in his veins.

"Though the mills of God grind slowly, yet they grind exceeding small. Though with patience he stands waiting, with exactness grinds he all."

III. PHILLIS WHEATLEY:—This remarkable colored

girl was brought, in 1761, on a slave ship from Africa to the Boston slave market, and purchased by Mrs. John Wheatley, a benevolent and cultured lady. When bought she was naked except a piece of dirty carpet around her loins. She was thin and sick from a rough, tedious sea voyage, for her constitution was delicate at best. Impressed by her intelligent countenance and modest demeanor, she was selected from a large number of slaves.

It was the intention at first to teach her the duties of a house servant; but clean clothing and good food wrought such a change for the better, that her mistress decided to instruct her in letters. She was only eight years old and proved a very apt pupil; in less than a year and a half she had mastered the English language sufficiently well to read the most difficult portions of the Bible. She also mastered writing with equal ease, and in four years from the time she was taken out of the slave market could carry on an interesting correspondence upon many topics. Her amiable disposition and budding intellect attracted the attention of the refined and cultured of Boston, who gave her encouragement by lending her books and conversing with her upon literary subjects. Having acquired a fairly good English education. she began the study of Latin, and soon became so proficient that she made an admirable translation of one of Ovid's tales, which was published in Boston and republished in England, where it was heartily commended by many of the reviews.

When asked what she remembered about her home in Africa she replied, "Nothing except the fact that every morning my mother poured out water before the rising sun." She could not help but contrast this with the worship of the true and only living God, and this child of Africa became deeply pious. In 1770, at the age of sixteen, she was happily converted and united with the congregation at the "Old South Meetinghouse." Four years afterwards, her master manumitted her. But the New England climate was too severe for one of her studious and sedentary habits, with delicate constitution, and she began to go into a decline. At the suggestion of eminent physicians, her adopted mother, for such she proved herself to be, sent her on a voyage to England, in care of her son, who was going on business. Some years previous to this Phillis had developed a great talent for poetry, which she had cultivated to the utmost. Indeed her reputation was well established, and had preceded her to England. Her rare conversational powers and charming demeanor took London by storm.

Soon the nobility, thoughtful people, and press, united in extolling the name of Phillis Wheatley, the African poetess.

Her poems were first published in Boston in 1770. But her admiring friends prevailed upon her to bring out a second and better edition in London in 1773. This was a small octavo volume of about one hundred and twenty pages, comprising thirty-nine pieces. It was dedicated to the Countess of Huntingdon, and contained a picture of the poetess, and a letter of recommendation signed by the governor and lieutenant-governor of Massachusetts, with many other reliable citizens of Boston, including her master; establishing the fact that all the poems contained in the book were written by Phillis. For the poems were so excellent, strangers were disposed to question their originality.

During Phillis' stay in England, Mrs. Wheatley grieved herself sick about her adopted daughter. She would talk to her picture by the hour, and pointing it out to friends, exclaim with all a mother's pride:

"See! Look at my Phillis! Does she not seem as though she would speak to me?"

When she could endure the separation no longer, she sent an urgent request to Phillis to return at once to Boston. This she hastened to do and found her kind benefactor at death's door. She was only able to comfort her for a short time before the end came.

Mr. Wheatley and his daughter soon followed her to the grave.

Young Mr. Wheatley made his home in England; so Phillis was alone in the "wide, wide world."

The historian Sparks informs us that "she soon after received an offer of marriage from a respectable colored man of Boston, named John Peters.

"In an evil hour, he was accepted; and though he was a man of talents and information, he proved utterly unworthy of the distinguished woman who honored him with her alliance."

Her married life was brief and unhappy. One babe gladdened her heart, only to die early. Having been tenderly brought up, she naturally expected the same treatment from her husband, but was doomed to a sad disappointment. Peters became jealous and morose, and subjected her to cruel treatment.

Her delicate constitution gave way, and she went into a hasty decline, from which she died December fifth, 1784, in the thirty-first year of her age, loved and mourned by all who knew her.

She was certainly one of the most remarkable characters in history. Her life reads more like a romance than the statement of historical facts. From a condition of nudity in a slave-ship she worked her way up until she conquered the social caste of Boston and London, and was dined, and praised by the cultivated and refined of two continents.

George W. Williams says of her, "She addressed

a poem to General Washington that pleased the old warrior very much. We have never seen it, though we have searched diligently."

Mr. Sparks says of it, in his Life of Washington, "I have not been able to find among Washington's papers this letter and poem addressed to him. They have doubtless been lost."

Thus we see a distinguished biographer, and no less distinguished historian, both "searched diligently for the poem and their conclusions were that it had "doubtless been lost." But we are glad to inform our readers that the poem in question was "not lost, but gone before," to the publisher; sent by Washington himself. And having obtained a copy at no little trouble and pains, we shall give it in full, but will first quote two letters germane to it.

"CAMBRIDGE, February 28th, 1886.

"MISS PHILLIS,—Your favor of the 26th of October did not reach my hands till the middle of December. Time enough, you will say, to have given an answer ere this. Granted. But a variety of important occurrences, continually interposing to distract the mind and withdraw the attention, I hope will apologize for the delay, and plead my excuse for seeming neglect. I thank you most sincerely for your polite notice of me, in the elegant lines enclosed; and however undeserving I may be of such encomium and panegyric, the style and manner exhibit a striking proof of your poetical talents; in honor of which, and as a tribute justly due to you, I would have published the poem, had I not been apprehensive, that while I only meant to give the world this new instance of your genius, I might have incurred the imputation of vanity. This and nothing else, determined me not to give it place in the public prints.

"If you should ever come to Cambridge, or near

E. J. COOPER,
Editor Colored American, Washington, D. C.

headquarters, shall be happy to see a person so favored by the Muses, and to whom nature has been so liberal and beneficent in her dispensations.   I am, with great respect, your obedient, humble servant,
"GEORGE WASHINGTON."

This is about the kind of a letter we would expect from a man who was noble enough to emancipate his own slaves, that they might enjoy that liberty for which he imperiled his life.

The following letter accompanied the poem, dedicated to Washington just before he took command of the Continental army.

"GENERAL WASHINGTON, Sir:—

"I have taken the liberty to address your excellency in the enclosed poem, and entreat your acceptance, though I am not insensible to its inaccuracies.   Your appointment by the Continental Congress to be Generalissimo of the armies of North America, together with the fame of your virtues, excites sensations not easy to suppress.   Your generosity, therefore, I presume, will pardon the attempt.

"Wishing your excellency all possible success in the great cause you are so generously engaged in, I am your excellency's most obedient, humble servant,
"PHILLIS WHEATLEY.

"Providence, October 26, 1775."

HIS EXCELLENCY, GENERAL WASHINGTON.

"Celestial choir! enthroned in realms of light,
Columbia's scenes of glorious toils I write;
While freedom's cause her anxious breast alarms,
She flashes dreadful in refulgent arms.
See Mother Earth her offspring's fate bemoan,
And nation's gaze at scenes before unknown;
See the bright beams of heaven's revolving light
Involved in sorrows and in veil of night.

The goddess comes, she moves divinely fair,
Olive and laurel bind her golden hair;
Wherever shines this native of the skies,
Unnumbered charms and recent graces rise.
Muse! bow propitious while my pen relates
How pour her armies through a thousand gates:
As when Eolus heaven's fair face deforms,
Enwrapped in tempest and a night of storms;
Astonished ocean feels the wild uproar,
The refluent surges beat the resounding shore;
Or thick as leaves in Autumn's golden reign,
Such and so many moves the warrior's train.
In bright array they seek the world of war,
Where high unfurled the ensign waves in air.
Shall I to Washington their praise recite?
Enough, thou knowest them in the fields of fight.
Thee, first in peace and honor we demand,
The grace and glory of thy mortal band.
Famed for thy valor, for thy virtue more,
Hear every tongue thy guardian aid implore.
One Century scarce performed its destined round
When Gallic powers Columbia's fury found;
And, so may you, whoever dares disgrace
The land of freedom's heaven-defended race.
Fixed are the eyes of nations on the scales,
For in their hopes Columbia's arm prevails.
Anon, Britannia droops the pensive head,
While round increase the rising hills of dead.
Ah! cruel blindness to Columbia's state,
Lament thy thirst of boundless power too late.
Proceed, great chief; virtue on thy side;
Thy every action let the goddess guide.
A crown, a mansion, and a throne that shine
With gold unfading, Washington, be thine."

IV. SOJOURNER TRUTH,—The Libyan Sibyl:—It is
not known when this remarkable woman was born,
as it was not customary to keep a record of such
trivial events as the birth of a slave-child. This much

is known, she was manumitted by an act of the legislature of New York in 1811, by which all slaves forty years of age were liberated at once, the others in 1828, and the children on reaching their majority.

Her former name was Isabella, that of her parents, James and Betsey, slaves of Colonel Ardinburgh, who belonged to that class called Low Dutch; he lived in Hurley, Ulster County, New York.

She remembered that her parents, Bomefree and Mau-mau-Bett, after having all their children, whom God had intended as the prop and stay of their declining years, sold away from them, were emancipated when they became old and well nigh helpless. But this was little more than liberty to starve or perish from cold, for they were given to understand that they could expect no help from the very people who had been enriched by thier unpaid toil for more than half a century.

At nine years of age, Isabella was sold for one hundred dollars to one John Nealy of Ulster County, New York. She thinks her sale was connected in some way with a flock of sheep. The trials of her life dated from this period, or as she expressed it, "Now the war begun." She knew nothing of the English language, while the Nealys could not talk Dutch. Mr. Nealy, however, could understand that language, but neither mistress nor maid could understand the language of the other. This naturally led to frequent misunderstanding, and punishment for poor Isabella. She was often slapped over for bringing the wrong article to her mistress. She suffered terribly from cold, her feet becoming badly frozen. And while they gave her plenty to eat, they also gave her plenty of whippings; often for no other reason than her inability to understand what she was told to do.

One Sunday morning she was sent to the barn,

where she found her master waiting for her with a bundle of rods in his hand. Stripping her to the waist, and tying her hands before her, he gave her the most cruel flogging she ever received. Her flesh was deeply lacerated, the blood streaming to the barn floor, the scars remaining to her dying day. And she never knew why she was so cruelly whipped.

Often afterwards she stated, "When I hear 'em tell of whippin' women on the bare flesh, it makes my flesh crawl, an' my very hair rise on my head! Oh my God, what a way is this of treatin' human bein's!" She now remembered her mother's instruction to pray to God in time of trouble, and at once obeyed, begging God to send her father, who was still living, and through him to provide a kinder master.

This prayer (and indeed *all* her prayers) was promptly answered. In a short time her poor old father came to see her. When he started away she followed him to the gate, and unburdened her heart.

He promised to do what he could and in a short time sent a rough but kind-hearted man, by the name of Schriver, who purchased Isabella of her master for one hundred and five dollars. Schriver lived about six miles distant, and owned a large farm, but left it unimproved, while he engaged in fishing, and keeping a hotel. He and his family were coarse, ignorant, and profane, but honest, kind-hearted people. Here Isabella was kindly treated, but learned from their example to swear like a trooper. Her work consisted of carrying fish, hoeing corn, bringing roots and herbs from the woods for beers, and going on errands to the Strand for a jug of molasses or liquor.

Naturally instead of improving in morals she retrograded, during the year and a half she spent there.

Her next master was John J. Dumont, to whom

she was sold for seventy pounds in the year 1810. He also lived in Ulster County, near the town of New Paltz. She remained with him until the fall of 1827. Mr. Dumont was a kind-hearted man, but his wife was not accustomed to Negroes and disliked Isabella from the first.

Mrs. Dumont employed two white girls; one of them, named Kate, became jealous of Bell (as they now called her for short) on account of the master's praise, and was very overbearing towards her. Thus she was praised and complimented by her master, who declared she could do more than half a dozen common people; while her mistress replied that "the reason she accomplished so much work, was because she did not half do it." In proof of which she called attention to the potatoes which Bell had cooked for breakfast, and showed that they had a dingy, dirty look; remarking, "This is a fine specimen of Bell's work, but it is the way all her work is done." Even the master scolded this time, and commanded her to be more careful in the future on pain of punishment, while Kate joined heartily in the censures, wishing to please the mistress.

Isabella had done her best to have those potatoes nice and clean, and was much distressed at her poor success, and inability to account for it. In this dilemma Mr. Dumont's daughter Gertrude, a kind-hearted girl of about ten years of age, offered her sympathy and aid. It was agreed between them that Gertrude should be called in the morning when Bell arose, and they would wash the potatoes thoroughly, and that Gertrude should watch them while Bell was milking. This plan was carried out in full; but presently Kate came into the room, requesting Gertrude to "go to her mother;" but she kept her place in the corner, watching closely. Presently she saw Kate pick up a large chip covered with ashes and deliberately dash them into the kettle. Then Gertrude cried out, "Oh, Poppee!" (her word for father.) "Poppee! Kate has been putting ashes in among the potatoes! I saw her do it! Look at those that fell on the outside of the kettle! You can now see what made the potatoes so dingy every morning, though Bell washed them clean!" Gertrude soon made the fraud as public as the censure had been. The master was prouder of Bell than ever, while the mistress and Kate were both deeply mortified. She tried after this vindication harder than ever to please her master, working almost night and day in the effort.

Some time after this a strong attachment sprung up between Bell and a slave named Robert, belonging to an English neighbor named Catlin. But the Englishman forbade him to visit Bell, and ordered him to take a wife from among his fellow slaves. Still Robert continued to follow his inclination, and make clandestine visits. One Saturday afternoon, learning that Bell was sick, he boldly went to see her. But Catlin and his son followed him, and as soon as he reached the object of his affections, they both fell upon him like madmen, cursing, and beating him over the head and face with heavy canes. The blood spurted from his face, and they would probably have beaten him to death had not the more humane Dumont interfered, telling the brutal ruffians they had beaten him already too much, they could no longer spill human blood on his premises; he would have "no nigger killed there."

The Catlins now took a rope and tied his hands behind his back so tight that Mr. Dumont compelled them to loosen it, saying that "no brute, much less a man, could be tied that way where he was."

Mr. Dumont also followed them home as Robert's

protector, and succeeded in cooling their wrath be, fore he left them.

Bell had witnessed the whole scene from her window, and was shocked at the cruel treatment of poor Robert, for whom she had the warmest affection, and whose only crime in the eyes of his master was his love for her.

Both now became obedient chattels, each marrying a fellow slave, if the farce of a union liable to be annulled at the caprice of the master can be called a marriage.

In process of time, she became the mother of five children; and carried the youngest in her arms when she "walked" away from Mr. Dumont's house in 1827.

By the conditions of the act of the New York legislature she would have been free July 4, 1828. Mr. Dumont, in consideration of the long years of faithful service, promised to give her free papers one year in advance of this date. But when the time came he backed out on the trivial plea that her hand had been disabled during the past year, and she could not perform as much work as formerly. In vain did she remind him of his own statement, that she did more work during those past years than several ordinary slaves. Surely working night and day for long years would more than make up for a disabled hand one year. But as he still refused, she determined to take the matter into her own hands, and without his consent. She started one fine morning just before daylight, her baby on one strong arm, a bundle of food and clothing on the other. Night found her at the home of Mr. and Mrs. Van Wagener, to whom she had been directed by a neighbor. Here she was kindly received and given employment. In a short time Dumont found her. She anticipated this and resolved to settle it with him at once. As soon as they met, his salutation was, "Well, Bell, so you've run away from me?" "No, I did not *run* away, I *walked* away by daylight, and all because you had promised me a year off my time." His reply was, "You must go back with me." Her decided answer was, "No, I won't go back with you." He said, "Well, I shall take the child." This also was as firmly denied. Mr. Isaac Van Wagener now interposed, and bought her service for the remainder of the year for twenty dollars. Dumont also exacted five dollars for the baby, and then left; but not until he heard Mr. Van Wagener tell Isabella not to call him master, adding, "There is but one Master; and he who is your Master is my Master." Thus ended her life as a slave.

"Sojourner once visited Mrs. Harriet B. Stowe at her home; in the course of a conversation the question was asked:—

"Well, Sojourner, did you always go by this name?"

"No, 'deed, my name was Isabella; but when I left the house of bondage, I left everything behind. I wa'n't goin' to keep nothin' of Egypt on me, an' so I went to the Lord an' asked him to give me a new name. An' the Lord give me Sojourner, because I was to travel up an' down the land, showin' the people their sins, an' bein' a sign unto them. Afterward I told de Lord I wanted another name, 'cause everybody else had two names; an' de Lord give me Truth, because I was to declare the truth to de people."

A few years after this, she felt called of God to labor for the salvation of souls, and the good of her own oppressed people.

Though never able to read or write, she kept her friends busy reading the Bible to her, and answering her numerous letters, She had a remarkable memory, learning long hymns by hearing them only once, and could repeat many chapters in the Bible from hearing them read a few times. Moreover she had marvelous power with God and man, and a natural eloquence and repartee seldom equaled.

On one occasion she was at a Woman's Rights Convention, where the ministers in the town turned out, and taking issue with the ladies, by their sophistries, turned the public sentiment against them, leaving the ladies and their cause in utter despair, when Sojourner stepped to the front and snatched a victory from the jaws of defeat. Hear her:—

"Well, chil'ern, what's all dis here talkin' 'bout? Dat man ober dar say dat women needs to be helped into carriages, and lifted ober ditches, an' to have de bes' place everywhar. Nobody eber help me into carriages, or ober mud puddles, or gives me any bes' place (and raising herself to her full height and her voice to a pitch like rolling thunder, she asked), an' ar'n't I a woman? Look at me! Look at my arm! (And she bared her right arm to the shoulder, showing her tremendous muscular power.) I have plowed, an' planted, an' gathered into barns, an' no man could head me—an' ar'n't I a woman? I could work as much, an' eat as much as a man when I could git it, an' bear de lash as well—an' ar'n't I a woman? I have born thirteen children an' seen 'em mos' all sold off into slavery, an when I cried out with a mother's grief, none but Jesus heard—an' ar'n't I a woman? Den dey talks 'bout dis ting in de head—what dis dey call it?" "Intellect," whispered some one near. "Dat's it, honey. What's dat got to do with woman's rights or niggers' rights? If my cup won't hold but a pint an' yourn holds a quart, wouldn't ye be mean not to let me have my little half-measure full?" And she pointed her finger and sent a keen glance at the minister who had made the argument. The cheering was long and loud.

"Den dat little man in black dar, he say woman can't have as much rights as man, cause Christ w'an' a woman. Whar did your Christ come from?"

Rolling thunder could not have stilled that crowd as did those deep, wonderful tones, as she stood there with outstretched arms and eye of fire. Raising her voice still louder, she repeated, "Whar did your Christ come from? From God and a woman. Man had nothing to do with him." Oh! what a rebuke she gave the little man!

Turning again to another objector, she took up the defense of mother Eve, and ended by asserting that "if de fust woman God ever made could turn the world upside down, all 'lone, dese togedder ought to be able to turn it back an' git it right side up agin, an' now dey is askin' to do it, de men better let 'em."

Hundreds rushed up to shake hands, and congratulate this glorious old mother and bid her Godspeed on her mission of 'testifyin' concernin' de wickedness of dis 'ere people."

While Parker Pillsbury was speaking at an abolition meeting one Sunday afternoon, and criticising the churches in regard to slavery, a furious thunderstorm came up. A young Methodist arose, and interrupting the speaker, said he was "fearful God's judgment was about to fall on him for daring to sit and hear such blasphemy; that it made his hair almost rise with terror." Here a voice was heard above the rain, wind and thunder, saying: "Child, do not be skeered; you are not goin' to be harmed. I don't speck God's ever hearn tell on ye."

She got up a fine Thanksgiving dinner, for the Battle Creek Colored Regiment, then encamped at

Detroit. While soliciting for the "boys," she met one man who refused to donate, making rude remarks about niggers, the war, etc. Much astonished, she asked, "Who are you?" "I am the only son of my mother," he answered. To which she replied, "I am glad der are no more," and passed on.

During the war she met an old Northern Democratic friend, who asked her what business she now followed. She quickly answered, "Years ago, when I lived in the city of New York, my occupation was scouring brass door-knobs; but now I go about scouring copperheads"

Just before the war she held a number of meetings in Ohio, and hit the apologists of slavery sledge-hammer blows. At one of these meetings a man interrupted her and said, "Old woman, do you think that your talk about slavery does any good? Do you suppose people care what you say? Why, I don't care any more for your talk than I do for the bite of a flea." "Perhaps not," she answered, "but the Lord willin', I'll keep you scratchin'."

Sojourner was an inveterate smoker. Some years before her death, a friend asked her if she believed the Bible. "Certainly," she answered. He continued, "The Bible says 'no unclean thing can enter the Kingdom of Heaven.' Now what can be more filthy than the breath of a smoker?" "Yes chile," she answered, "but de Bible also say, 'He which is filthy let him be filthy still.' Besides, when I goes to Heaven I 'spect to leave my breff behin' me." However, she soon became convinced that it was wrong, and discontinued it. When told it would affect her health, she answered, "I'll quit ef I die." She did quit and lived!

On another occasion she attended a large **reform**

meeting where there were a number of speakers of national reputation. But in spite of this fact, a long-winded person mounted the platform and worried the people until half had left, and the others were groaning in spirit. At last he paused to take a long breath; when Sojourner rose up in the back part of the audience and said, "Chile, ef de people has no-whar to put it, what is de use? Sit down, chile, sit down!" He sat down.

She made a fine point on the Constitution the year the weevil destroyed so much wheat. Said she: "Chil'ern, I talks to God, an' God talks to me. Dis mornin' I was walkin' out, an' I got ober de fence into de field. I saw de wheat a holdin' up its head lookin' very big. I goes up an' takes holt ob it. You believe it, dare was no wheat dare? I says, 'God,' (speaking the name reverently) 'what is de matter wid dis wheat?' an' he says to me, 'Sojourner, dare is a little *weasel* in it.' Now I hears talkin' about de Constitution, an' de rights ob man. I comes up an' I takes holt ob dis Constitution. It looks mighty big, an' I feels for my rights, but dar aint any dar. Den I says, 'God, what ails dis Constitution?' He says to me, 'Sojourner, dar is a little weasel in it.'"

Volumes were written about the Negro and the Constitution, but here was a volume in a few sentences.

Harriet Beecher Stowe says of her: "I never knew a person who possessed so much of that subtle, controlling personal power, called presence, as she." Wendell Phillips stated, that he has known a few words from her to electrify an audience. In proof of this he cites the question she asked Frederick Douglass, who was speaking in Faneuil Hall at one of the darkest periods of the abolition struggle. Douglass was sad,—almost ready to despair, when she lifted her long finger and asked, loud enough to be heard by all, "*Frederick, is God dead?*" That was all she said, but it was enough.

In Calvin Fairbanks' account of Sojourner's interview with President Lincoln, he states that he and a friend were standing in the White House, when she approached the marshal and said: "I want to see President Lincoln." "Well, the President is busy, and you can't see him now." "Yes, I mus' see him. If he knew I was here, he'd come down an' see me." Finally the marshal went to the President's room with a statement of the case, when the President said: "I do believe she is Sojourner Truth. Bring her up here."

Up she went, and we approached near enough to catch glimpses and hear the words of greeting. "Sojourner Truth, how glad I am to see you!" To which she replied, "Mr. President, when you first took your seat I feared you would be torn to pieces, for I likened you unto Daniel, who was thrown into de lions' den, an' ef de lions did not tear you to pieces, I knew dat it would be God dat had saved you; an' I said ef he spared me I would see you befo' de fo' years expired, an' he has done so, an' now I am here to see you for myself. I never hearn of you befo' you was talked of for President." He smilingly replied, "I had heard of you many times before that." The President purchased her book; then handing him a photograph of herself, she said, "It's got a black face, but a white back, an' I'd like one of yours, with a green back." No man enjoyed a joke more than President Lincoln; and putting his fingers into his vest pocket, he handed her a ten dollar bill, remarking: "There is my face with a green back."

The following is from one of her dictated letters: "He then showed me the Bible presented to him by the colored people of Baltimore, and it is beautiful beyond description. After I had looked it over, I said to him: 'This is beautiful indeed; the colored people have given this to the head of the government, and that government once sanctioned laws that would not permit its people to learn enough to enable them to read this book. And for what? Let them answer who can.'

"He took my little book, and with the same hand that signed the death warrant of slavery, he wrote as follows:

"'For Aunty Sojourner Truth, Oct. 29, 1864. A. Lincoln.'"

Sojourner remained a year at Arlington Heights, instructing the freed women in habits of economy, neatness and order. She sometimes addressed large numbers of them, and on one occasion exclaimed, "Be clean! be clean! for cleanliness is godliness."

She was disgusted with the Government's policy of giving food to the Negroes, without making any effort to teach them to be self-supporting. Her plan was to colonize the freedmen out West. She traveled over many states securing signers to a petition to Congress for her pet scheme.

Rev. George Schorb of Evanston, Illinois, heard her lecture at Topeka, Kansas, in the interest of her colonization scheme. He said, "She was more than a hundred years old, but her voice filled a large auditorium, and she held her audience with ease." In fact at this period she seemed to renew her youth, her hair turned black in streaks, second sight and second hearing came to her, her wrinkles vanished, and she looked younger than she did twenty years before.

She obtained thousands of signatures to her petition to Congress, and although that body took no action, her efforts gave an impetus to the exodus of the colored people to the West, a few years afterwards.

In reviewing her life we can but wonder what she might not have been, had she, when young, received kind treatment, and a thorough education. Referring to Horace Greeley, she said, "You call him a self-made man; well, I am a self-made woman." She certainly was, and the world was better for her long sojourn in it. For she went about doing good, until she passed to her reward from Battle Creek, Michigan, November 26, 1883.

MRS. FANNIE BARRIER WILLIAMS,
Member of the Chicago Woman's Club, Newspaper Correspondent and Author.

CHAPTER XVII.

THE CLUB MOVEMENT AMONG COLORED WOMEN OF AMERICA.

Afro-American women of the United States have never had the benefit of a discriminating judgment concerning their worth as women made up of the good and bad of human nature. What they have been made to be and not what they are, seldom enters into the best or worst opinion concerning them.

In studying the status of Afro-American women as revealed in their club organizations, it ought to be borne in mind that such social differentiations as "women's interests, children's interests, and men's interests" that are so finely worked out in the social development of the more favored races are but recent recognitions in the progressive life of the negro race. Such specializing had no economic value in slavery days, and the degrading habit of regarding the negro race as an unclassified people has not yet wholly faded into a memory.

The negro as an "alien" race, as a "problem," as an "industrial factor," as "ex-slaves," as "ignorant" etc., are well known and instantly recognized; but colored women as mothers, as home-makers, as the center and source of the social life of the race have received little or no attention. These women have been left to grope their way unassisted toward a realization of those domestic virtues, moral impulses and standards of family and social

MRS. HAYDEE CAMPBELL,
The Popular Kindergarten Directress, of St. Louis.

MISS HELEN ABBOTT,
Noted Kindergarten Teacher in St. Louis, Mo.

life that are the badges of race respectability. They
have had no special teachers to instruct them. No
conventions of distinguished women of the more
favored race have met to consider their peculiar
needs. There has been no fixed public opinion
to which they could appeal; no protection against
the libelous attacks upon their characters, and no
chivalry generous enough to guarantee their safety
against man's inhumanity to woman. Certain it is
that colored women have been the least known,
and the most ill-favored class of women in this
country.

Thirty-five years ago they were unsocialized, un-
classed and unrecognized as either maids or ma-
trons. They were simply women whose character
and personality excited no interest. If within
thirty-five years they have become sufficiently important to be studied apart from the general race
problem and have come to be recognized as an
integral part of the general womanhood of American civilization, that fact is a gratifying evidence
of real progress.

In considering the social advancement of these
women, it is important to keep in mind the point
from which progress began, and the fact that they
have been mainly self-taught in all those precious
things that make for social order, purity and character. They have gradually become conscious of
the fact that progress includes a great deal more
than what is generally meant by the terms culture,
education and contact.

The club movement among colored women
reaches into the sub-social condition of the entire
race. Among white women clubs mean the for-

ward movement of the best women in the interest
of the best womanhood. Among colored women
the club is the effort of the few competent in behalf of the many incompetent; that is to say that
the club is only one of many means for the social
uplift of a race. Among white women the club is
the onward movement of the already uplifted.

The consciousness of being fully free has not yet
come to the great masses of the colored women in
this country. The emancipation of the mind and
spirit of the race could not be accomplished by leg-
islation. More time, more patience, more suffering and more charity are still needed to complete
the work of emancipation.

The training which first enabled colored women
to organize and successfully carry on club work
was originally obtained in church work. These
churches have been and still are the great preparatory schools in which the primary lessons of social
order, mutual trustfulness and united effort have
been taught. The churches have been sustained,
enlarged and beautified principally through the organized efforts of their women members. The
meaning of unity of effort for the common good,
the development of social sympathies grew into
woman's consciousness through the privileges of
church work.

Still another school of preparation for colored
women has been their secret societies. "The ritual
of these secret societies is not without a certain social value." They demand a higher order of intelligence than is required for church membership.
Care for the sick, provisions for the decent burial
of the indigent dead, the care for orphans and the

enlarging sense of sisterhood all contributed to the development of the very conditions of heart that qualify women for the more inclusive work of those social reforms that are the aim of women's clubs. The churches and secret societies have helped to make colored women acquainted with the general social condition of the race and the possibilities of social improvement.

With this training the more intelligent women of the race could not fail to follow the example and be inspired by the larger club movement of the white women. The need of social reconstruction became more and more apparent as they studied the results of women's organizations. Better homes, better schools, better protection for girls of scant home training, better sanitary conditions, better opportunities for competent young women to gain employment, and the need of being better known to the American people appealed to the conscience of progressive colored women from many communities.

The clubs and leagues organized among colored women have all been more or less in direct response to these appeals. Seriousness of purpose has thus been the main characteristic of all these organizations. While the National Federation of Woman's Clubs has served as a guide and inspiration to colored women, the club movement among them is something deeper than a mere imitation of white women. It is nothing less than the organized anxiety of women who have become intelligent enough to recognize their own low social condition and strong enough to initiate the forces of reform.

MRS. ANNA J. COOPER,
Teacher of Latin in the Washington High School, and Author of the "Voice From the South."

The club movement as a race influence among the colored women of the country may be fittingly said to date from July, 1895, when the first national conference of colored women was held in Boston, Mass.   Prior to this time there were a number of strong clubs in some of the larger cities of the country, but they were not affiliated and the larger idea of effecting the social regeneration of the race was scarcely conceived of.

Among the earlier clubs the Woman's League of Washington, D. C., organized in 1892, and the Woman's Era Club of Boston, organized in January, 1893, were and are still the most thorough and influential organizations of the kind in the country.

The kind of work carried on by the Washington League since its organization is best indicated by its standing committees, as follows:

Committee on Education.
Committee on Industries.
Committee on Mending and Sewing.
Committee on Free Class Instruction.
Committee on Day Nursery.
Committee on Building Fund.

These various activities include sewing schools, kindergartens, well-conducted night schools, and mother's meetings, all of which have been developed and made a prominent part of the educational and social forces of the colored people of the capital.   The league has made itself the recognized champion of every cause in which colored women and children have any special interests in the District of Columbia.

The league is also especially strong in the personnel of its membership, being made up largely of teachers, many of whom are recognized as among the most cultured and influential women of the negro race in this country.

Mrs. Helen Cook, of Washington, was the first president elected by the league, and still holds that position. Mrs. Cook belongs to one of the oldest and best-established colored families in the country. She has had all the advantages of culture, contact, and experience to make her an ideal leader of the leading woman's organization of the colored race.

The Woman's League claims to have originated the idea of a national organization of colored women's clubs. In its annual report for 1895 there occurs the following language:

"The idea of national organization has been embodied in the Woman's League of Washington from its formation. It existed fully developed in the minds of the original members even before they united themselves into an association which has national union for its central thought, its inspiring motive, its avowed purpose—its very reason for being."

Having assumed a national character by gaining the affiliations of such clubs as the Kansas City League, the Denver League, and associations in Virginia, South Carolina and Pennsylvania, the Washington League was admitted into the membership of the National Council of Women of the United States.

MISS ANNA JONES,
Teacher in Kansas City High School; is an Alumnus of the
University of Michigan, a Brilliant Linguist
and a Most Successful Teacher.

MISS SARAH A. BLOCKER,
Principal of Normal Department of Florida Baptist College,
Jacksonville, Fla.

The league is very tenacious of its name and claim as the originator of the idea of nationalizing the colored women's clubs of America, but its claim has always been challenged with more or less spirit by some of the clubs composing the National Association.

The New Era Club of Boston was organized in the month of February, 1893. The desire of the cultured and public-spirited colored women of that city to do something in the way of promoting a more favorable public opinion in behalf of the negro race was the immediate incentive to this organization. The club began its work of agitation by collecting data and issuing leaflets and tracts containing well-edited matter in reference to Afro-American progress. Its most conspicuous work has been the publication of the Woman's Era, the first newspaper ever published by colored women in this country. This paper gained a wide circulation and did more than any other single agency to nationalize the club idea among the colored women of the country. The New Era Club has sustained its reputation as the most representative organization of colored people in New England. It has taken the initiative in many reforms and helpful movements that have had a wide influence on race development. This club has been especially useful and influential in all local affairs that in any way effect the colored people. Deserving young men and women struggling to obtain an education, and defenseless young women in distress have always been able to find substantial assistance in the New Era Club.

This Boston organization embraces a member-

MRS. JOSEPHINE ST. PIERRE RUFFIN,
Prominent Woman of Boston, Leader of the Club Movement Among Colored Women.

ship of about one hundred women, many of whom are prominent in the ranks of New England's strongest women.

Mrs. Josephine St. Pierre Ruffin has been the president of the Era Club all the time since its organization. She is an active member in many of the influential women's organizations in Massachusetts. She is a woman of rare force of character, mental alertness and of generous impulses. She has played a leading part in every movement that has tended to the emancipation of colored women from the thraldom of past conditions. Her husband, the late Judge Ruffin, held the first position of a judicial character ever held by a colored man in New England.

These two clubs, located respectively in Washington and Boston, were worthy beginnings of the many local efforts that were destined to grow and spread until there should be such a thing in the United States as a national uprising of the colored women of the country pledged to the serious work of a social reconstruction of the negro race.

But these two clubs were not the only examples of the colored woman's capacity for organization. The following clubs were thoroughly organized and actively engaged in the work of reform contemporaneously with the clubs of Boston and Washington:

The Harper Woman's Club of Jefferson City, Mo., was formed in 1890 and had established a training school for instruction in sewing; a temperance department and mothers' meetings were also carried on. The Loyal Union of Brooklyn and New York was organized in December, 1892. It had a membership of seventy-five women and was engaged largely in agitating for better schools and better opportunities for young women seeking honorable employment; the I. B. W. Club of Chicago, Ill., organized in 1893; the Woman's Club of Omaha, Neb., organized February, 189⁻· the Belle Phoebe League of Pittsburg, Pa., organized November, 1894; the Woman's League of Denver; the Phyllis Wheatley Club of New Orleans; the Sojourner Club of Providence, R. I., and the Woman's Mutual Improvement Club of Knoxville, Tenn., organized in 1894.

It will thus be seen that from 1890 to 1895 the character of Afro-American womanhood began to assert itself in definite purposes and efforts in club work. Many of these clubs came into being all unconscious of the influences of the larger club movement among white women. The incentive in most cases was quite simple and direct. How to help and protect some defenseless and tempted young woman, how to aid some poor boy to complete a much-coveted education; how to lengthen the short school term in some impoverished school district; how to instruct and interest deficient mothers in the difficulties of child training are some of the motives that led to the formation of the great majority of these clubs. These were the first out-reachings of sympathy and fellowship felt by women whose lives had been narrowed by the petty concerns of the struggle for existence and removed by human cruelty from all the harmonies of freedom, love and aspirations.

Many of these organizations so humble in their beginnings and meager in membership clearly

MISS LULU LOVE,
Prominent Teacher of Physical Culture in the Public Schools
of Washington, D. C.

MISS LUTIE A. LYTLE,
Teacher Law Department Central Tennessee College, Nashville, Tenn.

needed behind them the force and favor of some larger sanction to save them from timidity and pettiness of effort. Many of them clearly needed the inspirations, the wider vision and supporting strength that come from a national unity. The club in Mississippi could have a better understanding of its own possibilities by feeling the kinship of the club in New England or Chicago, and the womanhood sympathy of these northern clubs must remain narrow and inefficient if isolated in interest from the self-emancipating struggles of southern clubs.

As already noted some of the more progressive clubs had already conceived the idea of a National organization. The Woman's Era journal of Boston began to agitate the matter in the summer of 1894, and requested the clubs to express themselves through its columns on the question of holding a National convention. Colored women everywhere were quick to see the possible benefits to be derived from a National conference of representative women. It was everywhere believed that such a convention, conducted with decorum, and along the lines of serious purpose might help in a decided manner to change public opinion concerning the character and worth of colored women. This agitation had the effect of committing most of the clubs to the proposal for a call in the summer of 1895. While public-spirited Afro-American women everywhere were thus aroused to this larger vision in plans for race amelioration, there occurred an incident of aggravation that swept away all timidity and doubt as to the necessity of a National conference. Some obscure editor in a Missouri town sought to gain notoriety by publishing a libelous article in which the colored women of the country were described as having no sense of virtue and altogether without character. The article in question was in the form of an open letter addressed to Miss Florence Belgarnie of England, who had manifested a kindly interest in behalf of the American negro as a result of Miss Ida B. Wells' agitation. This letter is too foul for reprint, but the effect of its publication stirred the intelligent colored women of America as nothing else had ever done. The letter, in spite of its wanton meanness, was not without some value in showing to what extent the sensitiveness of colored women had grown. Twenty years prior to this time a similar publication would scarcely have been noticed, beyond the small circles of the few who could read, and were public-spirited. In 1895 this open and vulgar attack on the character of a whole race of women was instantly and vehemently resented, in every possible way, by a whole race of women conscious of being slandered. Mass meetings were held in every part of the country to denounce the editor and refute the charges.

The calling of a National convention of colored women was hastened by this coarse assault upon their character. The Woman's Era Club of Boston took the initiative in concentrating the widespread anxiety to do something large and effective, by calling a National conference of representative colored women. The conference was appointed to meet in Berkeley Hall, Boston, for a three days' session, July 29, 30 and 31, 1895.

In pursuance to this call the 29th day of July,

MARY C. JACKSON,
Assistant Principal Haines' Normal and Industrial School,
Augusta, Ga.

MRS. HENRIETTA M. ARCHER,
Principal of the Department of Latin and Music in A. & M.
College, Normal, Ala., and Associate with the
National Colored Woman's Association.

1895, witnessed in Berkeley Hall the first National convention of colored women ever held in America. About one hundred delegates were present from ten States and representatives of about twenty-five different clubs.

The convention afforded a fine exhibition of capable women. There was nothing amateurish, uncertain or timid in the proceedings. Every subject of peculiar interest to colored women was discussed and acted upon as if by women disciplined in thinking out large and serious problems. The following named women were elected as officers of the conference:

Mrs. Josephine St. P. Ruffin, president; vice-presidents, Mrs. Helen Cook, of Washington, and Mrs. Booker T. Washington; secretary, Miss Eliza Carter.

The sanity of these colored women in their first National association was shown in the fact that but little time was spent in complaints and fault-finding about conditions that were inevitable. Almost for the first time in the history of negro gatherings, this Boston conference frankly studied the status of their own race and pointed out their own shortcomings. They set for themselves large and serious tasks in suggestions of plans and work to redeem the unredeemed among them. The convention did credit to itself by sending far and wide a warning note that the race must begin to help itself to live better, strive for a higher standard of social purity, to exercise a more helpful sympathy with the many of the race who are without guides and enlightenment in the ways of social righteousness.

Of course the Missouri editor was roundly scored in resolutions that lacked nothing of the elements of resentment, but the slanderous article against colored women that was the immediate incentive to the calling of the conference, became of the least importance when the women came together and realized the responsibility of larger considerations. They very soon felt that a National convention of responsible women would be a misplacement of moral force, if it merely exhausted itself in replying to a slanderous publication. The convention, therefore, easily shaped itself toward the consideration of themes and policies more in keeping with its responsibilities to the thousands of women and interests represented.

The chief work of the convention was the formation of National organization. The name adopted was "The National Association of Colored Women." The first officers of the National association were as follows:

The importance of this Boston conference to the club movement among colored women can scarcely be overestimated. The bracing effect of its vigorous proceedings and stirring addresses to the public gave a certain inspiration to the women throughout the whole country. The clubs that already existed became stronger and more positive and aggressive in their helpful work.

The National association has steadily grown in power and influence as an organized body, composed of the best moral and social forces of the negro race. It has held three National conventions since its organization, in 1895: At Washington, D. C., in 1896; Nashville, Tenn., in 1897; and

Chicago, in 1899. At the Chicago convention one hundred and fifty delegates were present, representing clubs from thirty States of the Union. The growing importance of the National organization was evidenced by the generous notices and editorial comments in the press of the country. Fraternal greetings were extended to the Chicago convention from many of the prominent white clubs of the city. It is not too much to say that no National convention of colored people held in the country ever made such a deep impression upon the public and told a more thrilling story of the social progress of the race than the Chicago convention. The interest awakened in colored women, and their peculiar interests, was evidenced in many ways. The National association has made it possible for many bright colored women to enjoy the fellowship and helpfulness of many of the best organizations of American women. It has certainly helped to emancipate the white women from the fear and uncertainty of contact or association with women of the darker race. In other words the National Association of Colored Women's Clubs is helping to give respect and character to a race of women who had no place in the classification of progressive womanhood in America. The terms good and bad, bright, and dull, plain and beautiful are now as applicable to colored women as to women of other races. There has been created such a thing as public faith in the sustained virtue and social standards of the women who have spoken and acted so well in these representative organizations. The National body has also been felt in giving a new importance and a larger relationship

MRS. JOHN R. FRANCIS,
Member of the Board of Trustees Public Schools, Washington, D. C.

to the purposes and activities of local clubs throughout the country. Colored women everywhere in this club work began to feel themselves included in a wider and better world than their immediate neighborhood. Women who have always lived and breathed the air of ample freedom and whose range of vision has been world-wide, will scarcely know what it means for women whose lives have been confined and dependent to feel the first consciousness of a relationship to the great social forces that include whole nationalities in the sweep of their influences. To feel that you are something better than a slave, or a descendant of an ex-slave, to feel that you are a unit in the womanhood of a great nation and a great civilization, is the beginning of self-respect and the respect of your race. The National Association of Colored Women's Clubs has certainly meant all this and much more to the women of the ransomed race in the United States.

The National association has also been useful to an important extent in creating what may be called a race public opinion. When the local clubs of the many States became nationalized, it became possible to reach the whole people with questions and interests that concerned the whole race. For example, when the National association interested itself in studying such problems as the Convict Lease System of the Southern States, or the necessity of kindergartens, or the evils of the one-room cabin, it was possible to unite and interest the intelligent forces of the entire race. On these and other questions it has become possible to get the co-operation of the colored people in Mississippi and

Minnesota and of New York and Florida.   Such
co-operation is new and belongs to the new order
of things brought about by nationalized efforts.

Through the united voice of the representative
colored women of the country the interests of the
race are heard by the American women with more
effect than they were in other days.   There is certainly more power to demand respect and righteous
treatment since it has become possible to organize
the best forces of all the race for such demands.

The influence of the National association has
been especially felt in the rapid increase of women's
clubs throughout the country, and especially in
the South.   There are now about three hundred of
such clubs in the United States.   There is an
average membership of about sixty women to each
club.   Some have an enrollment of over two hundred women and there are but few with less than
twenty-five.   Wherever there is a nucleus of intelligent colored women there will be found a
woman's club.   The following is only a partial list
of the clubs composing the National association.

CHAPTER XVIII.

CLUB LIST.

NAMES OF THE CLUBS OF THE NATIONAL ASSOCIATION OF COLORED WOMEN.

ALABAMA.

Eufaula Woman's Club.
Greensboro Woman's Mutual Benefit Club.
Montgomery Sojourner Truth Club.
Mt. Meigs Woman's Club.
Selma Woman's Club.
Tuskegee Woman's Club.
Tuskegee-Notasulga Woman's Club.
Birmingham Sojourner Truth Club.
Ladies' Auxiliary, Montgomery.
Ten Times One, Montgomery.

ARKANSAS.

Little Rock Branch of National Association.
Woman's Club, Little Rock.

CALIFORNIA.

Los Angeles Woman's Club.

NORTH CAROLINA.

Biddle University Club.

SOUTH CAROLINA.

Charleston Woman's League.
Charleston W. C. T. U.

MRS. MARY CHURCH TERRELL,
President of the National Association of Colored Women.

COLORADO.

Denver, The Woman's League.

CONNECTICUT.

Norwich, Rose of New England League.

FLORIDA.

Jacksonville Woman's Christian Industrial and Protective Union.

The Phyllis Wheatley Chautauqua Circle, Jacksonville.

The Afro-American Woman's Club, Jacksonville.

GEORGIA.

Atlanta Woman's Club.
Harriet Beecher Stowe, Macon.
Columbus, Douglass Reading Circle.
Augusta, Woman's Protective Club.
Woman's Club of Athens.

INDIANA.

The Booker T. Washington Club, Logansport.

ILLINOIS.

Chicago, Ida B. Wells Club.
Chicago, Phyllis Wheatley Club.
Chicago, Woman's Civic League.
Chicago, Women's Conference.
Chicago, Women's Circle.
Chicago, Progressive Circle of King's Daughters.

KANSAS.

Sierra Leone Club.
Woman's Club, Paola.

MRS. HART,
Jacksonville, Fla., Promoter of a Monument to Commemo-
rate the Valor of Black Soldiers in the
Spanish-American War.

KENTUCKY.

Louisville, Woman's Improvement Club.
Echstein Daisy Club, Cane Springs.

LOUISIANA.

New Orleans, Phyllis Wheatley Club.

MASSACHUSETTS.

Boston, Woman's Era Club.
Boston, Lend-a-Hand Club.
Boston Female Benevolent Firm.
Boston, E. M. Thomas League.
Boston Calvary Circle.
New Bedford Woman's Loyal Union.
Salem, Woman's Protective Club.
Cambridge Golden Rule Club.
Chelsea, B. T. Tanner Club.
New Bedford, St. Pierre Ruffin Club.

MINNESOTA.

Minneapolis, Ada Sweet Pioneer Club.
Minneapolis and St. Paul, Twin City Woman's Era Club.
St. Paul, Woman's Loyal Union and John Brown Industrial Club.

MISSOURI.

Jefferson City Woman's Club.
St. Louis, F. E. W. Harper League.
St. Joseph, F. E. W. H. League.
St. Louis Suffrage Club.
St. Louis, Phyllis Wheatley Club.
St. Louis Woman's Club.
St. Louis Married Ladies' Thimble Club.

Kansas City Club.
Self-Improvement Club, St. Louis.

MICHIGAN.

The Detroit Willing Workers.
Detroit, Phyllis Wheatley Club.
Lima, The Booker T. Washington Club.
Grand Rapids, Married Ladies' 19th Century Club.
Battle Creek, The Sojourner Truth Improvement.
Ann Arbor, The Woman's Federation Club.

NEW YORK.

New York and Brooklyn, Woman's Loyal Union.
Buffalo Woman's Club.
Harlem Woman's Sympathetic Union.
Rochester Woman's Club.
New York and Brooklyn, W. A. A. U.

NEBRASKA.

Omaha Woman's Club.
Woman's Improvement Club.

PENNSYLVANIA.

Pittsburg and Alleghany F. E. W. H. League.
Woman's Loyal Union, Pittsburg.
Washington Young Woman's Twentieth Century
    Club.

OHIO.

Toledo Woman's Club. A. M. E., Columbus.

RHODE ISLAND.

Newport Woman's League.
Providence Working Woman's League.
Lucy Thurman W. C. T. U., St. Paul.
The Dunbar Reading Circle, Cleveland.

IDA GRAY NELSON, D. D. S.,
The Only Colored Lady Dentist in the Country. Graduate of
Ann Arbor, Michigan; is very popular and has a large
and lucrative practice in the City of Chicago.

BELLE GARNET,
Graduate Nurse of Provident Hospital and Training School,
Chicago, now Pursuing a Course of Medicine
in the Chicago Medical College.

413

TENNESSEE.

Knoxville, Woman's Mutual Improvement Club.
Memphis, Coterie Migratory Assembly.
Memphis, Hook's School Association.
Phyllis Wheatley, Nashville.
Jackson, Woman's Club.
Jackson, W. C. T. U.

TEXAS.

Fort Worth Phyllis Wheatley Club.

VIRGINIA.

Woman's League of Roanoke.
Richmond Woman's League.
Cappahoosic Gloucester A. and I. School.
Urbanna Club.
Lynchburg Woman's League.
Lexington Woman's Club.

DISTRICT OF COLUMBIA.

Washington, D. C., Ladies' Auxiliary Committee.
Washington League.
Washington, Lucy Thurman W. C. T. U.
Woman's Protective Union, Washington, D. C.

WEST VIRGINIA.

Wheeling, Woman's Fortnightly Club.

There are of course hundreds of clubs that are not yet members of the National association, but these outside clubs have all been brought into being by the influence of the National body, and have received their inspiration and direction from the same source.

A study of the plans and purposes of these clubs reveals an interesting similarity. They show that

S. J. EVANS,
Chief Stenographer in One of the Largest Mercantile Houses
in Chicago.

the wants, needs, limitations and aspirations of the Afro-American are about the same everywhere— North, South, East and West.

If the question be asked: "What do these clubs do; what do they stand for in their respective communities, and what have they actually accomplished? satisfactory answer will be found by studying them a little at short range.

The first thing to be noted is that these club women are students of their own social condition, and the clubs themselves are schools in which are taught and learned, more or less thoroughly, the near lessons of life and living. All these clubs have a program for study. In some of the more ambitious clubs literature, music and art are studied more or less seriously, but in all of them race problems and sociological questions directly related to the condition of the negro race in America are the principal subjects for study and discussion.

Many of the clubs, in their programs for study, plan to invite from time to time prominent men and women to address them on questions of vital interest. In this way club members not only become wide awake and interested in questions of importance to themselves and their community, but men and women who help to make and shape public opinion have an opportunity to see and know the better side of the colored race.

Race prejudice yields more readily to this interchange of service and helpfulness than to any other force in the relationship of races.

The lessons learned in these women's organizations of the country all have a direct bearing on the social conditions of the negro race. They are such lessons that are not taught in the schools or preached from the pulpits. Home-making has been new business to the great majority of the women whom the women's clubs aim to reach and influence. For this reason the principal object of club studies is to teach that homes are something better and dearer than rooms, furniture, comforts and food. How to make the homes of the race the shrines of all the domestic virtues rather than a mere shelter, is the important thing that colored women are trying to learn and teach through their club organizations.

Take for example one club in Chicago, known as the "Colored Woman's Conference," and it will be found that its aims and efforts are typical of the best purposes of club life among colored women. The special activities and aims of this particular club are the establishment of kindergartens, mothers' meetings, sewing schools for girls, day nurseries, employment bureau; promoting the cause of education by establishing a direct line of interest between the teacher and the home life of every child; friendly visiting and protection to friendless and homeless girls; and a penny savings bank as a practical lesson in frugality and economy. The special thing to be noted in this program is that colored women are not afraid to set for themselves hard and serious tasks and to make whatever sacrifices necessary to realize their high purposes.

A lack of kindergarten teachers more than a lack of money has retarded the work of establishing kindergartens, especially in the South, where they are specially needed. The progressive woman feels that an increased number of kindergartens would have a determining influence in shaping and moulding the character of thousands of colored children whose home lives are scant and meager.

The success of the kindergarten work in St. Louis, Mo., under the direction of Mrs. Haydee Campbell and her able assistant, Miss Helene Abbott, is a happy justification of the wisdom and anxiety of the colored club woman to extend these schools wherever it is possible to do so.

The mothers' meetings established in connection with almost every club have probably had a more direct and beneficial influence on the everyday problems of motherhood and home-making than any other activity. Meetings of this sort have been the chief feature of the women's clubs organized by the Tuskegee teachers among the women of the hard plantation life, within reach of the Tuskegee Institute. Thousands of these women in the rural life of the South continue to live under the shadow of bondaged conditions. There has come to them scarcely a ray of light as to a better way of how to live for themselves and their offspring.

It is to the credit of the high usefulness of the colored club woman that she has taken the initiative in doing something to reach and help a class of women who have lived isolated from all the regenerating and uplifting influences of freedom and education. It is the first touch of sympathy that has connected the progressive colored woman with her neglected and unprogressive sister.

In this connection especial word ought to be said in behalf of these clubs as agencies of rescue

MRS. C. S. SMITH,
Nashville, Tenn., Late Secretary of the National Association
of Colored Women.

and protection to the many unprotected and defenseless colored girls to be found in every large city. No race of young women in this country have so little done for them as the young colored woman. She is unknown, she is not believed in, and in respect to favors that direct and uplift, she is an alien, and unheeded. They have been literally shut out from the love, favor and protection that chivalry and a common pride have built up around the personality and character of the young women of almost every other race. The colored women's clubs have had heart enough and intelligence enough to recognize their opportunity and duty toward their own young women, and in numerous instances have been the very salvation of unfortunate colored girls.

An interesting example of the usefulness of these clubs in this rescue work was recently shown by the success of the Colored Woman's Conference, above mentioned, in saving a girl, friendless, and a victim of unfortunate circumstances, from the stain of the penitentiary by pledging to take her in charge and to save her to herself and society by placing her under good and redeeming influences.

These women's clubs have never failed to champion the cause of every worthy applicant for advice and assistance. They have made the cause of the neglected young colored woman one of commanding interest, and are interesting in her behalf every possible means of education, and are endeavoring to create for her a kindlier feeling and a better degree of respect, and to improve her stand·ing among young women generally. The clubs have entered upon this department of their work with great heartiness and have enlisted in behalf of young women new influences of helpfulness and encouragement.   Colored girls with poor homes and no homes are many.   Thousands of them are the poor, weak and misguided daughters of ill-starred mothers.   To reach out for and save them from a bitter fate; to lift them into a higher sphere of hopefulness and opportunity is a task altogether worthy of the best efforts of club women.

What has been said of the earnestness and prac-tical aim of colored women's clubs in behalf of kindergartens for the children and salvation for the girls may also be said of the practical way in which they have established and sustained sewing schools, mending schools and friendly visitations in behalf of neighborhood respectability and decency, and of their various committees that visit reform-atory institutions and jails in search of opportuni-ties to be useful.   Numerous and interesting in-stances might be given to show to what extent these women are realizing their desire to be useful in the social regeneration of their race.

This chapter on the club movement among col-ored women would be incomplete without some notice of the leaders of the movement.   Nothing that these club women have done or aimed to do is more interesting than themselves.   What a variety of accomplishments, talents, successes and am-bitions have been brought into view and notice by these hitherto obscure women of a ransomed race! Educated?   Yes, besides the thousands educated in the common schools, hundreds of them have been trained in the best colleges and universities

MISS MATTIE B. DAVIS,
President The Woman's Club, Athens, Ga.

MRS. MARY L. DAVENPORT,
President of the Chicago Woman's Conference.

in the country, and some of them have spent several years in the noted schools of Europe.

The women thus trained and educated are busily pursuing every kind of avocation not prohibited by American prejudices. As educators, fully twenty thousand of them are at work in the schools, colleges and universities of the country, and some of them teach everything required to be taught from the kindergarten to the university. Among these educators and leaders of Afro-American womanhood are to be found linguists, mathematicians, musicians, artists, authors, newspaper writers, lecturers and reform agitators, with varying degrees of excellence and success. There are women in the professions of law, medicine, dentistry, preaching, trained nursing, managers of successful business enterprises, and women of small independent fortunes made and saved within the past twenty-five years.

There are women plain, beautiful, charming, bright conversationalists, fluent, resourceful in ideas, forceful in execution, and women of all sorts of temperament and idiosyncracies and force and delicacy of character.

All this of course is simply amazing to people trained in the habit of rating colored women too low and knowing only the menial type. To such people she is a revelation.

The woman thus portrayed is the real new woman in American life. This woman, as if by magic, has succeeded in lifting herself as completely from the stain and meanness of slavery as if a century had elapsed since the day of emancipation. This new woman, with the club behind her and the

MRS. BOOKER T. WASHINGTON.
425

club service in her heart and mind, has come to the
front in an opportune time. She is needed to
change the old idea of things implanted in the
minds of the white race and there sustained and
hardened into a national habit by the debasing influence of slavery estimates. This woman is needed
as an educator of public opinion. She is a happy
refutation of the idle insinuations and common
skepticism as to the womanly worth and promise
of the whole race of women. She has come to
enrich American life with finer sympathies, and to
enlarge the boundary of fraternity and the demo-
cracy of love among American women. She has
come to join her talents, her virtues, her intelligence, her sacrifices and her love in the work of
redeeming the unredeemed from stagnation, from
cheapness and from narrowness.

Quite as important as all this she has come to
bring new hope and fresh assurances to the hapless
young women of her own race. Life is not a
failure. All avenues are not closed. Womanly
worth of whatever race or complexion is appreciated. Love, sympathy, opportunity and helpfulness are within the reach of those who can deserve
them. The world is still yearning for pure hearts,
willing hands, and bright minds. This and much
more is the message brought by this new woman
to the hearts of thousands discouraged and hope-
less young colored women.

It is a real message of courage, a real inspiration
that has touched more sides of the Afro-American
race than any other message or thing since the
dawn of freedom.

This is not exaggeration or fancy. Demonstration of it can be seen, heard and felt in the wide-spread renewal of hope and effort among the present generation of young Afro-American women.

These young women, thus aroused to courage, to hope and self-assertion toward better things, can find inspiring examples of success and achievements in the women of their own race. They have begun to feel something of the exaltation of race pride and race ideals. They have been brought face to face with standards of living that are high and ennobling, and have been made conscious of the severe penalties of social misdoings.

Around them has been created a sentiment of care, pride, protection and chivalry that is every day deepening and widening the distinctions between right and wrong in woman's relationship to man, child and society.

The glow of optimism has coursed so easily through this chapter concerning the work done and attempted by colored women that the importance of it all may seem somewhat exaggerated.

It, perhaps, should be confessed that in spite of the actual good already realized, the club movement is more of a prophecy than a thing accomplished. Colored women organized have succeeded in touching the heart of the race, and for the first time the thrill of unity has been felt. They have set in motion moral forces that are beginning to socialize interests that have been kept apart by ignorance and the spirit of dependence.

They have begun to make the virtues as well as the wants of the colored women known to the American people. They are striving to put a new social value on themselves. Yet their work has just begun. It takes more than five or ten years to effect the social uplift of a whole race of people.

The club movement is well purposed. There is in it a strong faith, an enthusiasm born of love and sympathy, and an ever-increasing intelligence in the ways and means of affecting noble results. It is not a fad. It is not an imitation. It is not a passing sentiment. It is not an expedient, or an experiment. It is rather the force of a new intelligence against the old ignorance. The struggle of an enlightened conscience against the whole brood of social miseries born out of the stress and pain of a hated past.

FANNIE BARRIER WILLIAMS.